Fast
and
Bonnie

To the memory of
my mother and father

FAST AND BONNIE

A History of William Fife and Son Yachtbuilders

MAY FIFE McCALLUM

ORIGIN

This edition published in 2022 by
Origin, an imprint of
Birlinn Limited
West Newington House
10 Newington Road
Edinburgh EH9 1QS

www.birlinn.co.uk

First published in 1998 by
John Donald Publishers

ISBN 978 191247 674 9

British Library Cataloguing-in-Publication Data
A catalogue record for this book is available from the British Library

Typesetting and origination by Geethik Technologies
Printed and bound by Bell & Bain Ltd, Glasgow

Contents

Foreword to the Third Edition

Nearly forty years ago, while working on a floating restaurant on the Forth and Clyde Canal, I first met the author. Little then did I know of her enthusiasm for all things maritime, her family connections or her knowledge of Ayrshire's most famous yacht builders. Now I am director of the Scottish Maritime Museum I appreciate all the work that she has undertaken to ensure a greater knowledge of maritime heritage and in particular of this famous Fairlie yacht builder.

The first and second editions of *Fast and Bonnie* have been used by every curator at the Scottish Maritime Museum and have been the main reference for countless exhibitions in Irvine, Scotland and around the world. This updated edition will be as equally valuable to coming generations of museum professionals, historians, sailors and enthusiasts alike. Over the last thirty years May's work at the museum cataloguing and interpreting all things Fife has been invaluable. This book brings that knowledge and her family history together.

There are more Fife yachts restored to their original condition today, either sailing or on display in museums, acknowledging the enduring appreciation and enthusiasm for their superb design and build. There is also an increasing number of replicas being built, ensuring that the name of William Fife and Son will be enshrined in the history of Fairlie, Ayrshire and around the world.

David Mann
Director, Scottish Maritime Museum
February 2022

Sketch of *Viola* from Benoit Leman, Peintre Officiel du Yacht Club de Monaco.

Preface

My earliest recollections of yachting date back to one balmy summer day in 1938. While playing on the beach at Fairlie I became aware that a large number of sailing boats were drifting majestically down Fairlie Roads towards a buoy which marked the Tan, a channel between the islands of Little and Great Cumbrae. Like graceful swans, they seemed to fill my small horizon and left a lasting memory.

Of course I was aware that yachts were built on the street where I lived. I had seen them being launched but they were inanimate wooden hulls which slid or more often had to be helped into the water at high tide. I went to school with the children of the men who built these craft and my grandmother was a member of the family who designed them. At that time I did not realise that this was perhaps one of the last sights of a gathering of such large yachts.

As I grew up my interest in sailing and the Fife yard developed. A family of three generations of designers and builders had given the world some of its most beautiful yachts, yet no one had recorded its history. Countless tales circulated about the yard and the boats built there. Some of them were false. I felt the record had to be put straight, and the true story recorded, as a lasting tribute to the three Williams.

The story is told in a matter of fact way. The Fifes were down-to-earth practical men, and flowery descriptions have been left to the writers of articles for the yachting press.

I have endeavoured to check all available sources of information and hope that the resulting story will interest anyone who loves sailing, and in particular anyone who has sailed or owned a Fife yacht.

Acknowledgements

The gathering of information for this book has taken many years and I am indebted to the people who have taken the time and trouble to provide me with material.

I am indebted to Mrs Jan Howard, the late Miss Ruth Swann, Mr John Swann and Miss Elspeth Swann for information and family photographs, and to Mrs M. Crowthurst for reminiscences.

Grateful thanks are due to the many correspondents in the UK and further afield who have enlarged the picture, namely, Mr Norris Bryson USA, Daina Fletcher and Kevin Jones of the Australian Maritime Museum Sydney, John Bilsey of Wollongong NSW, Bruce Stannard Australia, Mr D. Geaves for information on *Fiona,* Les Amis de Noirmoutier, Mr Terry Needham Belfast, Mr David Loomas, Mr Christopher Temple, Adepar St Malo, Monica Krzyzanowski and Grant Willoughby for photograph of the Bute Fifes, Bill Hamilton for Bute Fife family history and Sarah Goldie of Largs Historical Society.

In the village of Fairlie thanks are due to the late James Boag senior, the late Duncan, John and Archibald McMillan. I am also grateful to Miss Kate McMillan, John McFie, Sandy Neilands and John French.

Much of the material was obtained from archives and libraries and I wish to thank the staff of the following institutions for their kind assistance: the director and staff of the Scottish Maritime Museum Irvine, members of the Largs Historical Society, Dr William Lindt and Duncan Winning of the Ballast Trust, staff at Custom House Greenock, staff at the Mitchell Library, City of Glasgow Council Libraries and Archives, staff at Glasgow University Business Archive, staff at the Scottish Record Office, staff at the Liverpool Picton and Brown Memorial Library, Ann Dennison at the Harris Library Preston, staff at the Northumberland County Council Registrar's Office, Mrs Alison Roberts, archivist at the Royal Northern and Clyde Yacht Club, and former archivist Iain McAllister, the Earl of Glasgow for permission to examine archives of Kelburn Estate and to Mrs Irene Innes for assistance.

I was grateful for the opportunity to interview Mrs Jenny Cairns in her 93rd year and to hear her reminiscences of the Bute Fifes. Campbell McMurray, director of the Naval Museum Portsmouth, gave much encouragement when he was director of the Scottish Maritime Museum, Irvine.

Thanks are also due to Duncan Walker, of Fairlie Restorations, Hamble, for arranging a family day sail on *Altair* when she visited the Clyde.

I am grateful to the Royal Northern and Clyde Yacht Club for their contribution to the publication of the manuscript and for permission to use their archives. Thanks are also due to Benoit Leman, La Rochelle, for the sketches of *Viola*.

Posthumous thanks are due to Denis Cosgrove and Brian Barr for bringing *Fast and Bonnie* to the small screen. This film for BBC was made at the 2008 Fife Regatta and has wonderful shots of the yachts sailing in home waters.

Finally, I owe a tremendous debt to my family who have lived with this work for many years, in particular my husband Robert Kohn whose help in preparation of the manuscript was invaluable and who guided me through the intricacies of word processing. My daughter Particia Kohn provided the sketch of the Fife dragon on page 72. If I have omitted anyone, I have done so unwittingly and apologise.

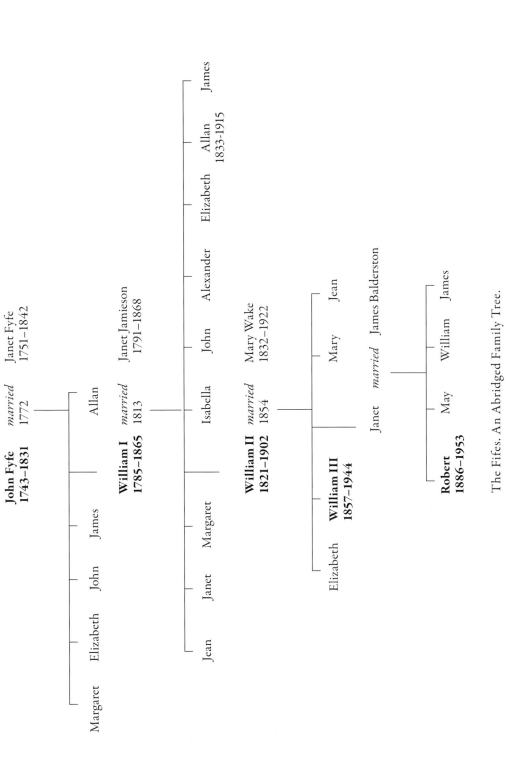

The Fifes. An Abridged Family Tree.

CHAPTER ONE
The Beginning

The village street is lined with mourners as the funeral cortège slowly makes its way to the Parish Church. It is August 1944 and villagers have come to pay their last respects to William Fife, the third generation of a remarkable family of yacht designers and builders.

Today there is nothing to indicate to a passing stranger that this forgotten corner of Ayrshire was once the birthplace of so many magnificent yachts. The only visible reminder is the weather vane on the church spire in the form of a gilded scale model of a yawl, *Latifa,* built in 1938.

To discover how the Fife yard came into being and how the term 'Fife built' came to mean a perfect yacht, just as the term 'Clyde built' was the mark of a superior ship, we have to start with events in the middle of the 18th century. These were troubled times. The Jacobite Rebellion of 1745 and the Austrian War of Succession were taking place and those events were influencing the lives of residents in Ayrshire and particularly the establishment of the yacht-building yard at Fairlie.

The land round Kilbirnie in Ayrshire was owned by Lord Crawford, whose family was related by marriage to the Earls of Glasgow, owners of the Kelburn estate, situated on the Ayrshire coast a few miles to the west of Kilbirnie.

In 1745 John, the Third Earl of Glasgow, was wounded and lost his hand at the Battle of Fontenoy whilst fighting in the War of Austrian Succession. A soldier from Kilbirnie carried him from the battlefield to safety and in gratitude the Earl gave him life-rent of a farm on the Kelburn estate. When Lord Glasgow died, his son George, the Fourth Earl, inherited the lands of Lord Crawford of Kilbirnie and became the feudal overlord of the two estates.

There are records of movement of employees between the two estates round about that time. John Fyfe, born in Kilbirnie in 1743, son of a small farmer or portioner, moved from Kilbirnie to work on the Kelburn estate as a wright in 1770. In 1772 he married Janet Fyfe, who may have been a cousin. They had several children, four of them sons – John, James, William and Allan – who all became wrights or carpenters.

The demand for skilled seamen during the American War of Independence (1775–1783) and the commencement of the Napoleonic Wars (1803) meant that merchant ships were in constant danger of losing their seamen to impressment by the Royal Navy. In 1778 some Glasgow merchants tried to avoid the loss of their crews to the press and ordered their ships returning from America or the West Indies to anchor off Fairlie, where most of the crew were sent ashore in longboats to make their way inland to Beith. Local farmers and smugglers usually alerted incoming vessels to the presence of the press gang.

It appears that John Fyfe junior, the eldest son of John, the wright on Kelburn estate, was building fishing boats at the beginning of the 19th century. Old customs records list fishing boats built by him at Fairlie and registered at Irvine, the local port of registration at that time. As a youth, William Fyfe, born in 1785, may have been attracted to his older brother John's business, and thus began his introduction to boat building.

At that time the river Clyde was not dredged and ships had to wait for high tide before proceeding upriver. Frequently they chose the sheltered haven behind the Isle of Cumbrae. This popular anchorage was used by both naval and merchant ships during the American War of Independence and the Napoleonic Wars, with additional movement from customs vessels stationed at Millport on the Great Cumbrae. The customs boats spent considerable time and energy chasing suspected smugglers. Smuggling, as elsewhere on the Clyde, was commonplace and frequently carried out by local trading vessels and fishing boats. This parade of passing ships caught William Fyfe's imagination and his interest in sailing boats grew as he watched the traffic in Fairlie Roads and observed the many vessels which anchored there. In order to inspect the ships at closer quarters, William built himself a small boat. It was so well made that he received an offer of purchase as soon as it was finished. He built another with equal success and so fate decided that his destiny lay in boatbuilding and not in millwright or cartwright work with his father. Working for himself would be more attractive than working as a lowly paid employee on the Kelburn estate.

The village of Fairlie was very isolated at this time. It had a population of about 140 people and was relatively inaccessible by land. The route from Glasgow was by sea or on land by cart on rough tracks. The overland route by Kilbirnie did not exist, and to catch a stagecoach to Glasgow necessitated a walk or ride across the moors to Dalry. Transport by sea was therefore very important for Fairlie as for other small communities on the shores of the Firth of Clyde. Building boats was an important occupation for the survival of these small villages. At first William and his brothers built fishing smacks and small trading vessels which plied between the Ayrshire coast, Arran, Argyll and Ireland. These boats carried butter and cattle and occasionally were engaged in smuggling Irish whiskey and salt. Payment in those days was usually by the barter system.

William Fyfe I (1785–1865). (Courtesy of Jan Howard.)

Early Ordnance maps of Fairlie show that there was a small smithy and sawpit on the foreshore. The smithy belonged to Adam French, the local blacksmith, and the sawpit was on the original boatbuilding site. It is likely that the yard began about 1803 when William Fyfe was 18 or 19 years of age. In the early days, the boats were built out in the open on the foreshore near the smithy and the land was rented from the Earl of Glasgow at the princely sum of one shilling per annum. Once the business had started to prosper this was raised to one pound. As the yard developed Mr French specialised in making high quality ironwork fittings for the yard boats.

It is remarkable that William Fyfe, a young man from an inland family, with no training in ship's carpentry, succeeded so well with his first boats. He came from a family of five woodworkers and had natural talent in this craft. Realising that he could produce a commodity which was in demand, he decided to free himself from working for a feudal superior who would have effectively kept him in thrall for the rest of his life.

It was an eminent Glasgow gentleman, James Smith of Jordanhill, who was initially responsible for encouraging young William Fyfe in his craft. Mr Smith had attributed his taste for yachting in early boyhood to sailing little cutters and schooners built by William Fyfe and his brothers. He wrote in one of his journals: 'Even in 1807, William Fyfe (then aged twenty-two) was distinguished for his taste in planning and workmanship in building sailing boats and had already built two for me.'

James Smith was in fact a gentleman of leisure whose father, a West India merchant, had established a company which was able to finance his son's

'Hard down!' in a stiff breeze – James Smith of Jordanhill at the helm of his yacht. (Courtesy of Glasgow City Council Libraries and Archives, Mitchell, Library, Glasgow.)

interests. These interests were varied. He was a keen geologist, archaeologist and President of the Andersonian University, an institution that John Anderson had founded in 1797 in defiance of his fellow academics at Glasgow University. He also wrote extensively on his researches into the Gospels of St Paul, whose journeys he had retraced in his yacht. The love of sailing was his main interest in life. His first cruise to the Western Isles was in 1806 in his yacht *Comet,* built by William Fyfe. He owned in succession the yachts *Amethyst, Raven* and *Wave.* His yachts were never large but always well planned and comfortable. They served him both as a place of study and a workshop when he dredged the Clyde to obtain samples for geological examination.

William Fyfe's first real yacht was the *Lamlash* of 50 tons, built in 1812 for James Hamilton of Holmhead and Captain James Oswald of Scotstoun. She was built expressly for pleasure and her owners took her cruising in the Mediterranean. Although a pleasure boat she was fitted with gun ports and if need be would be able to defend herself in foreign waters. *Lamlash* was named after the anchorage in Arran where her owner James Hamilton had a summer villa on Holy Isle. Mr Hamilton was also an early member of the Royal Northern Yacht Club and became Admiral of the club in 1826. *Lamlash* was the club's first flagship.

The eccentric Captain Oswald was said to have offered the skipper of the boat an umbrella if it started to rain when he was steering! No less striking a personality, Mr Hamilton became renowned for the punch which he served up at regatta meetings on the Clyde. By 1833 *Lamlash* was under new ownership and left Scotland for Van Diemens Land and the Sandwich Isles. She was obviously well built and able to withstand the rigours of ocean sailing.

The sport of yachting had not yet developed at the beginning of the 19th century. The men who owned yachts or sailing boats used them for practical purposes, namely to travel, collect scientific specimens, or even spectate or participate in naval battles.

Famine and trade depression were widespread after the Napoleonic Wars in the early years of the 19th century. Later the tide began to turn with the development of the coal, iron and steel industries, and the building of canals, railways and roads. This led to the River Clyde becoming a world leader in shipbuilding by 1830. The emergence of yachting as a leisure activity coincided with this Industrial Revolution and the enormous fortunes which were being made by a small elite. The people who made their money in industry and trade moved their families from the smoke and pollution of Glasgow during the summer months. Many of them built large villas on the coast of the Firth of Clyde, allowing some to indulge in the new sport that was developing – called yachting.

In keeping with the developing mechanical age, in 1812 a Scottish steam pioneer from Helensburgh named Henry Bell launched a steam-driven paddleboat, *Comet*, for the purpose of conveying passengers from Glasgow to Helensburgh. Initially he had difficulty in persuading a shipbuilder to build a hull for his steam engine but eventually this was carried out by John and Charles Wood in Greenock, a yard that was to experiment with many new ideas.

Soon afterwards a group of businessmen – William Croil, John Henderson and Dougald M'Phee from Dalry, a market town with hosiery mills 26 miles from Glasgow – persuaded William Fyfe and his brothers to build a similar vessel. In May 1814 the *Industry* was launched. She was built of oak from Kilbirnie, was 66 feet long and, in common with other early steamers, had a single cylinder side lever engine. This engine was built by George Dobbie of Glasgow. It is said that she was the first steamer to have a paddle box. Her paddle wheels were 10 feet 7 inches in diameter and were not connected directly to the crankshaft. The speed of the paddles was increased by spur wheel gearing. The spur wheels on the crank and paddle shafts made her very noisy, which earned her the nickname 'Coffee Mill' in her home port of Greenock.

Industry was one of the first steamers to carry cargo, mainly between Glasgow and Greenock. She was built with a shallow draught for the purpose of negotiating the sandbanks of the then undredged River Clyde. The river was dredged and deepened at a later date. *Industry* was mainly employed in taking sugar, which had arrived from the West Indies at Greenock, upriver to Glasgow, and returning with goods to be exported from Greenock, the deep-water harbour at that time. When not carrying goods she acted as a tug for sailing ships.

This remarkable boat had the distinction of being the oldest steamer on the Clyde, with a working life of 55 years. She was so well built that she outlived her first engine, and in 1828 Caird of Greenock fitted a second engine. She was later fitted with a folding funnel to enable her to sail upriver from Glasgow Bridge. After striking a rock off Renfrew in 1857 she sank, but was refloated and repaired. She was also involved in a collision in 1862 when she suffered damage to the hull, lost a paddle box and had a paddle wheel smashed. The boiler by that time also needed replacing so she lay for about a year in Greenock harbour. The owners, the Clyde Shipping Company, decided not to spend money and put her back into service. They gifted her to the City of Glasgow whose councillors had the idea of preserving her and locating her in the river above the weir at Glasgow. She was then moved to the harbour at Bowling at the western end of the Forth and Clyde Canal to await her move to Glasgow. In fact she lay in Bowling for 20 years. During this time the Provost of Dumbarton noticed her lying abandoned in Bowling harbour and approached the City of Glasgow councillors. He thought she would attract visitors if she was preserved and moored at the pier in Dumbarton. By this time, however, she was regarded as being too far gone for restoration. Her engine was removed and can now be seen in Glasgow's Riverside Museum. During her long working life her great age had earned her the honour of being allowed to enter any port on the Clyde without paying harbour dues. She was finally broken up in 1882. The *Dumbarton Herald* of 1882 printed a poem in her honour:

Industry, 1814. (Courtesy of Wotherspoon Collection, Mitchell Library, Glasgow.)

Industry's engine. (From *Clyde from the Source to the Sea*.)

Song of the *Industry*

I am an old and useless craft
Now lying by the shore,
Beside the waters of the Clyde,
Where I have splashed of yore.

My wooden sides are rotting fast,
My funnel lies below;

Industry at the Broomielaw. (Courtesy of Glasgow Museum of Transport.)

It stood both tall and straight at first –
Nigh seventy years ago.

Ah! Here I lie the oldest boat
That ever carried steam;
I'm going fast and sinking down
Beside my native stream.

I might have had a quieter place –
And more out of the way –
To lie and rest in peacefulness,
Than here in Bowling Bay.

But yet t'was here the old canoes,
Made by the Briton's hands,
Were found and dug some years ago,
Just from these very sands.

And by the fort of old Dunglass,
Where passed the Roman Wall,
To Henry Bell a pillar stands,
Who first did start us all.

And as the Western sun sinks down
Beyond Dumbarton grey,

Industry hulk in Bowling Basin. (Courtesy of Wotherspoon Collection, Mitchell Library, Glasgow.)

You will see a little further down,
Where the *Comet* launched away.

What fleets since then have followed fast
From yards both high and low!
And Clyde-built ships are just as staunch
As in days of long ago.

W.J.M.

The commercial success of *Industry* resulted in offers of capital to build similar vessels, and, had William Fyfe succumbed, the Fairlie yacht-building yard might never have existed. Happily, he consistently refused to build any more steamers in spite of offers of capital on advantageous terms. He said his ambition was to build and design yachts, which were 'fast and bonnie'.

His old friend, James Smith of Jordanhill, recognised the natural talents of William Fyfe and advised him that for self-improvement he should purchase the book *Naval Architecture* by Steele. The book was acquired and became a treasured possession. William recorded the birth of all his children on the inside of the front cover in the manner of a family bible. The book was a family heirloom and is still in existence today.

At that time, because orders for yachts were few and far between, the yard kept in business by building a superior type of fishing smack known as the Largs yacht. These were about 20 to 22 feet long and were sold for about £50. The fishing smacks and traders which Fife built were recognised as the best on the west coast for construction and speed. Even when the yard was fully established in yacht building, the second William Fife continued to build smacks or traders to keep the workforce employed when there were few orders for yachts. It appears that with usage the spelling of the family name changed in records from Fyfe to Fife with the birth of the second William Fife.

William's older brother, John Fyfe, was not only a boat builder but also a fisherman. The government had put a heavy duty on salt, which was required in quantity by fishermen to salt herring for export. As a fisherman it is likely that John Fyfe would take advantage of any tax-free salt which came his way. Early customs books for Largs and Irvine indicate that the Fyfe family were involved in the illegal trade.

In 1819, John Fyfe and the local innkeeper were questioned by the local customs officer about smuggled salt which had been hidden by one of John Fyfe's apprentices in the sawpit and also under an old boat. Both John Fyfe and the innkeeper were to have received some of the salt. Later, in 1830, a bag of flour, which had been picked up illegally from a wrecked cargo ship, was found on the *Industry* and seized.

As late as 1827 the Customs are still referring to John Fyfe *boat builder* at Fairlie, although by that time William had already established himself as a designer and builder of sailing yachts. According to James Smith sailing boats were being built by William and his brothers in 1807, so he was not working independently at this earlier date.

The first William Fyfe was a natural genius and an accomplished craftsman. A cheerful person, Ayrshire country bred, he was industrious and had a keen eye for business. The yard was essentially a family concern with William's brothers employed as the carpenters.

In 1813 he married Janet Jamieson. His success with *Industry* gave him confidence and financial security to contemplate marriage and support a family. William and Janet had ten children. The first three were daughters, which must have been a disappointment to William, who by now had a business which would benefit from the involvement of more younger male members of the family. Finally, in 1821 a son, William, was born who was to take the reputation of the Fife yard to all corners of the world. His three younger brothers, Alexander, Allan and James, were also to be closely associated with the building of his designs just as his uncles had been involved with his father.

Round about this time, in 1818, Charles Stuart Parker, a West India merchant with family connections in Liverpool and residing at Blochairn House in Glasgow, built a large villa in Fairlie, which he called Fairlie House. Three generations of the Parker family brought many benefits to the village, including a number of orders for yachts from the Fife yard. One of Charles Parker's sons, George, was a keen sailor and spent much of his time in Fairlie.

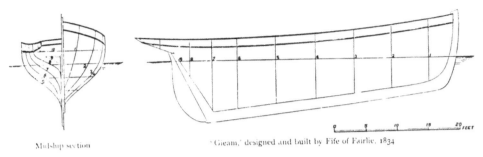

Midship section   'Gleam,' designed and built by Fife of Fairlie, 1834

Gleam, 1834. (Courtesy of Badminton Library of Sports and Pastimes.)

In one of his journals he records a voyage to the Hebrides in 1839 in *Phantom.* She is described as being built in 1833 by John Fyfe at Fairlie. He goes on to say: 'This man was a builder of coarse herring boats of between eight and twelve tons and from eighteen to twenty feet. The boat was built entirely by eye and was of clinker construction. There was a sort of cabin at the bows planked over without much attention to elegance or tightness.' The journal also makes criticism of the construction saying: 'The prevailing fault in all his boats was the shallowness at the stern . . . and we were frequently annoyed by the leakiness arising from the deficiencies in the thickness of the planking.' George Parker conceded that there was satisfaction in having 'a common herring boat', in that she had a deeper keel made of cast iron at the stern and was longer in proportion to her tonnage, which gave her considerable advantage when beating to windward. Her white sails (fishing boats usually had tanned sails) gave her an elegant appearance. The ballast was behind the mast and consisted of smooth round stones gathered on the Little Cumbrae shore. She was furnished with a small punt, rounded at both ends which could lie amidships when sailing. This description of a boat built by William's brother John is anything but flattering. Although the brothers worked together, William must have been a superior craftsman because from then on there is little more heard of John.

In 1832 the first William Fyfe launched *Gleam,* a cutter of 35 tons, for Captain Henry Gore-Booth. Built in the fashion of the day with 'a bluff cod's head and a mackerel tail' she was described in 1835 as 'the crack of the Clyde'. The following year he launched *Meteor,* regarded as the fastest boat on the Clyde. In the previous year, 1834, the second William Fife had been apprenticed to his father at the age of 13.

At this time boats were still being built to the old '94' rule or tonnage rule which had been introduced in 1794. Only the length of the keel and the breadth of the boat were taken into account, as external fin metal keels were unknown. Internal ballast was provided in the form of stones or iron ore. Gradually builders increased the draught and the amount of ballast and narrowed the beam in order that a boat of the same tonnage could be longer and carry more sail. Some lead was introduced on the outside along with internal ballast and eventually all the ballast was placed outside in the form of an iron or lead keel.

During the second William Fife's years of apprenticeship with his father, it seems that there were few yachts built. Times were hard. There were trade depressions in 1816 and 1825 followed by the potato famine in the west of Scotland in 1836 and 1837. People in rural areas were poor, farm servants earned about 10 shillings a week, labourers six shillings and sixpence and skilled artisans about 13 to 30 shillings. In this climate the yard found it difficult to expand and build larger boats. Capital was not available to invest in woodworking machinery to increase output without substantially increasing the workforce. It is said that the first William's daughter, Jean, a dressmaker, gave her savings to her father and brother to help purchase the required powered machinery to modernise the yard. It was indeed a family business.

Eventually, in 1839 William Fyfe decided to hand over the yacht-building side of the yard to his son, William Fife, 'because he had no use for it as it didn't make any money'. It is ironic that the man who turned down the opportunity to build more steam paddle boats because he wanted to build fast and beautiful yachts should give up his dream eventually because it could not provide an income. At the age of 54 he had eight sons and daughters unmarried and took financial responsibility for his brother's widow and her unmarried daughter. A guaranteed income from the building of fishing boats and traders was indeed necessary. He could ill afford to indulge in dreams and he had to return to the sturdy work-boats with which he had established his reputation. The years from 1839, when he took over the yacht-building side of the yard, till 1848 were difficult ones for young William and it was not until he designed *Stella* in 1848 that his fortunes were to change.

CHAPTER TWO
Parker, the Proa Man

The early years of the 19th century brought riches and prosperity to many Glasgow businessmen. Trade with America and the West Indies was thriving and a group of business elite was formed. This group met to discuss trade; they socialised together and frequently intermarried. The Parkers of Blochairn House just north-east of Glasgow were one such family. In 1818 Charles Stuart Parker obtained ground in Fairlie where he built a substantial villa as his summer residence. After this villa was built, his brothers-in-law Hugh Tennent and Robert Brown followed suit, and friends nicknamed the houses the 'Clyde Clapham'. The Parkers belonged to the group of West Indian, East Indian and Baltic merchants of Glasgow who had money to spend in the days of the first William Fyfe. Not only were they closely associated in business, but marriage between their families was common and recommendations on where to have one's yacht built would be by word of mouth. The association of Fife's yard with the Parker family spanned three generations.

George Parker, the second son of Charles Parker, appears to have been a young man with time to spare from his duties with the family firm of West India merchants. They imported sugar and rum, the goods arriving at Greenock by sailing ship. Samples were shown at their stock rooms in Greenock. The products were then sold and transported upriver to Glasgow. Young George spent much of his time in Fairlie and sailed regularly, visiting the Isle of Little Cumbrae, which was eventually owned by the family. In 1831 at the age of 25, George was experimenting with the design of proas or catamarans. He discussed this with the first William Fyfe while at the same time he was having a hull built at Port Glasgow by John Wood, 'the Flying Proa man'. This was the same Wood who had built the hull for the *Comet*. The hull of this proa was 22 feet long with an 11-foot-long outrigger projecting 15 feet on one side of the canoe. The beam of the main hull was two-and-a-half feet wide, draught three feet. The outrigger was 11 inches broad and about one foot deep. Mr Fyfe had drawn a sail plan and the mast was made at Steele's yard in Greenock. This first proa was named *Flying Fish* and was launched on 29 July 1831. The boat was then taken to Fairlie, where a whole day was spent trying out the rig of the proa. At the first attempt, with Fyfe aboard, the mast snapped

William Fyfe letter to George Parker offering to fit out Parker's proa. (Courtesy of Liverpool Record Office.)

six feet from the top. After repairs and setting a yard at the top of the sail, and with a punt lashed to the outrigger, the proa sailed about in Fairlie Bay with a crew of Fairlie boys. Again, the top yard fastening gave way and the boat capsized.

This did not stop George Parker experimenting and developing his proas, which much later became what we now know as 'twin-hulled catamarans'. He had a new mast made at Steele's shipyard and ordered a topsail from

Orr, a sailmaker, both in Greenock. Sailing this proa still proved to be difficult even with several crew on board. The boat was taken back to Steele's yard to have the mast lightened. After the alterations were completed, the return sail to Fairlie in heavy swell brought more problems; ropes broke and had to be replaced. Again, there were still fears for the safety of the mast.

George Parker, a determined man, went back to Fyfe's in November to collect a model for a new boat. In June of the following year he again visited Steele's and made a model of a canoe. At that time he also started to investigate the use of lateen sails.

In 1832 a larger and more ambitions project was the proa built by Fyfe to George Parker's design. According to George Parker's journal it had achieved a speed of ten knots. This vessel, the *Ruby Queen,* was about 60 feet long and rigged with lateen sails. The following year, after discussion with Fyfe, it was altered and made lighter – and the improved proa was faster than the old Largs steamers.

One of George Parker's regular crew was a local man by the name of William Duff. Apparently the exploits of the adventurous young man with his odd craft in Fairlie Bay had not gone unnoticed by the village. The frequent capsizings and breakages made everyone nervous, and William Duff had to inform George Parker that his parents did not want him to have anything more to do with the proa. This did not deter the intrepid Mr Parker, and the experimentation continued – but this time with friends Duncan Darroch, Robert Tennent and Captain Hay as crew. The following year he had a smaller proa built at Steele's which attracted comment in the *Glasgow Courier.* The article stated that the *Flying Fish* had spawned, producing a proa junior, while the writer declared that it would give him satisfaction to see her owner turn his perseverance and ability to improving and constructing more useful craft!

George Parker married in 1836 and cruised to the Western Isles with his wife and father-in-law, Professor Traill, from Edinburgh, in *Phantom,* built by John Fyfe. As already described, although she was a good sailing boat, she was not particularly well built or comfortable.

In 1840, with a young family to accommodate, George designed the *Doria,* a 58-foot schooner with three masts, which he had built by Fyfe. By 1845 he was discussing alterations, and in 1846 a new stern was fitted. In 1849 he decided to have the stern altered again and lowered it about ten inches.

George Parker and his family emigrated to America. Sadly, in 1852, his children died in Canada, and George died in New York in 1860. An intrepid sailor, his life must have been in danger many times in the quaintly rigged proas which he designed himself, not always successfully. He did, however, discuss some of his plans and projects with the first William Fyfe who carried out alterations. In practice he did not always take Mr Fyfe's advice. George

Parker's circle of young friends who shared his love for sailing included his brother James, who married a daughter of James Smith of Jordanhill, and Archibald Smith, her brother. Other friends were William Thomson, later to be known as Lord Kelvin, and Hugh Blackburn, Professor of Mathematics at Glasgow University. Major Duncan Darroch, whose family estate was at Renfrew, and who was to become his brother-in-law, was a frequent sailing companion. Robert Brown QC, and Hugh Tennent, owner of Wellpark Brewery in Glasgow, were his uncles in whose larger yachts he sailed as a young boy.

This tightly-knit social group, related by marriage and business interests, all owned yachts, some of them built by Fyfe or were hauled up for the winter in the Fairlie yard. James Smith of Jordanhill, a man of many scientific interests, who had encouraged the first young William Fyfe, must have been responsible indirectly for many of the orders for the young boat-builder. *Gleam,* a 30-ton cutter, was one of the first yachts built by the yard for his son-in-law, Henry Gore-Booth. By that time the yard was already established, with a reputation for good craftsmanship.

Later, as a result of the Industrial Revolution, even larger fortunes were made by Victorian businessmen. This period coincided with the development of yacht racing as a sport, and many would come to the small village on the Clyde coast to order the best racing yachts that money could buy.

CHAPTER THREE

Uphill Struggle

In the time of the first William Fyfe, Fairlie, which is situated on a bay on the North Ayrshire coast, was very different from what it is today. The Hunterston peninsula to the south-west of the village gave shelter to a vast stretch of shallow water which dried out at low tide and was known as Southannan Sands. These sands were reclaimed in the 1970s for building a deep-water ore terminal and are no more. In front of the yard these shallows extended to just north of the village, some 200 yards seaward from high-water mark. In 1608 Timothy Pont described the area as having an island close to the shore. This was probably the large sandbank which eventually became the site of the old railway pier at the north end of the village.

In the early days, when the first Fyfe started to build fishing boats, there was a small tidal harbour near the site of the yard. It is said that the stones from this harbour were used as a foundation for what is today Allanton Park Terrace, immediately adjacent to the yard. Because of the shallowness of the waters access by sea was not easy. Even the ferry grounded at low water and passengers had to wade ashore or be carried by the ferryman. Launching of shallow-draught fishing boats would not have been a problem, but later, when the yard began to build larger yachts with deeper keels, greater care had to be taken to avoid grounding on sandbanks during launching. At the beginning of the 19th century direct access from the sea was therefore only possible at high tide. Originally the yard built boats of local timber from the Kelburn or Kilbirnie estates, but as business grew, timber had to be brought in by sea. Many years later, when external keels replaced internal ballast, lead and other heavy equipment was also delivered by sea.

In spite of all these disadvantages the Fifes developed a boat-building business in this remote area, which was difficult to access and certainly had problems for launching larger vessels. The first and second William Fifes overcame these problems entirely using natural genius, talent, business acumen and dogged determination.

When the first William handed over the yacht-building side of the yard to his son times were hard and he said he had 'no use for it as it made no money'. Later, in January 1884, at a Royal Northern Yacht Club dinner held at the St Enoch Hotel in Glasgow, the second William Fife was honoured by the presentation of a portrait in oils. In his speech of thanks he stated that until he was 28 years of age the yacht-building side of the business made no money. He also mentioned that his fortunes changed in 1848 when he is recorded as saying 'a good friend loaned him money', thus enabling the business to prosper. It is likely that this good friend may have been Dr Hugh Morris Lang, of Largs – a banker who was known for his philanthropic gifts of bursaries to the local school, and who made a large fortune from railway shares, many of them overseas. His expert advice helped William to put his business in order and gave it financial security. Wherever the money came from, in 1848 it enabled William to build the 40-ton schooner *Stella* on speculation. She was not launched till 1851 when, in the event, she was purchased by Dr Lang.

The second William Fife's designs are recorded from 1839, and it is known that the yard also built boats to other designs, such as the George Parker-designed *Doria* and some of his proas.

Up until about 1854 sailing ships were measured by the tonnage rule or builders' measurement as it was also called. This rule was also applied to leisure yachts with slight modifications. The rule was based on the length of the keel taking the ground, the beam and the depth was calculated to be half the beam. The beam was therefore involved twice in measurement, and gradually yachtbuilders discovered that if they increased the draught and the amount of ballast, they could reduce the beam, and a boat of the same tonnage could be longer and carry more sail. About the 1830s ballast was increased by fitting external lead or iron keels.

This measured tonnage could also be reduced by shortening the length of the keel and by raking the stern post, thereby leaving the length of the waterline the same. Eventually, in 1854, the Royal Thames Yacht Club introduced a new parameter: the length of the keel was to be measured between the stem and stern post on deck and this became known as 'Thames Measurement'. Well before the Thames Measurement was introduced, James Smith of Jordanhill, the first William's patron, was actively experimenting with the measurement rules of the time. He kept a sketchbook of contemporary yacht lines and measurements, including those of *Amethyst,* his own boat. There were a series of projections of the stern from the after-part of the stern post for several boats. *Gleam, Oitha* and *Fanny* were at least one foot longer than *Amethyst, Dream, Falcon,* or *Sylph*. His sketchbook ideas were tested practically, as can be seen from an article in the *Glasgow Courier* of 1833, which reported that *Amethyst* was in Fife's yard 'to be lengthened aft and have a new raised deck fitted'. The article also remarked that the deck was fixed in an ingenious manner: 'doweled and without a carlin'. At this stage yacht owners, in search of optimum performance within the rules, were themselves continuously experimenting by altering lengths of bows and sterns, and the Fife yard was already noted for its unusually fine workmanship.

Three years after she was built *Stella* was also lengthened by six feet at the bow. After his success with *Stella* the young William Fife produced *Aquila* in 1851. An improvement on *Stella,* she was a 43-ton cutter. Unfortunately, because of her sharp ends and deep draught her builder was the only one to believe that this was not a hazardous experiment. She was regarded as a toy by experienced yachtsmen and as a coffin by fishermen. However, she proved to be a fast and excellent sea boat, crossing the Atlantic and surprising those who had predicted disaster.

Aquila's design was a great improvement on any yacht built on the Clyde or in Great Britain at that time. Most of her racing was against *Stella,* who had the older-styled, fuller bow. She was not so fast when running or reaching, and so William Fife added six feet to the bow to give her more length. Immediately afterwards, at the Kingstown and Queenstown regattas, she sailed away from the opposition. *Aquila* eventually became the property of Lord Brassey, a well-known yachting figure who owned her during the years 1853–1859. This improvement must have helped Fife when he produced *Cymba* in 1852. A 50-ton cutter, she had a considerably raked stern post and a 3-ton lead keel in addition to internal ballast. Owned by Mr Rowan of Glasgow and skippered by Robert McKirdy of Largs she was never beaten in her first season.

In 1853 *Cymba* won the Queen's Cup on the Mersey. Her skipper was William Jamieson, a cousin of William Fife. It is said that Jamieson asked a well-known English skipper 'What would they say in the Solent about *Cymba?*' The skipper, Penny, replied, 'They would not say anything, they would just laugh. But, my word, she would bring tears to their eyes before you had her there very long!' This remarkable vessel had a long career, latterly as a pilot boat on the Irish coast, and was finally broken up in 1899.

Skipper William Jamieson, two years older than his cousin, the second William Fife, was the son of Fairlie innkeeper John Jamieson, a brother of William's mother. At the age of 13 he left home to join the yacht *Kite.* By the time he was 30, he was an experienced skipper, sailing mainly yachts built by his cousin William. *Coralie, Cymba, Ithona, Surge, Surf* and *Fiery Cross* were a few of his charges. When he died in December 1901, a month before his cousin, he was one of the oldest skippers on the Clyde.

Fife's yard was indeed a family business. William was the eldest son, and, as was the custom in Scottish tradition, inherited the charge of the yard. Like his father before him, William's brothers Alexander, Allan and James worked beside him as carpenters. The eldest in the family was his sister Elizabeth, a dressmaker, who is accredited with giving financial help to her father and brother to purchase machinery for the business. There were two other sisters – Janet who died at the age of 18, and Margaret who married a local man, Alexander McNair.

Bute Fyfes at Ardmalish. (Courtesy of Monica Krzyzanowski & Grant Willoughby.)

It is little wonder that the first William found it difficult to make ends meet with such a large family to support. There is evidence that he also helped his less fortunate relations. A cousin John, who was a carpenter in Ardrossan, and his wife, both died about the same time, and an uncle in Ardrossan took care of their three sons. Apparently these orphaned boys were not happy in this household and walked from Ardrossan to Fairlie, a distance of about ten miles, to throw themselves on the mercy of their father's cousin. He took them under his wing and employed them as apprentices. On completion of their apprenticeship they crossed to the island of Bute where they set up a successful boat-building business at Ardmaleish.

The second William Fife was a remarkable man. Like his father before him he had no formal training. He learned his craft and practical experience from his skilled father. A perfectionist, he would often take down a frame which did not satisfy him and replace it with one which met with his approval. He did not work from drawings but from wooden half models, which he made and from which lines could be transferred to the lofting floor. He gradually improved his racing yachts by lengthening them and introducing fine ends, as can be seen in *Stella, Aquila, Cymba* and *Oithona*. This development shows

William Fife II (1821–1902).

that William was working out a more advanced racing-yacht hull design similar to that of the *America* before she came across the Atlantic to astound British yachtsmen in the Solent in 1851. The experimentation continued, and success with the lengthening and narrowing process was obvious in *Fiona, Neva* and *Annasonna*. Fife told the story of how he asked a Largs man what he thought of his new long sharp bows. The man answered, 'Weel I woudna like tae say ouer muckle, she's whaup nebbit aneuch anyway' ('whaup nebbit' = with a beak like a curlew).

Like his father, William had a natural instinct for design and no slipshod work was permitted. Every boat leaving the yard had to be perfect. In spite of ruling his workforce with a firm hand, from all accounts the second William Fife was a likeable man, popular with his employees and held in great esteem by all. On one occasion he was presented with a silver tea service at a gathering of yachtsmen in Largs. As mentioned previously, the Royal Northern Yacht Club presented him with his portrait in oils. He was active in public life. He served on the Parish and County Councils and the local

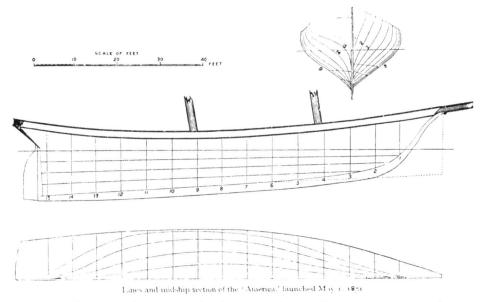

Lines of *America*. (Courtesy of Badminton Library of Sports and Pastimes.)

School Board and was an elder of the Parish Church. Although he received worldwide recognition for his designs and eventually made money, he remained basically an Ayrshire country (as opposed to 'county') person. His reticence and modesty meant that there was little written record of himself or his business. He obviously gloried in his work, refused to cut corners, and set a high standard even if it meant losing money. On one occasion, with no orders in prospect, he had built a schooner 'on spec'. A prospective buyer agreed to take the boat if it was fitted with three-feet-high bulwarks. The reply was, 'I hae kept her a long while, but I'll keep her a while yet, raither than make a common cairt o' her at the feenish.'

He built yachts for the rich, but they were not always prompt in settling their accounts. A yacht was built for a client who had been sailing it for a year and still had not paid for the boat. In the interval William had built another yacht for a neighbour of the first client. This boat was superior to the first one in races and the original client then suggested when his account was presented to him that it should be reduced, as he had a slower boat!

Lack of concern about money was also evident in a story told of how he had received a cheque in payment for a boat and was so engrossed in finishing a particular job that by the time he presented the cheque for payment the client had become bankrupt. His generosity was shown on another occasion, when a client who had been a good patron in his early years had some business misfortunes and could not pay the balance of his account: so Mr Fife quietly cancelled the debt. There is evidence that he expected the best from his men but that he was a fair employer. On one occasion when work

Allan Fife, brother of William Fife II.

was scarce he had the chance to build a large schooner at a fixed price. This meant that the men would have to take reduced wages. He told them of the offer and said he would leave them to consider the proposal. Before he left the yard they told him they had unanimously agreed to build the boat.

The workforce was composed mainly of local families. Fathers, sons and brothers following family tradition worked in the yard. The yard was the main employer in the village and many families depended upon it for a living. Yacht building was by its nature a seasonal activity lasting from September till the end of May, during which time men were employed building, repairing, or altering boats. What happened in spring when the last yacht slid down the ways? The men were paid off, hopefully to be re-employed at the end of the summer.

As a result, the majority of able-bodied men signed on as professional crews on racing yachts for the summer season. If the owner followed the racing circuit, they might begin by attending regattas at the Royal Thames Yacht Club before the cross-Channel races, subsequently proceeding to

Building yachts on the shore. (From *Fairlie Past and Present.*)

racing on the south coast of England and then on to the Mersey. By the month of July they were back in home waters attending the Royal Northern Yacht Club, Mudhook, Clyde Corinthian and Royal Clyde regattas in what became known eventually as Clyde Fortnight. The 'grand tour' continued when the boats left the Clyde to cross the Irish Sea to the Royal Ulster at Belfast and the Royal Irish at Dublin. The culmination of the season was the final gathering at Cowes Week. At the end of the year's racing the men would return to Fairlie in the hope that competition on the water that summer would have intensified the rivalry between owners to the extent that they would order a new racing machine from their yard for the following year.

The members of the Fife family who were employed in the yard had a similar way of life. Brother Allan, almost as knowledgeable on design and building as his brother William, was a noted racing skipper, sailing many of his brother's designs to victory. The youngest brother James was also a carpenter in the yard. Brother Alexander, who never married, did not go to sea in summer. He is nevertheless credited with most of the building of the *Pearl.* William said that 'Alexander built her in his spare time, ahint the big shed and mainly by the licht o' the mune.' *Pearl,* built in 1873, skippered by Allan Fife, had an extremely successful racing record. She was a five-tonner, 25 feet long and built for Mr Alan Buchanan of Glasgow, who had a large holiday villa in Fairlie. Apart from her first race, *Pearl* was undefeated for three seasons until she raced against G.L. Watson's first five tonner *Clothilde,* and lost.

William Fife & Son was a real family business from design, through building, to the actual sailing of the end product. The combination of the

William Fife II at the yard. (Courtesy of *Yachting News.*)

various skills of each member of the family contributed to attracting prospective clients and to the continuation of yard orders.

In 1854 at the age of 33, the second William Fife married. His wife, Mary Wake, from Felton in Northumberland, was a governess and ten years his junior. The Fife family was now living in Croftend House, just opposite the entrance to the yard on the foreshore. At this time there were no covered building sheds and boats were still being built in the open. A contemporary map shows a blacksmith's forge and two other small sheds. The sheds may have housed the steam box and possibly small power-driven saws. Most other work was carried out with hand tools at this time.

CHAPTER FOUR
Establishment

The Victorian era began in 1837 when the young queen ascended the throne. The Industrial Revolution also began about this time. The British colonies were developing, overseas trade was expanding very rapidly, and the demand for manufactured goods, both at home and abroad, grew apace. All this led to the formation of a new class of very wealthy merchants, professionals and industrialists. The very nature of industry at that time generated untold pollution in cities and wherever the industries were established. As a result, many who had to remain close to these new industrial centres sought to escape to more pleasant out-of-town surroundings at weekends and in the summer months. In a very short time this led to a proliferation of large villas on the shores of the Clyde estuary, where refuge was sought from the smoke and grime of the city. Concurrently, there was a slow emergence of sailing as a leisure activity, closely followed by the establishment of yacht clubs and yacht racing.

At the time when the first William Fyfe was starting in business, records show that in 1812 there were about 50 pleasure yachts afloat in British waters. These were generally built for cruising. In 1824 a group of Scottish and Irish yachtsmen in Belfast established the Northern Yacht Club. This arrangement combined yachting interests on Belfast Lough and on the Clyde. As the membership grew, in 1828 separate Scottish and Irish sections emerged. In 1831 a royal warrant was issued giving permission for members to fly a blue ensign on their vessels and the club became the Royal Northern Yacht Club. A few years earlier, at Cowes in England, 'The Yacht Club' had been founded in 1815 and became 'Royal' in 1820. In 1833 it was given the title of 'The Royal Yacht Squadron'.

The Crimea War (1853–56) and the economic collapse of the winter of 1856–57 led to many bankruptcies in the United States. This severely affected transatlantic trade and two main Glasgow financial institutions, the Western Bank and the City of Glasgow Bank, both closed. It is interesting to note that during this period, 1853–56, there are no records of yachts being built by the Fairlie yard. The Crimea War had a serious effect on the yacht-racing season of 1854. Although many yacht owners were in the services, the patriotic *Times,* the newspaper of the day, appealed for yachts to be laid up in order to free crews for service in the Royal Navy.

In 1856 the family business was first registered as a company, William Fife & Son. In the same year, which was just after the war, a new club, the Clyde Model Yacht Club appeared on the Clyde. This was not, as the title suggests, a club for people who sailed model or toy yachts. The constitution proposed 'to take in yachts under eight tons only, being the smallest acknowledged by the Royal Northern Yacht Club'.

There were obvious implications in this proposal. Inevitably there was an element of superiority in belonging to a 'Royal' club, which tended to cater for the wealthy aristocracy, landed gentry and close friends. The aim of the Clyde Model Yacht Club was for those people with 'small' businesses and 'smaller' means to enjoy regular regattas and yachting as a sport. The first elected Commodore of this new club was none other than James Smith of Jordanhill, who had long been interested in yacht design and performance and who we have seen was closely connected with the first William Fyfe. Apart from connections with the club, James Smith's daughter had married James Parker, brother of George, whose family were clients of Fife's yard. The patron of the club was the Hon G.F. Boyle, later to become the 6th Earl of Glasgow, and who was William Fife's feudal landlord. William Fife, together with another Fairlie resident, Captain Hay, who was a good friend and neighbour of the Parkers, was one of the first people to apply for membership of the Clyde Model Yacht Club. He was accepted in January 1857. At the end of the first club season, the Challenge Cup of 50 guineas for the closing cruise and race was won by Mr James Grant junior in his Fife-designed *Fairy Queen*, an eight-ton cutter built in 1857. This scaled down version of *Cymba* was completed by the yard in only six weeks.

After this event the club members decided to have an another race under the new American sail area rule. The same boats took part with the adjusted American handicap measurement system, which made little difference to *Fairy Queen* as she was again the winner. This first season concluded with a dinner at the Globe Hotel in Glasgow, after which Mr Fife reported that he had received an order for a 25-tonner from one of the members. This was presumably *Moonbeam*, which was built the following year. Forty years later, in 1898, *Moonbeam* won the Channel race from Plymouth to Fowey. She was 'as sound as the day she was built'.

From 1858 onwards there seems to have been no lack of orders for the yard. Between six and eight yachts were launched every year. The majority were of size to qualify for membership of the Clyde Model Yacht Club, with some notable exceptions. *Oithona*, built in 1856, was a 79-foot cutter built for Mr J.M. Rowan, the previous owner of *Cymba*. In 1858 the yard also built *Surge*, a 50-foot yawl, for C.T. Couper. Her skipper was Captain William Jamieson, William Fife's cousin. In 1861 she won £420 in prize money, and three years later her owner replaced her with another Fife boat, *Aeolus*, a 60-ton cutter.

At the end of 1861 *Aeolus* was lengthened by two feet aft and had a new owner, J. Houldsworth. It would seem that drawing out the length of the boat was still favoured as a means of getting the best out of the existing measurement rules. Soon after these alterations were made, Mr Houldsworth exchanged her for the Royal Northern Yacht Club's *Mosquito* and *Aeolus* remained as the club boat for 20 years. She must have been a particular favourite of Fife, as he is recorded as taking her back as part payment for the new club boat *Ailsa* that he built for the Royal Northern Y.C. She would prove her worth to the Fifes some years later. In 1864 *Aeolus* had been valued at £1,200 and Fife reduced the price of *Ailsa* by £400 in 1885 when he took her back.

By the 1860s the yard had acquired a reputation as a yacht-building establishment. Regular clients were ordering new boats every two to three years. Among them were D.W. and A. Finlay, heirs to the merchant Kirkman Finlay. The Finlay brothers sailed their own boats with amateur crews and produced designs for *Torch* and *Kilmeny*. When asked to build them, Fife objected to these two designs as he felt that they would not carry canvas well and would not be good sea boats. His criticism was that *Torch* was too lengthy. The Finlays insisted that he build to their design, and so the yard built *Torch* and the long narrow hull was successful. William Fife acknowledged his mistake, and *Torch* continued to win prizes for the next 20 years. Fife frequently refused to comply with client design requests; in most cases he was right, although in this instance he learned a valuable lesson.

In 1862 C.T. Couper, previously the owner of *Surge,* ordered another yawl, *Surf.* The following year another notable vessel, *Fiery Cross,* a 53-ton schooner built for Mr J. Stirling of Vale of Leven, was launched. She was a successful racing yacht skippered by Captain William Jamieson and she also had the distinction of cruising as far as the Faroes. The owner presented William Fife with a beautiful silver spirit kettle to mark the year of her launch. It is inscribed '*Fiery Cross,* 8 July 1863'.

Eighteen sixty-five was a significant year for the second William Fife. That year saw the launch of *Fiona,* a beautiful cutter of 80 tons. She was extremely long in proportion to beam, measuring 73 feet 6 inches by 15 feet 9 inches. Constructed of oak, teak, and mahogany she sailed for over 30 years and had an extremely distinguished racing career with Captain John Houston of Largs at the helm.

Fiona, the 'Fawn o'Fairlie', the 'terrible' *Fiona,* had an interesting history. She was built to order originally for a Mr Mosley who traded between Liverpool and the USA and who ran the blockades of the American ports during the Civil War. His fortunes declined, and *Fiona* was taken over by H. Lafone of Liverpool when half-completed. Mr Lafone traded with South America and had the idea of populating one of the Falkland Islands with

The 'terrible' *Fiona* (1865), nicknamed the 'Fawn o' Fairlie'. (From *Fairlie Past and Present*.)

men and cattle. One of his trading ships was called *Lafonia* from which the name *Fiona* was derived. There is still an area in the Falklands called Lafonia, where one of the last battles in the Falklands War of 1982 was fought.

Misfortune was to occur again when halfway through Fiona's first season Mr Lafone ran into financial difficulties and she was bought by a cousin, Mr Emmanuel Boutcher. The new owner kept her in a state of perfection. She was even hauled up for maintenance at Port Glasgow in 1867, unusual for a boat of her size. In her first season she won the Ryde to Cherbourg race, prompting Hunt's *Yachting Magazine* to comment that she was the fastest cutter in the world. She had a habit of carrying away spars and rigging. This may have been due to the boldness of her skipper, who, if need be, would cut away spinnakers to save time when racing and occasionally even threatened to lock the owner in his cabin when he suggested the skipper should be more cautious in a race! This colourful character, skipper John Houston, is said to have shared the champagne from

Half model of *Fiona*. (Courtesy of John McFie.)

the launching bottle with Mr Fife and refilled it with water for the launching ceremony of *Fiona*. The substitution does not seem to have had any effect on her performance.

For eight seasons *Fiona* was top-scoring boat in her class. She won six Queens Cups, three Albert Cups and many thousands of pounds in prize money. In her tenth season she also led the list of prizewinners. Although she officially won six Queens Cups, she had actually won seven, but was disqualified on Merseyside because her racing flag was smaller than the regulation size. It had been torn by the wind but was kept aloft as a good-luck banner. Perhaps the opposition, unable to defeat her on the water, had finally found a way to have her disqualified. Equally successful in Channel racing, she won the Ryde to Cherbourg and Ryde to Plymouth races. At the Plymouth regatta she carried away her topmast and bowsprit in a squall. This prompted the yachting journalists of the day to suggest a heavier rig for the following season. It was also noted that no one had ordered a similar yacht to her design when the reputation of the Clyde builders never stood higher and when patronage by a Glasgow millionaire might inspire even greater results. It was reported that William Fife had sustained the reputation of the Clyde for yacht building for many years, often in discouraging circumstances, and it was surprising that he had not received an order for another *Fiona*.

In 1879 Mr Boutcher had another *Fiona* built, this time by Camper and Nicholson. To this day, the family continue to name their boats after the 'terrible' *Fiona*. The latest in a long line is *Fiona VII*, ex *Local Hero*.

After she had been 20 years in retirement, Mr David Rait of Glasgow restored *Fiona* in 1899. She had been laid up for all of this time. In her first racing season after restoration she won the Cowes Cup, and in 1900 she came second in the Dover to Heligoland race, crossing the finish line only minutes behind the winner. She was the smallest and oldest boat in the fleet. It was a down-wind race in which spinnakers were carried for 320 miles. The following year she won the Dover to Heligoland race as well as the one from the Nore to Dover. Her success continued in 1902, 1903 and 1906 when she continued to win the Dover to Boulogne Cup. She was finally broken up in 1909 after a long and successful racing career of 22 years. The Dover to Boulogne Cup was presented to the Royal Thames Yacht Club and her mast was the flagpole of that club for many years. Her tiller can still be seen today over the stairs in the Royal Thames Yacht Club in Knightsbridge.

The launch of *Fiona* had brought fame to the yard. Established with a reputation for excellent craftsmanship, the success of *Fiona* brought more clients to Fairlie. William's success with *Fiona* was overshadowed by the death of his 80-year-old father in August 1865. Before his death the first William must have been proud of his son's success as a renowned yachtbuilder and designer. His dream of building 'fast and bonnie yachts' had been realised by his family and would continue for another generation.

At the time of his father's death the second William had a family of his own – a son and three daughters. Another daughter was born three years later. His only son, then aged eight and also named William, was to follow in his father's and grandfather's footsteps to become a designer of international repute.

CHAPTER FIVE

The Golden Age of Yachting

Fiona was launched in 1865. The launch of this boat appears to have been the turning point of the second William Fife's career. Till his death in 1902, William never lacked clients. The market for his designs grew to such an extent that it reached worldwide demand.

Fifteen miles south of Ayr, and about 50 miles further down the Ayrshire coast from the village of Fairlie, lies Culzean Castle, seat of the Marquis of Ailsa. The Marquis was a great yachtsman. When he inherited the estate in 1870 he commissioned Fife to design and build for him both the 36-ton *Foxhound* and the 141-ton schooner *Lady Evelyn*. *Foxhound* had a good racing career, started by winning Her Majesty's Cup at Cowes in 1871. Although *Foxhound* was a very good boat she was too small and outclassed to race against the English 40-ton boats, and therefore she was reluctantly replaced three years later by *Bloodhound,* a 40-ton cutter, also designed and built by Fife.

Bloodhound further established William's reputation as a builder and designer of large racing yachts. In 1875 she was the leading yacht on the Clyde. As befitted a keen racing owner, she had no cabin fittings except a seat on either side of the cabin sole. After ten years of successful racing the Marquis replaced her in 1881 with *Sleuthhound,* another 40 tonner from the Fairlie yard. *Bloodhound* then passed into the hands of a Mr A. Bain, who sailed her for 13 years, up to 1902. Finally, having had several other owners, she was bought by Sir Thomas Dunlop, the Vice Commodore of the Royal Clyde Yacht Club.

The Royal Clyde Yacht Club had started off as the Model Yacht Club, founded in 1856. Its name was subsequently changed to the Clyde Yacht Club in 1863. After a long process Queen Victoria granted a royal charter, and in 1872 the club became known as the Royal Clyde Yacht Club. Sir Thomas was a great supporter of this club; he remained Vice Commodore for 30 years and was elected Commodore in 1934. During the First World War he was Lord Provost of Glasgow.

In 1907 Sir Thomas put *Bloodhound* into the Fairlie yard with orders to break her up. This must have upset the Marquis of Ailsa, because he bought her back and refitted her. Regretfully the following year she was sunk on the starting line by *L'Espérance* at a race in the Solent. Nevertheless, she was raised and repaired. In 1909 the Marquis started to experiment with her. He modernised the rigging and the sail plan and adapted her to a more scientific era of yacht racing.

This experimentation was successful. During the five years up to 1913 she raced in the handicap class and won a total of 208 flags, of which 116 were firsts. Sadly, in 1922, after an active life of 48 years, a fire at White's yard in Southampton destroyed her. Although the boats no longer exist, half models of all the Marquis's yachts can be seen on display at Culzean Castle, now a property of the National Trust for Scotland.

In 1874 William Fife excelled himself. Together with *Bloodhound* he also produced two other high tonnage yachts, *Cythera,* a 116-ton yawl for Mr D. Richardson of Greenock, and *Neva*, a 60-ton cutter. All had very successful racing careers, and these three yachts consolidated Fife's reputation. *Neva* was commissioned by an English yachtsman who died before she was completed. She was then taken over by Mr Robert Holms-Kerr of Largs, a successful stockbroker who was a member of the Glasgow Stock Exchange.

Neva's first skipper was Captain John Houston, of *Fiona* fame. He is said to have told Mr Holms-Kerr to put 'as much lead on her bottom as she will carry and if you can afford it, a strip of gold beneath the lead'. When Mr Fife heard this he said, 'Ach, never mind a' Houston says, you'll soon be trying to eat a' you see, he's lead daft.' By all accounts Captain Houston was quite a character. His almost total disregard for safety during racing when he pressed boats and crew to their limits was probably the reason for him wanting 'as much lead as she can carry' under her keel. At this time yachts were being built longer, narrower, and with increased weight on keels to allow more sail to be carried. Rigging technology was not keeping pace with these developments and this often resulted in broken spars and sails carried away.

Neva sailed 95 races under another skipper, Captain Lemon Cranfield, and won 57 prizes. In 1876 she won the first Royal Cup presented to the Royal Clyde Yacht Club. In 1877 she was first in the class for high-tonnage yachts at the Royal Merseyside regatta. Pressed hard in a challenge match from the Mersey to Barrow she lost her topmast. That year she was sold to a Mr Cowan, who refitted her in 1885. Her skipper was now Captain John Boyd of Fairlie. From 1891 to 1898 she lay neglected in Greenock, and finally was discovered to have dry rot and was broken up.

Cythera was said to be Mr Fife's favourite boat and one of the finest racing yachts he ever built. At the Royal Merseyside regatta she came second to *Neva*. In 1878 she took part in the first Clyde Week along with four other high-tonnage yachts, not one being less than 100 tons. They were *Lufra, Jullanar, Condor* and *Formosa*. That year the Royal Clyde, the Royal Northern and the Mudhook Yacht Clubs decided to work together for the improvement of the sport and amalgamated their regattas into what became known as

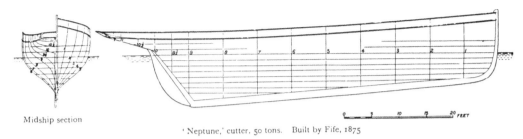

Midship section

'Neptune,' cutter, 50 tons. Built by Fife, 1875

Neptune (1875). (Courtesy of Badminton Library of Sports and Pastimes.)

Clyde Week. They also introduced the Royal Yachting Association's scale of time allowances based on those originally drawn up for the Royal Alfred Yacht Club.

Originally designed as a cutter, *Cythera* was re-rigged in 1879 as a yawl with a suit of new sails from Lapthorn. Having crossed the Atlantic some time before, she left New York in March 1884 with a crew of 14 on board on a voyage to the West Indies. She was never seen or heard of again. Did she disappear in the infamous Bermuda Triangle? We shall never know.

The phenomenal success of the big trio in 1874 led to the yard building eight more boats the following year. In fact, the yard was so overwhelmed with work that Mr Fife had to turn down the building of a large yawl for the famous Lancashire cricketer Mr A.B. Rowley. Mr Rowley insisted that he wanted a Fife boat, so William Fife designed *Latona,* a 165-ton yawl which was built by J.S. White at Cowes. This was the first time that William had designed a boat without actually working on it himself. The success of *Latona* showed that he could have made his mark as a designer alone. In 1880 *Latona* won the race from Dover to Boulogne and back to Dover.

Another notable boat was launched from the yard in 1880: *Neptune,* a 50-ton yawl for Mr N.B. Stewart of Keil. Mr Stewart died that year, but his family continued to sail *Neptune.* In 1885, under different ownership, *Neptune* was still in the front at races round the Isle of Wight, and, skippered by Captain Robert Gomes, raced on till 1896.

Although by now the yard had more orders for yachts that it could cope with building, William never forgot its humbler origins. He continued to build fishing smacks and traders. The Fife traders were valued for their construction and speed.

In 1870 the *Jessie Kerr,* built for Walter Kerr of Millport, cost £250 complete with sails and gear. Mr Fife lost on the transaction and is reported as saying, 'Walter, when you ordered this boat it would have paid me to have given you £10 and you go away.' Mr Fife chartered her for her first passage to bring a cargo of 25 tons of lead to the yard. He is also reported as saying, 'If she makes a cupful of water I'll take her back.' She was eventually wrecked inside Horse Island while trying to enter Ardrossan Harbour. A few years later the

Jessie Kerr (1870) on the right, at Millport harbour. (Courtesy Wotherspoon Collection, Mitchell Library, Glasgow.)

Mary Kerr and later, in 1876, the *Lady Margaret* were also built for Walter Kerr. In fact, before the sport of yachting became popular, there were annual sailing matches in Fairlie Roads between the fishing smacks built by Fife's.

William Fife senior was a canny businessman. Not only did he build trading smacks but also occasionally had a share in some boats, perhaps as part payment. He is recorded as being the managing owner of *Crusader,* a 66-foot, two-masted trader built in the yard in 1856. In 1875 he built the *Bee,* a 66-foot smack in which he had shares, along with his cousin, Captain William Jamieson, and John Ferguson, a master mariner from Kilmun. He left his shares in the *Bee* to his son-in-law, James Balderston, who eventually sold them to John Ferguson.

About this time the second William Fife's son, William Fife junior, as he was known, left Brisbane Academy at the age of 15 and began his apprenticeship in the yard. He could not have begun his career at a more auspicious time. His father had acquired a formidable reputation as a yacht designer and builder, the yard was in full employment and the craftsmanship of the workforce was of the finest. A skilled group of men from two generations ensured that every boat that left Fairlie was perfect in construction and finish.

Young William, unlike his father and grandfather, was not a skilled time-served woodworker. He was first and foremost a designer. In 1875, with his father, he contributed to the design of the five-tonner *Clio* and the following year a similar design was produced named *Camellia*. It is said that these are

Mary Kerr. (Courtesy of The Ballast Trust.)

the first two yachts in whose design William junior shared. *Camellia* was to show her paces against another five-tonner designed by a young man whose reputation for yacht designing was growing. This five-ton class had been racing for a number of years, and in fact one boat called *Pearl,* designed by William Fife senior, kept her position at the head of the fleet for three years. Mr Fife owned her himself and after she stopped racing in the Clyde she turned up in France, where she still gave a good account of herself.

The season of 1876 saw the addition of three new boats to the class, *Camellia,* designed by W. Fife and his 19-year-old son; *Vril* by G.L. Watson; and *Freda* by D. Hatcher of Southampton. *Camellia* and *Vril* were almost identical apart from draught; *Camellia* drew five feet and *Vril* six feet of water. In addition, *Vril* had all her ballast in an external keel, a novelty at that time. Because the three boats came from different designers, a match was organised off the coast of Holyhead Island, a locality not familiar to any of them. *Freda* sailed against *Vril* and *Camellia* separately, and the yacht, which won two out of each of three races, was to be the winner. In the first races, sailed in very dirty weather, *Freda* won two races and then won three against *Camellia.* William Fife was no longer the undisputed doyen of Clyde yacht designers.

The Marquis of Ailsa, who was also keen on boatbuilding, had a small building facility in the bay below the castle where small boats were built regularly. He decided to expand this interest and opened a

Ketch (1892), coasting vessel. (Courtesy of The Ballast Trust.)

boatyard at Maidens, south of the Castle. In 1877 the Marquis' yard built the ten-ton *Beagle* to a design by William senior. Unfortunately *Beagle* had a short life. At the close of the opening race of the Royal Clyde Yacht Club she was run down and sunk by the schooner *Nyanza*. The accident occurred because the finish mark for the race had been changed from the end of Tighnabruich pier to a marker boat with a flag. *Nyanza,* a large steel-framed schooner built by Steele's of Greenock and belonging to James 'Paraffin' Young, the distinguished chemist, did not notice this till the last minute and in order to prevent a gybe luffed sharply round the mark, resulting in a collision with *Beagle,* whose port side burst open. She filled with water and sank immediately. On board *Beagle* were William Fife senior, his son William and William senior's brother Allan Fife. Fortunately they managed to scramble over the rail of the *Nyanza* before the boat sank.

The year 1877 was nearly the end of the Fife dynasty. In addition to the accident on *Beagle,* when the two senior members of the family and the heir were nearly drowned, William junior later in that same month nearly lost his life at sea. The 20-year-old had gone to Largs in a lugsail towing a punt.

John Clark of Curling Hall, Largs. (Courtesy of *Baillie Magazine*.)

His 17-year-old cousin, William, son of Allan Fife, and William Boyd, son of the model yachtbuilder David Boyd, accompanied him. Having delivered the punt, they left Largs to return to Fairlie at about seven o'clock in the evening. A strong south-westerly breeze sprang up and the boat capsized off Keppenburn, north of Fairlie. Fortunately some men on the shore saw what happened, launched a boat, and eventually rescued the young men who by now were much exhausted. Had these two incidents in 1877 ended in tragedy, then there would have been no more magnificent yachts launched from the Fairlie yard.

The following year, the last of William junior's apprenticeship, saw the launch of *Condor,* a 159-ton yawl for John Clark of Paisley. Mr Clark a mill owner, had purchased Curling Hall, a summer residence in Largs. Known to be an aggressive businessman, he was Lord Provost of Largs from 1883 till 1887.

Condor was the largest vessel built in Fairlie up till that time. She had 14 tons of lead bolted onto the greenheart keelson and the flooring was cast

Mohican (1885), built by D. & W. Henderson. (Courtesy Royal Northern & Clyde Yacht Club.)

iron. No expense was spared in the interior decoration of the saloon and staterooms. The saloon was panelled with yellow pine relieved by white and gold decoration. The cabin furniture was black ebony decorated with gold, and the stairs and passageways were of oak. Sofas were covered in blue silk repp and there were electro-plated silver lamps. This luxury yacht had a crew of 14.

As a keen yachtsman, Mr Clark was a member of the syndicate which built *Thistle,* designed by G.L. Watson in 1889 as a challenger for the America's Cup. In addition to owning sailing boats, Mr Clark had a magnificent steam yacht, *Mohican,* 704 tons, built in 1885 for himself and his brother William. With a party of friends, Mr Clark crossed the Atlantic to watch the races between *Thistle* and *Volunteer.* On another occasion he cruised to Iceland and the voyage is recorded in a delightful book entitled *The Mohican in Iceland.* This steam yacht was eventually sold to the German government in 1896 for £17,000.

Mr Clark, Commodore of the Royal Clyde Yacht Club from 1887 to 1894, donated £100 to provide stained-glass windows for the new club premises at Hunter's Quay. He also donated a hospital to Largs and spent money on the construction and endowment of the Clark Memorial Church in the town.

Two years after the launch of *Condor,* John Clark, who had been impressed by the ability of the young George Lennox Watson to design such winners as *Vril* in the five-ton class, commissioned him to design the 90-ton *Vanduara*.

After her successful first season of 13 firsts, two seconds and three thirds, young Watson's design reputation was established. Mr Clark continued to have all his future yachts designed by Watson. This was the beginning of a period of rivalry between the old-established firm of William Fife & Son and the young up-and-coming George L. Watson.

CHAPTER SIX
Friends and Rivals

For many years William Fife senior had been the only man in the north to uphold the honour of yacht designers on the Clyde against competition from the south coast. This started to change when the young designer George Lennox Watson came to the fore. Watson, born in 1851 (the year that *America* won the famous cup) was the son of a Glasgow doctor. Later he was to become one of the Clyde's most prestigious designers. As a young man Watson served his apprenticeship in the shipbuilding yard of Robert Napier, where he too worked 'at the tools', learning how to handle wood and iron, and gaining a good grounding in iron shipbuilding. He completed his training with the firm of A. & J. Inglis at Pointhouse, Glasgow, and owed some of his success to the guidance of Mr John Inglis. In 1871 he designed a small cruising yacht for himself, the *Peg Woffington*. Built in a joiner's yard, she was remarkable for that time in having all her ballast fitted externally in the form of a lead keel with a novel midship section 20 years ahead of its time. As is so often the case with radical new ideas, she was an object of ridicule to the 'knowledgeable' critics of yachting. These ideas of tentatively replacing some of the internal ballast with outer fixed keels was already being tried by other designers, but *Peg Woffington* appears to be one of the first boats to have no internal ballast but a heavier external keel.

The then current measurement tonnage rule restricted the design above the water line. Watson studied below-water-line sections to try and improve performance and initially he was one of the first to realise that the forefoot of a boat was not as important as canvas aloft. His first design for a five tonner, *Clothilde,* built in 1875, raced against W. Fife senior's *Pearl. Pearl* was built by his brother Alexander and sailed by another brother Allan, the best helmsman of small yachts in the Clyde at that time. Until she met *Clothilde, Pearl* had been thought to be unbeatable. However *Clothilde* won and established George Watson as a new and challenging designer.

The five-ton cutter *Vril,* designed by Watson and owned jointly with his friends John Lawrence and Charles Hilliard, took part in a match with the second William Fife's *Camellia* and Dan Hatcher's *Freda*. This was a hard fought match. *Freda* won, and *Vril* took second-line honours. Fife now had competition from another Scottish designer. Although Watson's innovations were making their mark, yet another younger yacht designer came to the fore on the competitive scene. This time it was back to Fairlie and the young William Fife the third.

Three years after the match between *Vril* and *Camellia* two new five-tonners began to do battle. This time it was between *Cyprus*, designed by William Fife junior when he was 22 years of age, and *Nora*, by George Watson. *Nora* was a very different design built for Messrs Allan, keen racing yachtsmen. *Cyprus* appeared to have an edge, winning 13 firsts out of 15 starts in 1879. *Cyprus* was kept in the Fife family during her racing career on the Clyde and was always helmed by her designer. After a racing career of five years she was bought by the Revd G.L. Blake, who raced her but fitted her out for cruising. When he bought her she had no fittings below deck at all. A particularly novel idea was a transparent compass binnacle fitted into the deck space ahead of the cockpit and lit from below by a lamp in the cabin. There was a small, watertight, lead-lined cockpit and no other comforts. Eventually she was bought by an American yachtsman and ended up sailing on the Great Lakes.

Yacht design was constantly changing due to technical advances, scientific theories and rule changes which, as today, tried to keep abreast of development. Historically, prior to 1820 those few yachts which existed were similar to fishing vessels, having round, barrel-like bottoms, full round bows, built of timber and with internal ballast of gravel or stones. After the visit of *America* in 1851, new long bows were built onto old boats and *America's* midship section, which was flatter, was copied. Gradually internal ballast was replaced by external lead keels. In 1860 iron framework, combined with wooden planking, was developed, and became a method favoured for building the China clippers. Robert Steele's yard in Greenock, famous for its clippers, also built yachts and *Nyanza* was constructed in this way. Apart from lengthening and deepening yachts, no great changes were made in design for some time. Prior to 1870 little was known about resistance to bodies moving through water. In 1866, in his *Shipbuilding Theoretical and Practical,* McQuorn Rankine concluded that resistance to movement through water of a vessel was due to surface friction, and, at higher speeds, waves were an additional resistance factor. About 1874 William Froude studied the effect on resistance of towing different shapes through water at different speeds and confirmed Rankine's deductions.

Although well documented, this scientific evidence was ignored by many shipbuilders of the time. These builders were superb craftsmen and could work alongside their men but few were able to analyse or interpret the results of speed curves or calculations. There was one, however who had the benefit of Rankine's tuition and began to estimate the resistance of ships. This was John Inglis of Pointhouse.

Froude's experiments were confirmed by towing actual ships and comparing this with models. As a result, Froude's law of comparison was stated, i.e. 'The equivalent speed of a ship and the model it represents will vary as the square root of their lengths'. Froude also distinguished between surface friction and friction due to eddies and waves.

George Watson, working in the Pointhouse yard with John Inglis, had early access to the results of Froude's experiments. He designed *Clothilde* without cutting away too much, but enough to have people mock her and compare her to a cartwheel. However, her sailing performance must have spurred him to greater efforts and he continued to develop his designs with confidence, producing the ten-ton *Verve* for Mr Robert Wylie, who had first helped the young designer with a commission. She was one of the first yachts to have chain plates and rigging screws instead of deadeyes and lanyards.

The young 29-year-old Watson was finally recognised as a designer and he acquired a rich patron, Mr James Coats of Paisley, a threadmill owner. For him he designed the ten-ton *Madge* in 1880. Another Paisley thread manufacturer, Mr John Clark commissioned the 90-ton *Vanduara* built by Henderson's of Meadowside. This was Watson's first big cutter design which sailed away from all her competitors and firmly established G.L. Watson as a genius in yacht design. In his eagerness to apply scientific principles, Watson occasionally over-reached himself. He received a commission to design the America's Cup challenger of 1877. His patron, John Clark, was a member of the syndicate headed by Mr James Bell, Commodore of the Royal Clyde Yacht Club, which put forward a challenge with *Thistle*. The desire to reduce friction from the surface resulted in not having enough boat to hold her to windward, and, although she sailed as fast as *Volunteer,* she drifted to leeward and lost the challenge.

William Fife & Son did not ignore these developments. The 29-year-old William Fife junior travelled to New York on the *City of Rome* and was present along with George Watson, Sir James Bell and Tom Ratsey when *Thistle* was in the Eirie Basin dry-dock prior to the America's Cup races and he had ample opportunity to study her underwater lines.

Watson's fame had spread and commissions followed, which confirmed his superiority as a designer – *Britannia* for the Prince of Wales and the *Valkyries* for Lord Dunraven. Unlike the Fifes, Watson also designed several elegant steam yachts and was a consulting designer to the Lifeboat Service. At the height of his fame in 1894, when Watson was only 42 years of age, William Fife senior was 73 years old, and, as has been shown, had been ahead of his time when he designed boats such as *Stella* before the arrival of the *America*. Energetic young Watson, with the design of *Peg Woffington* and the application of the results of William Froude's experiments, was following a similar pattern of development and innovation to William Fife senior.

The difference between the two designers is difficult to pinpoint. Both

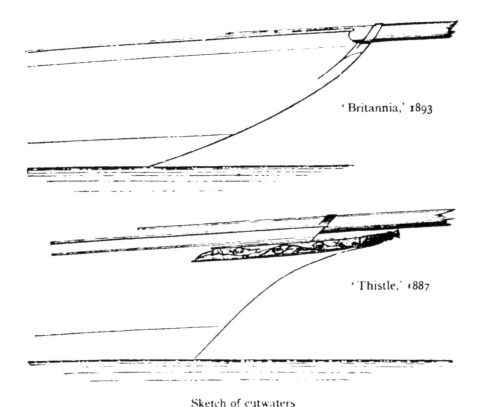

Sketch of cutwaters

Bows of *Britannia* and *Thistle*. (Courtesy of Badminton Library of Sports and Pastimes.)

produced successful and graceful yachts. Perhaps William Fife senior was more set in his ways, cautious, and resistant to change. Tyrrel Biddle, in his book of 1881, *The Corinthian Yachtsman,* had this to say of him:

> Fyfe is one of those practical men from whom more may be learnt in a day than from others of his calling in a week. A believer in well-known and well-tried principals, Fyfe will not waste either his or your time in discussing the possibility of this or that theory being correct but will at once give his opinion without circumlocution and his opinion will be found not far from wrong in the end.

In spite of this he did experiment successfully within the old tonnage rule and Thames Measurement rule and not only designed and built yachts but sailed them and carried out management duties for the firm.

George Watson, on the other hand, worked as a designer with a good grounding in practical construction. A much younger man, he was exposed to the new ideas of Froude when he was in his early twenties. He was also predicting the use of aluminium alloys in the framework of yachts as early as 1881. On account of his age he was more receptive to the many changes in design and rules of measurement. He had the vision to move forward and experiment for himself. In 1904 he died at the age of 53, whereas William Fife senior died two years earlier, a much older man at the age of 81. Although William Fife junior took over the designing of Fife yachts during his father's latter years, William senior continued to have a keen and active interest in the yard right up to his death. The characters of the two rivals were completely different. George Watson was grave and staid, polite, and with a courteous manner, thought by some to be distant. He only seemed to come alive when talking about anything to do with yachting or listening to criticisms of design. William Fife senior, on the other hand, had a genial, loveable personality and was fond of storytelling and singing. He had great consideration for his workmen and enjoyed a good relationship with them.

William Fife senior had great respect for the young designer Watson. At a dinner of the Largs Yacht Club in 1883 he said of his rival that he was pleased to think that he no longer had a single-handed battle to fight against the south-country builders, and while he had always done his best, sometimes not always as well as he would have wished, he felt his younger friend (Mr Watson) would maintain and increase the fame of Clyde building yards. His prediction came true, and although they were keen rivals in designing winning yachts, they remained friends.

The Royal Yachting Association was founded in 1875 to standardise yacht-racing rules and to classify yachts for racing. In 1881 it introduced a new tonnage rule – the 1730 Rule, which gave rise to an undesirable hull shape known as 'plank on edge'. The previous Thames Measurement Rule and this new rule meant that a vessel with greater beam had a high rated tonnage and a greater handicap in racing. The result was that boats were built with deep keels weighted with lead to compensate for narrow beam, and in addition they carried enormous areas of sail. Stays could not be set up properly because of the narrow deck, and so there were many breakages and loss of gear, and a number of these 'lead mines' or 'lead coffins' disappeared beneath the waves.

In 1886, these extreme designs prompted the RYA to adopt a rule proposed by the designer Dixon Kemp. This rule was based on length and sail area only and called Linear Rating. The rule formula was:

$$\text{Rater} = \frac{\text{Length} \times \text{Sail Area}}{6,000}$$

The boats designed to this rule became known as raters, '40 raters' (60 feet long with 4,000 square feet of sail), '20 raters', etc. The rule was further refined in 1896 and became known as the Linear Rating Rule to avoid extreme designs of a very light undercanvassed yacht with excessive overhangs. This extreme rule was perhaps suitable for small ½- to 2½

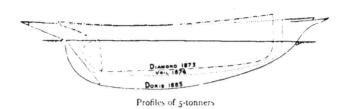

Profiles of 5-tonners

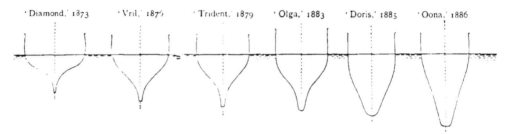

Sections showing decrease of breadth and increase of depth in 5-tonners—under 94 and 1730 Rules

Development of plank on edge design. (Courtesy of Badminton Library of Sports and Pastimes.)

raters which were only used as day boats, but for 5 raters upwards the boats were not as good as those built before 1890. They were expensive to build and handle and were only good for one or two seasons' racing before being broken up since they were unsuitable for cruising. Yachtbuilders felt so strongly about this that they sent a joint letter to the RYA deploring the extreme effect which rendered ex-racers unsuitable for cruising. The RYA took the view that owners of racing yachts wanted speed and the yachtbuilders withdrew their original suggestions for improving the rule, which was not revised till 1896. The signatures on the original letter included those of George L. Watson and William Fife junior.

CHAPTER SEVEN

New and Old Generations

The Fairlie yard continued to prosper even when business was slack elsewhere. The *Glasgow Herald* of 25 April 1879 stated that the Clyde yards were half empty – 'a howling wilderness' in contrast to Fife's yard. Fairlie was 'at the present time the cheeriest sight on the Clyde'. It is to be noted that even then a few fishing smacks were still being built to 'fill up the book'.

Just after William junior completed his apprenticeship in 1878 he spent some time at J. Fullarton & Co., shipbuilders in Paisley, where he gained experience in the use of metals in boat construction. This must have been useful to him when he later designed the composite hull of the America's Cup challenger *Shamrock I*.

This method of construction, where iron framework is combined with wooden planking, was adopted on the Clyde for the construction of clipper ships about 1860. Steele's yard at Greenock built many of these clipper ships and yachts. They used this method in the construction of the sailing yachts *Nyanza* and *Silene* and also large steam yachts. Iron was eventually replaced by steel, and as early as 1881 George Watson was suggesting aluminium alloys as an ideal alternative material, which at that time was prohibitively expensive. Nickel-steel was cheaper and held out a better promise; it was used by W. Fife junior for the frames and beams of the 20-rater *Dragon III* in 1893.

In 1883 Culzean Ship & Boatbuilding Company, which was started by the Marquis of Ailsa in the early 1870s underneath the shadow of Culzean Castle, moved to Maidens to allow the Marquis to build larger boats. Three years later, at the age of 27, the younger Fife was invited to become manager and partner of this yard when he left Fullarton's to further his career. Meanwhile, the Fairlie yard was as busy as ever. On Sundays people would walk from Largs to Fairlie, a distance of three miles, to see what was building in the Fife yard. Mr Fife was inclined to think the real purpose of the travel was to obtain 'refreshment', since the licensing laws, which were still in force up to the 1960s, prevented residents who were not bona fide travellers from purchasing intoxicating liquor in their local hostelries. It was therefore necessary to 'travel' in order to qualify for the purchase of alcoholic refreshment. The boats they might have inspected were well worth the walk.

William Fife II on the *St Bryde* (1879). (Courtesy of *Baillie Magazine*.)

The *St Bryde,* a schooner of 40 tons, built in 1879 for Sir John Douglas of Greenock and later owned by Mr Holms-Kerr of Largs, was the background for a sketch of Mr Fife senior, which appeared in the *Baillie Magazine* of 1884. *Neptune,* a ten-tonner built the following year, was still in the forefront of races ten years later. On average, the yard was now building seven yachts a year, some of them very large indeed.

One of William senior's successes was the 40-ton *Annasona,* built in 1881 for Mr J. Hedderwick, a member of the Royal Clyde Yacht Club. Her skipper was an Irishman, William O'Neill. Her name in Gaelic means 'Happy Anna' and in spite of a late appearance on the racing scene in her first season and misfortunes such as breaking the jaws of her gaff, and on another occasion having her bowsprit carried away by a steamer, she won 44 flags in her first two seasons; 41 of them were firsts.

Although he owned and operated his own boat yard, managed by young William Fife junior, the Marquis of Ailsa still ordered yachts from William

Fife senior. In the same year that Fife senior launched *Annasona, Sleuthhound* (40 tons) was built for the Marquis to replace *Bloodhound* in competitive racing between the 40-tonners. Miss Jean Fife, William senior's youngest daughter, who was 13 years of age, launched her in May. It must have been quite a thrill for the teenager to launch a 64-foot yacht for such a prestigious client of her father's. However, she was no stranger to the launching ceremony, having launched the 50-ton *Thora* the previous year when she was only 12 years old. Her brother, then a partner and manager in the Marquis' boatyard, probably had some say in designing *Sleuthhound*. Meanwhile, the Fairlie yard at this time was still fully under the control of William Fife senior. At the age of 60, he showed no sign of handing over the running of the business to his son or ceasing his design work.

Down in Maidens young William was also designing yachts, which would be built at Fairlie. A ten-ton cutter, *Ulidia,* built in 1883 for an Irish yachtsman, Mr Corry, nearly missed the traditional launching christening. On this occasion, Mr Fife senior had just announced 'success to the *Ulidia*' when he missed the razor sharp bow with the ribbon-bedecked bottle of wine. Fortunately an alert lad on board the boat managed to jerk the string and succeeded in breaking the bottle. After a single season she was sold to an American in 1886 and taken to New York on board the steamer *Richmond Hill.*

As always, the yard was a family business. William senior was in charge and his brothers Alexander, Allan and James worked as carpenters. In addition, Allan was a skipper of racing yachts in the summer season. Away from home young William was gaining experience before rejoining his father and taking over the running of the yard. He had four sisters, Elizabeth, the eldest in the family and a year older, and three younger sisters – Janet, Mary and Jean, the youngest. Mary was eventually to become William's secretary when he became head of the firm, and Janet, the tomboy of the family, enjoyed sailing with her brother in spite of suffering badly from seasickness. Janet was the only one of the family to marry. Her husband was James Balderston, a threadmill manager from Paisley. He too was fond of the sea and was one of the party aboard John Clark's steam yacht *Mohican* when she cruised to Iceland in 1886. When William junior was a young boy and his father was carrying out alterations on Mr Clark's *Condor,* which lay at Largs, he had to walk the three miles from Fairlie to Largs to deliver his father's lunch. In 1886 a son, Robert, was born to Janet and James Balderston. He was later to go into partnership with his uncle as a business manager. Janet and James had two more sons and a daughter. In 1902 Clark dismissed James Balderston from his position as a mill manager because he had objected to the lowering of the mill girls' wages. As a token of appreciation for his support the mill workers presented him with a clock.

Carpenters, Fife's yard, late 1800s. (From *Fairlie Past and Present*.)

At this time many changes were occurring in the village of Fairlie. The railway works, begun in 1878, were completed in June 1880, thereby opening up the village to the outside world. During construction of the railway, the influx of workers raised the population from 672 to 967; and 80 of the new residents were Gaelic-speaking. Special services in Gaelic were held in the Free Church and a 'shelter' was opened for the navvies and their families by the more prosperous members of the community whose committee was headed by Mrs Hunter of Hunterston. In 1877 there were reports of chaos due to general drunkenness in the village on the day the navvies received their pay. A pier was built in 1882 at the railhead of a short branch line from the main Largs to Glasgow route. This railway opened passenger and cargo trade, not only to and from the village, but also further afield through shipping to islands and elsewhere. The herring fleets also used this railhead as a port of call.

The Fife family took part in village life to the full. In 1879 the first Fairlie Annual Gathering was held. This took the form of a supper ball in Boag's new hall. The following year Mr Fife was chairman. The Misses Fife played the piano, there was dancing to a quadrille band and speeches and songs. The Fife sisters also entertained at the Parish Church Sunday school soirées. Mary Fife was the accompanist for the singers and played duets with her sister Jean. William senior, as a member of the County Council, was frequently involved in village affairs. During the years 1884–85 he tried to solve the problem of sewage pollution of the shore from the drainage pipes which led directly from the houses onto the beach. Apparently much of the problem was caused by the summer influx of people occupying 'the better class of houses'.

Fife's was not the only boat-building establishment in Fairlie. On the foreshore, just north of Fife's yard, was Boag's yard. Started by a former employee of the yard, it specialised in fishing skiffs but also built steam launches which were used for trips round the Isle of Cumbrae, and screw steamers and numerous yachts for the Coats and Clark families.

Another boat-building family with a difference was the Boyds. This time, however, the boats were model yachts, and again it was a truly family business. David Boyd assembled the hulls from strips of yellow pine, and spars were varnished by drawing them through a cloth soaked in varnish. A boy stepped the masts and the women cut the sails and set up the rigging. There were between 20,000 and 30,000 model yachts made over a period of 50 years. The smallest class 1 boat cost sixpence and the largest class was 2 feet 6 inches long and cost £2.

Model yacht racing was encouraged by William Fife senior, who watched open regattas from his yacht *May*. In spite of his skill in designing racing yachts it was always a sore point with him that he never managed to design a winning model yacht. Those designed and built by his workmen always won.

William senior did not have the opportunity to travel as widely as his son. However, he was interested to see other designers at work and to observe their construction methods. When William junior was a boy he took him to Cowes to see the *Fanny* under construction. She was built in 1829 for Mr James Meiklan, a member of the Royal Northern Yacht Club and a Scottish member of the Royal Yacht Squadron. *Fanny* was the first Cowes-built English-manned yacht to appear at the Clyde regattas. In fact William Fife senior had no need to travel – people came to see Mr Fife at Fairlie. The Marquis of Ailsa is said to have spent the good part of a year in Boag's Inn just across the road from the yard during the building of *Bloodhound*. She had been on the stocks for a Glasgow businessman who died while she was still in the framing stage. The Marquis asked Mr Fife not to part with her without first consulting him, and eventually he became the owner.

One of William senior's contemporaries was William Thomson, later to be known as Lord Kelvin. A keen yachtsman, in 1875 he had a villa built in Largs for summer vacations. When staying at Netherhall, he frequently visited Fife at Fairlie and discussed theory of design. Kelvin was interested in the behaviour of wetted as opposed to dry surfaces in motion. One day, on the beach, Lord Kelvin drew in the sand the lines of a yacht, which he said would beat all others. At the same time William senior outlined his ideas. Both were built, and it was said that Fife's design always beat Lord Kelvin's!

The senior Clyde yachtsmen by now held Fife in great esteem. At a dinner

Ailsa (1885). (Courtesy of Royal Northern & Clyde Yacht Club.)

in the St Enoch's Hotel in Glasgow in January 1884, the members of the Royal Northern Yacht Club presented him with a portrait in oils.

For a long time, while William junior was managing the Maidens boatyard, his father continued to design yachts at Fairlie. The Royal Northern Yacht Club came to William senior for a new club yacht. *Ailsa,* 60 tons, built in 1885, was, according to William senior, 'a bonnie round boat'. He still could not reconcile himself to the long lean look of new hull designs. Beautifully finished, as were all the Fife yachts, the upholstery was by Wylie and Lochead, a superior furniture company in Glasgow. The total cost of the boat was £2,400. The former Royal Northern Club yacht *Aeolus* was accepted in part payment by Mr Fife senior and brought back to Fairlie after 20 years.

Members of the Royal Northern Yacht Club were allowed to hire the club yacht for £5 per week and she came with a master, mate, steward and three paid hands. Her launch was not without problems, as she stuck at the end of the ways, something which happened frequently at Fairlie due to lack of water. In 1918 she was broken up, but her rudderhead and tiller can still be seen in the vestibule of the Royal Northern and Clyde Yacht Club at Rhu. Alongside *Ailsa,* a beamy smack was taking shape. Once the mainstay of the

William Fife III as a young man.

yard, these fishing boats were in less demand. In those early days trawling had already begun to damage the herring fishing industry on the Clyde.

The younger Fife was already setting his sights well beyond the Clyde and the small village of Fairlie. In a letter to the American journalist W.P. Stephens at the end of 1886, he included the lines of a cutter, deck and sail plans, and requested Mr Stephens to publish them in his magazine. The letter also expressed a desire for orders on the other side of the Atlantic and a suggestion that he would be willing to travel there and supervise building if necessary.

With the establishment of other designers, James Coats deserted Fife as a designer and turned to George Watson. However, he still had some of Watson's designs built at Fairlie. *Cruiser*, a 12-tonner, was built in 1886, and in 1888 the yard built another Watson design for him – the *Puffin*. Craftsmanship of Fairlie-built boats was still very desirable even if the design was not Fife's.

Meanwhile William junior was building some of his own designs at the Maidens yard. Mr J. George Clark of Paisley, Vice Commodore of the Clyde Corinthian Yacht Club, ordered a 20-tonner, *Clara,* which was launched in July 1884. Both she and the other yachts in the yard were launched behind schedule because of a winter hurricane which twice destroyed the shed with iron-working machinery. Together with *Lenore* she was one of Fife junior's most successful 'plank on edge' designs and easily defeated the crack English 20-tonner *Freda.*

The following year *Clara* was sold and raced in southern waters. She was then purchased by a Mr Charles Sweet, a barrister at Lincolns Inn, and taken to America by her sailing master, Captain John Barr of Gourock. She won the only race she sailed in her first season on the other side of the Atlantic. In the following year, 1886, she won all her races. The crew were all from the Clyde and her outstanding performance made the Americans sit up and take notice of Clyde designs, Clyde yards and the abilities of Clyde racing crews.

Still out of the Maidens yard, William junior produced another successful boat, *Vagrant.* A small two-ton racing yacht, 18 feet on the waterline, she was built in 1884 for Thomas Trocke to race in Dublin Bay. This was a perfect example of a 'plank on edge' design and greatly over-canvassed. Twenty-two feet overall and only five feet wide, she had a bowsprit 15 feet long. This was in two sections. Her keel was cast iron, which gave her stability and has helped to keep her from sagging over the years as a softer lead keel might have done.

This type of yacht soon became obsolete and the Dublin Bay Class ceased racing as a class in 1888. *Vagrant* still continued to sail in Irish waters and eventually was laid up in a boatyard near Dun Laoghaire. In 1979 Hal Sisk, a keen yachtsman and then chairman of the National Maritime Museum of Ireland, discovered her. He traced her history back to the Culzean boatyard at Maidens and decided to restore her. The restoration was carried out in the yard of Jack Tyrell at Arklow, the same yard which built Sir Francis Chichester's *Gipsy Moth.* To celebrate her 100th birthday, in 1984, Sisk sailed her back across the Irish Sea to Maidens. She then joined the fleet of preserved boats at the Scottish Maritime Museum at Irvine and is the oldest surviving Clyde racing yacht.

Still working at Maidens, William junior then produced a large 150-feet-long steel auxiliary steam yacht, the barquentine *Black Pearl.* She was owned by Lord Pembroke and taken to Fairlie for internal fitting. This may have been to assist his father in giving work to his employees in a lean year when the only new boat building in the Fairlie yard was the one ordered by the Royal Northern Yacht Club. The following year, at Maidens, Fife junior built *Cassandra*, another large steam yacht, for George Clark.

Round about 1886 William seems to have returned to the Fairlie yard and

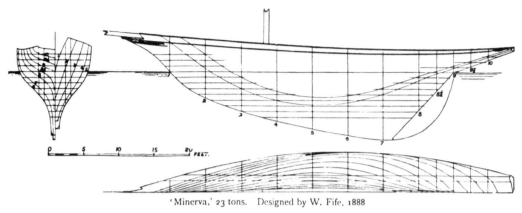

'Minerva,' 23 tons. Designed by W. Fife, 1888

Minerva (1888). (Courtesy of Badminton Library of Sports and Pastimes.)

entered into true partnership with his father, who was by now 65 years of age.

The following year William junior sailed to New York on the *City of Rome.* This vessel was a prototype of the three-funnelled liner. She had auxiliary sails and was regarded by some as the most beautiful ship of the whole era of steamships. While not the fastest ship to cross the Atlantic, her sleek lines and schooner bow united the grace of the clipper ship with the power of steam – a fitting ship to travel on for the designer of so many graceful yachts! William was accompanied by a friend, Mr James Grant, whose father had owned *Fairy Queen* and who now himself owned the Fife 20-tonner *Lenore,* built in 1882. They no doubt enjoyed the luxury of the gentlemen's smoking room with its parquet floor, pigskin upholstery and walls decorated with Japanese watercolours of birds and flowers. Was one of the purposes of the visit to where the New York Yacht Club held the America's Cup contest to study local weather and sea conditions? The young William may have been assessing the conditions under which an America's Cup challenger would have to sail. Mr James Grant, had his business in Glasgow and also a residence in Millport on the Isle of Greater Cumbrae. His father had been an original member of the Clyde Model Yacht Club and a faithful client of the Fairlie yard.

Lenore's nickname was 'Last of the Mohicans' because she was one of the last 'plank on edge' designs on the Clyde and had few similar boats to race against. However, in 1883 she maintained the reputation of the Clyde by thoroughly beating the flying *Freda*, best of the 20-tonners from the south. Her skipper at that time was Captain Hugh Morris of Fairlie, a nephew of the second William Fife. Following the tradition of yard carpenters, Captain Hugh Morris spent the slack summer building season on board racing yachts. The village was small, families large, and they intermarried without travelling

W. Fife III as an older man.

away from home. As a result the yard employed many 'members of the family'.

The success of *Clara* in American waters and the personal visit of Fife to New York may have been responsible for the order for *Minerva* in 1888. Built for Charles H. Tweed of New York, an associate of Charles Sweet, owner of *Clara,* her total cost was £1,000. At 40 feet on the waterline, and narrower and deeper than her American counterparts, she was to confound them with her speed for a number of years until an American designer, Nathanial Herreschoff, produced *Gloriana* to beat her.

Young William's reputation was now firmly established on both sides of the Atlantic and he was delighted with the reports of *Minerva*'s success sent to him by W.P. Stephens, the yachting journalist. In his reply to Mr Stephens he even offered to write something which might interest the readers of his journal. In the letter Fife added: 'Of course you can appreciate I have very little spare time on my hands.'

Indeed, from now on the yard was again extremely busy. There was a great increase in yacht building on the Clyde after a disastrous lull. The new linear rating Royal Yachting Association's rule with untaxed beam gave rise to new 20-raters which were large enough to put an old rater inside them. One such boat built that year was *Dragon*. A 20-rater, for Mr F.C. Hill, she had no trouble in winning against Watson's *Oreda* at the Clyde regattas, and later that season Fife junior sailed her in the south of England.

In 1889 William junior designed 18 boats, only two of which do not seem to have been built in the Fairlie yard. Some were fairly small, such as the 1½-raters for local racing, or the 2½-raters for the Bangor Yacht Club.

William was, of course, also a good helmsman. Anxious that his designs would be seen to be successful, he often sailed them himself for the owner, thereby ensuring that his design showed its best points and the client was satisfied that he had a fast boat. William junior had been disturbed by the fact that *Yvonne*, a 10-rater, had a very poor racing season. William was confident that his boat design was not to blame, and asked to be allowed to race her. He won three races out of four, and was delighted to show that it was not the fault of his design.

By now William junior was quite satisfied with the new YRA rule and in another letter to the journalist W.P. Stephens he urged him to try to persuade yachtsmen in America to adopt a classification by corrected length and similar to the Seawanhaka rule.

His hopes for exporting boats to America were dashed, as the resulting costs of freight and duty were too expensive, and he considered that a 40-foot boat was too small to sail across the Atlantic. One suggestion was to export the boat to Canada, pay an import duty of 10 per cent, and then sail the boat south to New York. However, he thought that the American Customs would put a stop to that. The conclusion was that it would be cheaper to have hulls built locally to his designs. His design fees were based on building costs at 7½ per cent of the first £5,000 and 5 per cent on anything above that sum.

At the end of 1889 William junior was still writing to W.P. Stephens in an attempt to get him to influence the Americans to adopt a measurement rule similar to that of the RYA, using length and sail area. He felt very strongly that the measurement of sail area gave room for cheating and that the square root of sail area was not the actual square root. He maintained that the current UK rule was a fair one and he suggested, as with the Seawanhaka rule, that actual sail area instead of square root of sail area would be better.

CHAPTER EIGHT

Down Under

In the 16th century Francis Drake had set out to circumnavigate the world and find *Terra Australis Incognita*. He never did find Australia, but two centuries later, in 1771, Captain James Cook landed at Botany Bay during his survey of the eastern Australian seaboard. Australia was first used by the British as a penal settlement. In 1788 the first settlers were the unhappy prisoners of the First Fleet destined for the penal settlement at Port Jackson, New South Wales. About 1820, free settlers began to arrive in this area. The last convict ship to Australia discharged her prisoners in Western Australia in 1868.

In the beginning, most of the non-convict settlers were naval, military or administrative personnel. Given the sea-faring nature of the colonists, it is not surprising that the first sailing races were held in the magnificent 12 square miles of sheltered waters within Port Jackson Heads. In the early days of sailing in these waters, small open boats with centreboards were popular. As the new colonists acquired wealth, the boats became larger and yacht clubs were formed, some of which were very exclusive. The first yacht clubs in Australia were the Royal Sydney Yacht Squadron, founded in 1863, and the Prince Alfred Yacht Club in 1867.

It is a long way from the small village of Fairlie in Scotland to Sydney, Australia. In 1864 the 20-ton *Vivid,* designed by William Fife senior and built at Fairlie, made the passage in a record-breaking time of 119 days, which included an 11-day stop at the Cape of Good Hope. She had been built in 1859 as *Scourge* for an Irish yachtsman and won the Irish Cup that year. Subsequently, in 1861, two Dublin Bay yachtsmen bought her, after which she was sold to Mr Sydney Burt of Sydney, who wanted to race her against Australian-built boats. *Vivid* left Liverpool on 31 October and met every variety of weather from calms to hurricanes. Her enforced stay at the Cape was caused by repairs to leaking fresh water tanks, and the voyage was marred by the on-board death of the first mate before reaching the Cape. In spite of all these setbacks *Vivid* covered the 16,000 miles, averaging 134.5 miles per day – a fitting tribute to the craftsmanship of the Fairlie carpenters and the sound construction of Fife boats.

Back in Britain, in 1875, the application of new scientific theories in naval architecture and yacht design had resulted in E.H. Bentall's daring and innovative design of *Jullanar,* with cut-away ends. British yachtsmen regarded this as a 'first'. However, seven years previously, in 1868, and 16,000 miles away in Australia, Richard Hayes Harnett had already designed *Australian,* with cut-away ends. Dan Sheehy, of Wooloomooloo Bay, built *Australian* for a Mr French. Because she was radically different she was not accepted for measurement under the old Thames Measurement Rule.

The Sydney Yacht Squadron register rule was specific in declaring that boats had to measure to the old Thames Measurement Rule; *Australian* was not eligible to register. The consequence was the formation of the Prince Alfred Yacht Club, which catered for smaller boats. There is a familiar ring to this, as with the formation of the Clyde Model Yacht Club for owners whose boats did not measure up to the Royal Northern Yacht Club specifications of the day.

In 1874 a Scot by the name of Robert Logan emigrated to New Zealand with his wife and six children. He had been a boat builder in Steele's yard on the Clyde and was reputed to have served his apprenticeship at Fife's yard in Fairlie. When he fist arrived in New Zealand he worked for a local boat builder before establishing his own yard at Auckland in 1878. Surrounded by a plentiful supply of excellent timber and with the knowledge of boat building he acquired on the Clyde, it is little wonder that he became known as the 'Fife of Australasia'. In fact he built boats to Fife designs, and it is reasonable to suppose that his own designs would mirror those of the Fife yachts constructed in his yard.

Across the water in Australia there was an abundant supply of suitable wood for boat construction. Although cedar, white mahogany and gum were suitable for the hulls and frames, Kauri pine for decks had to be imported from New Zealand.

In 1884, George Ellis of Sydney built a truly remarkable design, *Kelpie,* using teak on blue gum frames. *Kelpie* was built in the same year as *Vagrant,* which was built in Scotland at Culzean. Both were typical 'plank on edge' designs. Apparently the owner of *Kelpie,* John Fairfax, was not happy with the result, and never took delivery of this boat. After languishing in the Ellis yard for nine years she was re-launched in 1893. The new owners were the Scottish brothers, Eric and Russell Sinclair, a doctor and an engineer.

After a period of 86 years, numerous refits, alterations, and sailing in the really testing conditions of the waters between Australia and Tasmania, *Kelpie* was sold in 1979 to John and Helen Wood. She was re-launched in 1988 after a complete restoration, which took three years. Further restoration was delayed till 1990, and she is now sailing again. It is the hope of her owner that she will one day be preserved in the Sydney Maritime Museum. Her counterpart, *Vagrant,* is at the Scottish Maritime Museum in Irvine, Scotland.

Another Fife yacht imported to race with the Sydney Yacht Squadron in 1886 was *Iolanthe,* built in 1883 to the order of a Mr Howard. A modified 'plank on edge' design, she was sailed from Fairlie to Liverpool, and then made an easy passage on the deck of a ship to Australia. She had plenty of freeboard, a long counter, and was expected to provide strong competition for the local boats.

George Clark, Vice Commodore of the Clyde Corinthian Yacht Club together with his brother Norman, set out on a round the world cruise in 1889 on board their steam yacht *Cassandra. Cassandra* was designed by William Fife junior and built at Culzean in 1886. Norman Clark took along with him his small lugsail *Nellie,* which was stowed on deck. This lugsail was also designed by Fife junior and built at Fairlie. When the brothers reached Sydney, *Nellie* distinguished herself by beating the Sydney Harbour lugsails. This was yet another advertisement for Fife-designed yachts, and more orders for Fife designs followed.

J.G. Fairfax, one of the proprietors of the *Sydney Herald,* commissioned a Fife design in 1891. *Bul-Bul,* a 2½-rater was built by T. Cubbit at Sydney. This class provided excellent racing and matches were arranged between *Bul-Bul* and *Bronzewing,* designed by G.L. Watson. That same year J.G. Fairfax also had the 80-ton auxiliary steam yacht *Isis* built to a Fife design by W. Reekes at Sydney. The following year William Fife junior sent the design of the 31-foot *Alexa* to A.P. Wyly, who had it built locally in Australia.

It was not only in Sydney that Fife boats made their mark. In Hobart, Tasmania, F.N. Clarke was a faithful client and ordered no less than five individual designs which were built by R. Inches' yard at Hobart. The first, in 1894, was a cutter, 21 feet on the waterline, and appropriately named *Fairlie.* The second, built in 1896, was a similar yacht called *Ailsa.* In 1898 a design for a 25-foot waterline cutter was obtained, and again built by Inches. In this case the ironwork and frames were shipped out to Tasmania. This boat was *Fairlie II.* A fourth design, received in 1901, was for a 30-foot waterline yawl, and the last one, in 1902, was for a 30-foot waterline cutter named *Fairlie III.* Perhaps Fife designs were popular in Australia because they could stand up to the pounding received when sailing in their big seas and the frequently stormy weather encountered on the Eastern seaboard and in the waters between Australia and Tasmania.

By now, in 1895, Robert Logan, who had established his boatyard at Auckland, New Zealand, received a Fife design, which he built for a Mr Turnbull. His yachts were in great demand and it is possible that he may have tried to emulate the Fife design in his own boats. They were of an unusual triple diagonal construction, normally only found in lifeboats in this country and were able to with stand the stormy Southern oceans. One such design may have been the 43-foot *Yeulba* ('Flying Snake') built in

1909 and said to be a Fife design although there is no record of it in Fife's yard book. Even though boats were not built at Fairlie, designs which were sent abroad were usually listed.

Western Australia was not to be outdone by the older New South Wales colony on the Eastern seaboard. A yacht club was eventually established in Perth. A Mr Burnside and a Mr Stevens ordered a Fife design for a 30-foot waterline cutter, *Genesta,* which was built by A.E. Brown of Perth in 1895. R.B. Burnside was a Chief Justice and Commodore of the Royal Perth Yacht Club. *Genesta* was sailed till 1947, when she was scrapped and sunk in ten fathoms off the yacht club.

Meanwhile, in the state of Victoria, another Fife design was being built for Mr G.F. Garrard at McFarlane's yard in Port Adelaide. This 38-foot waterline yawl was named *Sayonara.* In 1903 her owner, Alfred Gollin, issued a challenge to New South Wales for a cup to be donated by himself – the Sayonara Cup. It was won that year by *Sayonara* herself, and from then on has been a trophy competed for by Victoria and New South Wales. *Sayonara* retained the cup in 1907 and 1909. She would not be the last Fife boat to win this trophy.

Over the years a number of Fife designs found their way to Australia and were built by local yards. In the early years of the 20th century two remarkable designs were built in Sydney. The first, *Awanui* (1907), was owned by A.C. Saxton, a timber magnate and one-time Vice Commodore of the Prince Alfred Yacht Club. Because he was a timber merchant his boat builders were allowed to have the pick of Kauri pine imported from New Zealand.

Awanui, a 36-rater, won numerous prizes in ocean racing and in 1910 was sold to a Walter Marks, eventually passing to two further owners while undergoing a partial rebuild in Tasmania in 1928. In 1967 she was bought as *Eun-na-Mara* by a Mr Norman Cocks, member of Perth Yacht Club. He carried out more alterations and she continued to win races. In 1987 he held an 80th birthday party for her, when she was toasted in champagne and beer by those on board 'until the sun was way down below the yardarm'.

Mr Saxton had several racing yachts, all called *Awanui.* In 1925 he had another Fife design, *Awanui IV,* built for offshore racing by Hays and Son at Sydney. Sadly she was to be the cause of his death. In 1926, while racing off the south coast of New South Wales, he was struck on the head by the boom and fell overboard; his body was never recovered. After this she had several owners and eventually, in 1993, her name was changed to *Carina.* The present owners acquired her in 1980 and she is still afloat. It is interesting to note that all her hull planks are full length with no joints, a bonus for the shipbuilder who had his pick of the timber available.

Another Fife yacht with a distinguished career, no longer sailing in Australia

Morna (1913). (Courtesy of John Bilsey.)

but cherished by her owner, John Bisley, is *Morna,* a magnificent 64-foot auxiliary cutter originally built for the distinguished surgeon Sir Alexander McCormick by Morrison and Sinclair of Sydney in 1913. She was named after his daughter, who later became Lady Anderson, wife of Sir Colin Anderson of the P & O Line. Sir Alexander used her as a day sailer and her racing career did not start till the thirties. When Sir Alexander McCormick left Australia in the 1920s she passed to a new owner, newspaper tycoon Sir Frank Packer, and then to Sir Claude Plowman, a radio manufacturer. Sir Claude raced her in the Sydney to Hobart race in 1946, 1947 and 1948, achieving the fastest time in each race.

In 1954 the brothers F. and J. Livingston bought her and renamed her *Kurrewa IV.* From 1954 till 1960 they entered her in six Sydney to Hobart races and achieved the fastest time in four of the races. After that she retired from racing, and until 1977 the boat was laid up and not maintained. Fourteen years of hard racing had affected her frames but the present owner hopes to be able to restore her, and hopefully there will be another veteran Fife lady to grace Australian waters.

Before he left Australia, Sir Alexander McCormick had acquired another Fife-designed yacht built in Fairlie, the 73-foot schooner *Ada,* which he sailed back to Australia. The Stuart brothers sailed her in Sydney harbour in the early 1950s. Subsequently purchased by Mr P. Warner in the late 1950s and renamed *Astor,* she raced in the Sydney to Hobart race 1960–64, taking line honours three times. Restored to first-class condition she is now owned by Richard and Lani Straman of Newport Beach.

Prior to the First World War the metre classes were beginning to be popular in Europe, and the Commodore of the Royal Sydney Yacht Club imported plans and specifications of these new classes but no one was interested. Metre boats did not begin to appear in Australia till after the war. Fife-designed *Vanessa II,* an eight-metre, built by Hayes at Sydney for Percy Arnot, was raced against other eight-metres and local designs which were slightly larger.

Money was scarce after the war, and with the depression looming the sailing fraternity started to look at smaller boats. On 7 July 1933 the Sydney Yacht Racing Association met and resolved that 'the necessary steps be taken by the delegates from the associated clubs to establish a six-metre one-design class, such design to be that of Messrs William Fife and Son and numbered 790'.

Fife Yard Number 790 was *Toogooloowoo II* for W.S. Dagg of Melbourne, and built by J.J. Savage. Bill Dagg had been trying for some time to win the Northcote Cup for the state of Victoria from the holders, New South Wales. In 1931 he challenged with *Toogooloowoo II,* and was narrowly beaten after sailing into a wind hole and was becalmed near the finishing line. The following year he won the cup. In 1935 *Toogooloowoo II* successfully defended the cup against the six-metre *Sjo Ro.* From the start of the Second World War in 1939 there was a lapse of 11 years before there was another challenge match, and at the end, in 1946, *Toogooloowoo II* held off the challengers but lost the match in 1947 to a Norwegian-designed six-metre *Avenger.*

The Sayonara Cup was responsible for the appearance of another Fife-designed eight-metre in Australia about 1954. *Saskia I* was brought to Australia by William Northam for the express purpose of challenging for the Sayonara Cup. She succeeded in winning the cup on several occasions.

Saskia I was built in 1931 for Arthur S. Young, when he successfully defended the Seawanhaka Cup for Britain against the Americans. The crew was composed of Arthur Young, John G. Stephen, Major Charles MacAndrew and two paid hands. In 1936, under the ownership of Mr K. Preston and Mr R. Steele, she was chosen to represent Britain at the Olympic Games. Unlike the other Olympic contenders, she did not undergo any trials. It was judged that her record of 15 firsts, 13 seconds and six thirds out of 60

Saskia (1930). (Courtesy of Sandy Neilands.)

starts was sufficient for her to qualify and represent Britain in the eight-metre class. Unfortunately she did not win an Olympic medal. After the Games she was sold in 1937 and eventually made her way to Australia. The man responsible for her appearance down under was W. ('Bill') Northam, an alderman of the City of Sydney Council. An all-round sportsman, Northam had been a racing driver in the 1920s and 1930s, and gave up in about 1932 and became a very good golfer. It was not until 1952 that he actually took up sailing. In 1953 he decided to challenge for the Sayonara Cup, which was held by the state of Victoria and had not been challenged for 24 years. *Saskia I* was purchased because the boat which challenged had to sail to Victoria and a Fife-built eight-metre was considered fit for the challenge.

The challenge took place in 1955. The journey to Melbourne was made in dreadful conditions with 65 mph gales and took 13½ days instead of seven. In spite of this, *Saskia* easily defeated the Victorian defender and another Tasmanian challenger.

The following year she beat the Victorian and Tasmanian challengers again. Northam decided to turn his attention to the Sydney to Hobart race and sold *Saskia* to R.E. Jeffreys. Her ultimate owners in Australia were Drs John and Michael Steffen.

CHAPTER NINE
The Golden Age

The beginning of a new decade saw the yard at its busiest. Men were no longer paid off in spring at the end of May and work carried on throughout the summer. The second William Fife's fame had spread abroad and in addition to design commissions from America he was now designing and building for European clients. This busy period started in 1890 when the yard built 14 boats, and in addition William junior designed nine others which were built in the USA, Finland, Southampton and in other Clyde yards. At the same time many enquiries came from America but indecision about measurement rules resulted in orders coming to nothing. Although this was fortuitous – the yard was overwhelmed with work and some designs were still being delivered late. This situation annoyed William junior, as he did not want this fact to be made public.

One satisfied client was Mr Allen Ames of New York, for whom he designed the 40-foot class cutter *Yama*. He had to turn down the request to have the frames made at Fairlie, again because the yard was too busy. The journalist W.P. Stephens undertook to supervise the construction of *Yama* carried out by Wintringham at New York. This successful arrangement led William to try to persuade him to supervise the building of a 40-foot cutter for Mr J. G. Beecher. Mr Stephens kept on sending potential clients in his direction and William was delighted to send quotations, but always, as a canny Scot, refused to disclose critical design dimensions until firm orders were received. Never one to let the grass grow under his feet, the younger Fife was off to America at the beginning of August to see how *Yama* performed in the Lakes races, and he made a request to sail at least one match on her. His journey across the Atlantic was once again on the luxurious three-funnelled liner *City of Rome,* owned by the Anchor line. Was he a creature of habit or did he prefer to travel on a liner with an acre of glistening sail rather than on one of the new completely steam-driven vessels?

Great changes were taking place in the yard. Over the years there had been a reluctance to make any kind of alteration to the hallowed ground where so many splendid boats had been built. It was almost as though there was a superstition that to make changes would alter the spell which ensured that Fairlie yachts would continue to be fast and successful. However, in 1890 the yard was modernised. A draughting loft, new office accommodation and covered working areas were built. The yard was also completely surrounded by a palisade of planks. The younger Fife was now moving with the times and modernising the business. It is reasonable to suppose that the greatly increased workload contributed to the new layout of the yard. His father was now nearly 70 years of age, still designing a few boats and helping to meet the yard's increased commitments. The main responsibility of running the business now rested with William junior. Truth be told he would have preferred to have someone else managing everyday detail and problems while freeing him to work at the drawing board. Times had changed in more ways than one. The designing of yachts was now committed to paper instead of lines being taken from wooden half models, or using a bar of soap, as in the case of *Fidelio,* a 110-ton yawl designed by Mr Tennant, a partner in a chemical business in Glasgow.

Fife designs were popular with Irish yachtsmen. Robertson's of Sandbank built four Belfast Lough One Designs for the Bangor club. These were 18-foot 1-rater lugs with iron ballast and comparatively small sails built at a cost of £60. One of these little boats, *Miss Mollie,* was owned by Colonel R.G. Sharman-Crawford, a keen Irish yachtsman who became the Vice Commodore of the Royal Ulster Yacht Club. He was so delighted with this boat that he became a regular client of the Fifes. He was on board both the Fife-designed *Shamrock I* and *Shamrock III* with his fellow countryman, Sir Thomas Lipton, during the America's Cup races.

There was more than one class of Belfast Lough One Design. Class I had a waterline length of 25 feet, an overall length of 37 feet, a cutter rig, and was designed by William Fife in 1897. Eight were built by J. Hilditch at Carrickfergus and named after birds.

William Fife also designed a 15-feet waterline, 24-feet overall class referred to as Class II, which were built by A. Hutchinson & Co., John Hilditch and P. McKeown. Among the Fife-designed Class II boats were *La Poupée* and *Shulah.*

Linton Hope describes a Belfast Lough One Design class II which was designed by A. Mylne and which had a waterline length of 20 feet, an overall length of 31 feet and a sloop rig, also built by Hilditch.

The Dublin Bay Sailing Club introduced another popular Irish one design class in 1898. The boats were very similar to the Belfast Lough type, with a waterline of 25 feet, an overall length of 38 feet, and had cutter rig. They too were designed by William Fife.

Earlier, in 1887, the Water Wag Association had been founded in Dublin Bay with the object of racing in identical boats – one of the first attempts to form a one-design class. These small centre-board boats were 13 feet long and were sharp at both ends, with flattish bottoms to enable them to be beached easily. The Fife-designed *Rose* enjoyed a very successful season in

Belfast Lough One Design 25 Feet LWL. (Courtesy of Royal Northern & Clyde Yacht Club.)

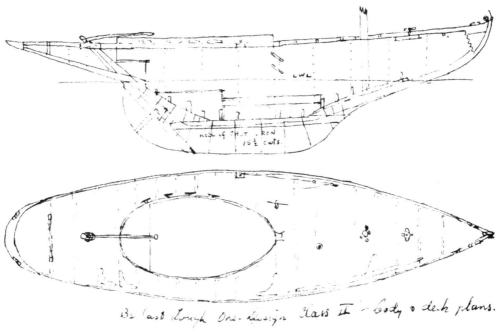

Belfast Lough One Design 15 Feet LWL. (Courtesy of Terry Needham.)

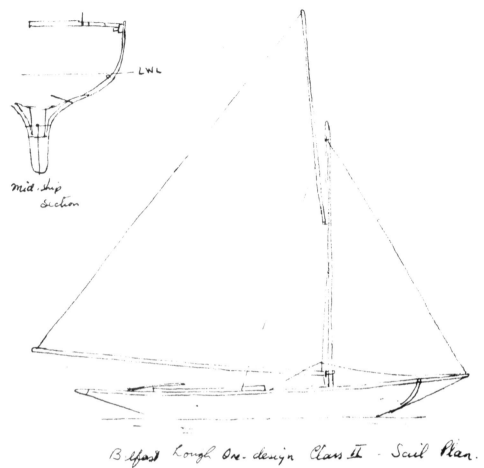

LWL

mid.ship Section

Belfast Lough One-design Class II - Sail Plan.

Belfast Lough One Design 15 feet LWL sail plan. (Courtesy of Terry Needham.)

1890. In 1900 a class of 'New Water Wags' was developed, designed by J. Doyle of Kingstown. They were 14 feet long and had a transom stern.

William Fife was responsible for the design of another Irish Class, the Dublin Bay 25-foot class, in 1892. Other Dublin Bay classes were designed by Doyle, Kingstown, who was responsible for the 'Colleens' in 1897, and Mylne, who produced the 21-foot class in 1902.

The following year was yet another bumper one for the yard. Twenty-five designs were produced, but the yard had only the capacity to build 12 of them. This huge workload meant that many were built elsewhere. Small-boat racing was also becoming more popular on the Clyde. Sons of the 'big boat' owners were eager to race against each other in something smaller, which could be sailed by themselves as amateurs without paid hands. Being smaller, the boats could be replaced yearly to obtain the required performance and results. Five 2½-raters were built for the young keen racing set, which included the brothers W.C. and J. Connell, R. Inglis and N. Clark.

Dragon II (1891) later named *Molly*. (Courtesy of Royal Northern & Clyde Yacht Club.)

In 1891, *Dragon II,* for F.C. Hill was launched. This new *Dragon* was four feet longer on the waterline, had nine square feet less sail area, but a much larger mainsail than the 1889 *Dragon.* Faster on every point of sailing, and commanded by Captain Ben Parker, with a crew from Itchen Ferry, she had 27 firsts and three seconds in 30 races. She lost her mast and bowsprit in one of the races when in the leading position, but still managed to come in second.

William Fife had been very disappointed that *Dragon I,* when two years old, was attracting offers of only £750, which he thought was below market price. He therefore looked across the Atlantic and tried to get his friend Stephens to persuade some American yachtsmen to offer at least £800 for the 20-rater. She was eventually sold in 1891 to Mr T. Ellis and renamed *Idalia.*

William was now beginning to experiment with composite structure. *Thalia,* a 40-rater, built for Mr J.A. Inglis of the Pointhouse yard, had alternate frames of wood and angle steel strengthened by steel diagonals. The deck was of teak and finished to the usual high standard. Launched by means of the new patented dock at high water at midnight, she slipped smoothly into the water, watched by a crowd of people from Largs and Fairlie. Such was the pride in yachts built in the yard that all the villagers took keen interest in launches and the subsequent performance of the boats.

Yacht in floating dock. (Courtesy of Scottish Maritime Museum.)

Launching of larger craft had always been a problem at Fairlie due to shallow water, even at high tide. In 1894 the 20-rater *Luna,* for F.B. Jameson, was launched by floating her off the beach using two pontoons. Never wasteful, the Fifes had constructed these from the hull of the 50-ton *Aeolus,* built 33 years previously for C.T. Couper and then owned by the Royal Northern Yacht Club for 20 years. She was taken back by the Fife yard as part payment for the club's new boat *Ailsa.* Later, the launching problem was solved by moving the boat into a shallow draft, flat-bottomed, wooden dry dock that could be floated and towed to deeper water. This finally avoided embarrassment when vessels became stuck in the sand during the launch, just after the ceremony had been performed.

Still recognised today, the fine craftsmanship of the Fairlie carpenters was one of the main features of boats built in the yard. A 23-foot Clyde lug class built for Mr Adam Teacher had its planks so perfectly fitted that no caulking was required, except a single strand of cotton along the centre of the planks. From then on, the Teacher family had all their boats built by Fife.

A schooner on yard slip. Probably *Ada*. (Courtesy of Scottish Maritime Museum.)

The loss of a friend and client of the Fifes occurred in May 1891, with the death of Mr James Grant, owner of *Lenore,* one of the few remaining original members of the Clyde Model Yacht Club. That same year, the end of the racing season brought more orders. The phenomenal success of *Dragon II,* and the fact that designs were being sent abroad to be built by local boatbuilders, resulted in a further 21 boats originating from the drawing board in Fairlie. Two were built by H. Staunton of Toronto, one in Nova Scotia, one in New York and one in Australia. The colonies were not William's only source of foreign orders. Other designs were commissioned to be built in Ireland and Germany. Sharman-Crawford ordered a 5-rater, *Red Lancer,* which turned out to be a crack racer in 1893. Mr Peter Donaldson, a faithful client ordered a new 10-rater, *Yseult.* He and his brother Robert had owned a string of small racing yachts from the yard.

Continued success on the racing scene also ensured a full order book for 1893, again not all built in Fairlie. *Lais,* a 40-rater for John Gretton, was built by Hanson & Sons at Cowes. *Calluna,* William junior's first really big racing cutter of 106 feet on the waterline, for a syndicate headed by Peter Donaldson, was built at Pointhouse. *Infanta,* a cutter for an American client, was built at Rhode Island. Two of the best boats in the racing circuit that year were built at Fairlie. Both were 20-raters for keen racing men, and both enhanced William's reputation even further. *Dragon III* was the champion 20-rater in her first season, when she won 31 prizes in 34 starts. She was built to replace *Dragon II* for F.C. Hill. During that season she was also

Bow carving of the Fife Dragon. (Courtesy Patricia Kohn.)

shortened by ten inches and had 45 square feet of sail added to match the alterations made to her formidable adversary *Deirdre. Zinita,* another 20-rater from 1893, for W.C.S. Connell, a partner in the Cunard line, was, according to Fife, 'the best sort of boat by a long way, being fast, very strongly built and a wonderful sea boat with a fair amount of accommodation inside'.

To date, one of the distinguishing features of a Fife-designed yacht built at the Fairlie yard is that of a dragon's head carved on the bow, continuing as a thin line to the stern, where it ends in a wheatsheaf. The whole carving is gilded. The dragon is not seen on early Fife boats, and in fact makes its first appearance about the time when the series of *Dragons* were built for Mr Hill.

An interesting comment is made in *The Field* magazine of 1890: 'All yachts at Fairlie have fiddle bows. As a consequence some carving is wanted for stem heads. Indeed ships carvers after a long depression are having a boom in this artistic form of business.'

The dragon can be clearly seen on white painted hulls, and in fact until about 1898 yachts were usually varnished and painted black or another dark colour. Photographic records of Fife boats suggest that white marine paints were first used c. 1890. It may have been the phenomenal racing success of the three *Dragons* which prompted William to use the dragon logo as his trademark. Worldwide, even today, a yacht sporting the golden dragon immediately draws the eye to its graceful lines, and it is instantly recognised as a boat built by William Fife & Son.

The 1893 season was one which would go down in history as a memory of the 'Golden Era' of yachting. The Fife yard, as always, was in the forefront of competition to produce the best results. *Calluna* had been built with the intention of defending various cups in the Solent against the American Herreschoff-designed *Navahoe* and as a trial horse for *Valkyrie II,* Lord Dunraven's challenger for the America's Cup. Fife called her 'my unlucky boat'. The skipper was Archie Hogarth, who had proved adept at handling smaller craft, but this was his first big racing yacht. She won only ten prizes in 36 races, and it was felt that she would have performed better if she had had a narrower beam and an extra two feet on the waterline.

The *Navahoe* did no better on the British side of the Atlantic. She had been built as a cruising boat and was not a racing machine. That year saw a revival of big cutter racing, which was soon to disappear. Five large boats appeared on the racing circuit. The Watson-designed *Britannia,* for the Prince of Wales, *Valkyrie II,* for Lord Dunraven, *Satanita,* designed by Mr J. Soper for A.D. Clark, and the Fife-designed *Calluna* and *Iverna,* which was designed by Alexander Richardson for the Irish yachtsman, Mr John Jameson, who fitted her out that year, to complete the quintet.

The opening regatta of big-cutter racing was held in May at the Royal Thames Yacht Club on the Thames estuary. The first contest showed that the two new Watson boats, *Britannia* and *Valkyrie II,* were evenly matched. Embarrassingly *Calluna* went aground and stuck in the mud. All through the season *Britannia* and *Valkyrie II* battled it out, and often, in their anxiety to vie with each other, forgot that the rest of the boats in the race would take advantage of their private contests. At the end of the season *Britannia* was held to be the best all-round boat.

That season was also remarkable for the number of broken masts and spars. *Britannia* had to replace three masts, one topmast, two bowsprits and a gaff; *Calluna,* two masts, one main boom and one gaff; *Valkyrie II,* one mast, one topmast, one boom and one bowsprit; *Satanita,* one bowsprit and one boom. Such occurrences added to the enormous cost of maintaining boats of that size and their crews. Travel round the coast to each event could only be afforded by the very rich. The very keen competition between owners resulted in pushing boats and crews to the limit when racing, thereby increasing the chance of broken gear. The year 1893 was particularly bad for breakages, and poor quality wood was blamed. It is therefore understandable that big-cutter racing would be on the decline.

The America's Cup challenge by Lord Dunraven with *Valkyrie II* had been accepted. The reappearance of the big cutters then followed, and was probably due to a desire to give *Valkyrie II* some good racing before she went across to America. In addition perhaps, owning a large yacht, which raced with the Prince of Wales's yacht, gave opportunity to owners to mix socially with royalty, which they could not otherwise hope to do in the normal course of events.

The culmination of the yachting season that year was the America's Cup races held in October. Lord Dunraven with his *Valkyrie II* challenge had a full summer of competitive racing before undertaking the 30-day voyage across the Atlantic. The sea crossing had to be undertaken because of the racing condition which included the requirement that the challenger should sail across the Atlantic. This meant that challenging British boats had to be much sturdier and more seaworthy than anything the Americans might build for coastal racing. Public interest in the contest was worldwide and intense. It has been reported that in New York the stock market was deserted and business was at a standstill during the races. Lord Dunraven, a notable sportsman and yachting enthusiast, was a popular contender for this contest. Because of the popularity of this event, waters where the races took place were crowded with spectator craft, and police boats had to keep them away from the start. They could not have been very effective because *Valkyrie*'s crew had to hold up a large notice saying 'Keep further off'. The American defender *Vigilant* won all three races. With a view to continuing the contest in 1894, *Valkyrie II* was left to winter in America.

Valkyrie II's sails were greatly admired in America, which enhanced the reputation of the sailmakers Lapthorn and Ratsey. This sail loft was so advanced that the sails of *Britannia,* the best all-round yacht of the big cutter quintet, kept their shape till the end of the season in spite of all the hard sailing throughout that year. On the other hand, the British found little to admire in American yacht design. All the American challengers had lifting keels and the British were not convinced that this gave any advantage over fixed keels. The conditions under which the challenge was accepted were also considered to be unfair, especially the requirement to sail across the Atlantic. It annoyed the British that the America's Cup rules were framed in such a way as to put the challenger at a disadvantage. Two years later a second challenge was to prove even more embarrassing for the British yachting fraternity, and in particular for Lord Dunraven.

CHAPTER TEN
'The Auld Mug'

It has been said that sport is 'war without weapons' and 'all is fair in love and war'. These sayings could not be truer in the case of the America's Cup races. Over the years no other sporting event has aroused so much emotion, so much public interest in the outcome, or caused so much money to be expended in order to win a mere piece of silverware.

Lord Dunraven was an eminent sportsman and one-time war correspondent of the *Daily Telegraph.* He frequently sailed on other top-class racing yachts such as *Irex,* owned by a friend, the prominent Irish yachtsman John Jameson, and is perhaps better known for his attempts to win the America's Cup in his trio of *Valkyries.*

In 1888 Lord Dunraven challenged for the America's Cup through the Royal Yacht Squadron, and although the challenge was accepted it fell through because of conditions imposed by the New York Yacht Club. *Valkyrie I,* which was a good racing cutter, and built for this challenge which never took place, was eventually sold to the Archduke Carl Stephen in 1892.

In the summer of 1892 the determined Lord Dunraven negotiated again with the New York Yacht Club and this time the challenge was accepted. *Valkyrie II,* designed by G.L. Watson, was dogged by misfortune. Before the challenge the boat was raced at summer regattas in British waters. She had a number of accidents which involved broken gear and the loss of a crewmember overboard but still she proved to be faster than *Britannia* and *Satanita.* Although the performance of *Valkyrie II* had been excellent in British waters, the races for the America's Cup were disappointing due to the general lack of wind during the event, and also because she unfortunately split her spinnaker twice in the last race. Although *Valkyrie II* did not bring back the cup, Lord Dunraven's challenge had succeeded in altering some of the conditions for future challengers. After wintering in America, *Valkyrie II* returned to the Clyde, where she met with her last and final accident. She was sunk by *Satanita* in 17 fathoms of water off Hunters Quay at the start of the Mudhook Yacht Club regatta at Clyde Week. At this stage Lord Dunraven had become a popular figure on both sides of the Atlantic. As war correspondent for the *Daily Telegraph* he made friendships with Generals Sherman and Sheridan, and the Americans admired him for his spirit. He was an active sportsman with other learned qualities in addition to his journalistic writing. He held an extra masters ticket, he wrote works on navigation, his expertise extended to designing some of his yachts, and he was a national hero because he had challenged for the America's Cup. What followed after his challenge in 1895 with *Valkyrie III* was unexpected and totally unsportsmanlike. Another side of the popular yachtsman's character was revealed.

During the challenge, in the first race, Lord Dunraven complained about obstruction by the spectator fleet on the starting line. This was perfectly within reason as there were no official patrol boats to keep the vast numbers of spectator boats at a reasonable distance from the competing yachts. The constant movement of these craft added to the obstruction by causing very broken water. At the start of the second race *Valkyrie III* hit *Defender* and carried on to win the race. Naturally *Defender* protested, and the protest was upheld. *Valkyrie III* clearly had been in the wrong. There were plenty of witnesses and photographic evidence as proof. It is surprising that such a good sportsman as Lord Dunraven should have sailed on without first verifying that there was no damage to *Defender*. After the disqualification, *Defender* offered to re-sail the race but this was turned down by *Valkyrie's* owner.

Then came the unpleasant event of the series. After crossing the starting line in the third race, *Valkyrie III* retired because Lord Dunraven accused *Defender* of adding additional ballast after the boats had been measured, giving *Defender* the advantage of another three or four feet on the waterline. He insisted on re-measurement, which was carried out the following day, and it was found that there had been no change. Lord Dunraven persisted with his accusations after he returned to Britain. An enquiry was held by the New York Yacht Club, and subsequently *Defender* was found to be innocent, and Lord Dunraven's name was removed from the list of their club members. He had already sent his resignation to the club before this occurred.

In spite of losing the challenge and losing the respect of his American friends, Lord Dunraven still had supporters who felt he had been wronged. Perhaps they could not accept that someone who knew so much about the sport should stoop so low as to try to win by means other than fair sailing. There was no evidence whatsoever that *Defender* had added extra ballast, and it is thought that the repacking and distribution of ballast before the race was misconstrued. The one good outcome of all this was that the US Senate passed a bill to keep spectator boats away from racing yachts in the America's Cup, thereby improving conditions for future challengers.

It was against this background of acrimonious international rivalry that Thomas Lipton was to take the stage as the next long-running contender for the cup. Lipton was a self-made man who had become a millionaire. He owned tea plantations and pork-packing factories which supplied his chain of grocery shops. He had come a long way since his days as a New York dock labourer. In early life he had shown no particular interest in yachting, which was not surprising considering he was personally responsible for the vast business empire he created. In 1887, the year before Lord Dunraven made his first challenge, Lipton had expressed a desire to sponsor an 'all Irish' challenge for the cup. At that time his dream was to have a boat designed and built in Ireland and crewed by Irishmen. Unfortunately he was unable to find an Irish designer with relevant experience and the scheme was abandoned.

In 1898 Lipton's became a public company and Thomas had much more time to himself to pursue his interests. He bought the steam yacht *Aegusa*, which had been built two years earlier by Scott and Co. of Greenock, and renamed her *Erin*. That same year he issued his first challenge for the 'Auld Mug' to the New York Yacht Club. Although he was a member of the Royal Clyde Yacht Club his challenge was issued through the Royal Ulster Yacht Club. A special committee from the club accompanied him to New York to discuss the conditions of the challenge. Among those present were the Vice-Commodore R.G. Sharman-Crawford and William Fife junior, who had been chosen by Lipton as the designer. It may be that Colonel Duncan Neil or Sharman-Crawford may have influenced Lipton in his choice of designer.

The challenger *Shamrock I* was designed by Fife and built by Thornycroft and Co. in 1899. Lipton chose to have the boat built by this firm on the Solent as it was experienced in composite construction as used on lightweight torpedo boats. *Shamrock I* was of composite metal construction with steel frames, manganese bronze plating below the waterline, and aluminium alloy topsides. She was launched on 26 June by Lady Russell, of Killowen and towed by *Erin* from the Solent to Fairlie, where she arrived on Sunday, 23 July. As she dropped anchor in Fairlie Bay the church bells were ringing for morning service. Such was the excitement and pride of the villagers in 'their' designer and yard that the local population lined the beach to watch the arrival of *Shamrock I* instead of going to church. Small boys jumped into all available rowing boats and raced each other to see who could be first to touch the hull. She then proceeded to the James Watt dock at Greenock, where she was strengthened internally with added bracing in preparation for the voyage across the Atlantic. Although 89 feet on the waterline, she had been built specifically light for racing and would not have been strong enough to withstand anything the Atlantic might throw at her on the way to New York. The voyage to America took 15 days.

Before leaving Britain *Shamrock I* had little preparation for racing. She only raced twice against *Britannia*, which was a smaller yacht, and the rigging was not tested for suitability before the event. The skipper chosen for the challenge was Archie Hogarth, assisted by Capt. Robert Wringe. Mr Archibald

Shamrock I (1899). (Courtesy of Royal Northern & Clyde Yacht Club.)

McMillan senior, foreman rigger at Fife's, accompanied the boat to America and wore the distinctive green and yellow cowl of *Shamrock*'s crew.

The defender *Columbia* easily won all three races, which prompted the journalist John Spears of the *New York World* to write that '*Shamrock* would have been better off if Mr Fife had stayed at home' and suggested that failure was due to overconfidence of the designer. The untested spars proved to be too light for the powerful sails and caused the steel gaff to buckle, which cost the second race, and the crew was criticised for not being trained to work together. In spite of defeat, Tommy Lipton came up smiling and endeared himself to the Americans. His cheerfulness in the face of defeat, his sense of fair play and honesty were in contrast to the previous challenger's ungracious behaviour. Lipton was a self-made man and not a member of the aristocracy, and this probably brought him closer to a nation that had fought to become independent not so long before.

What were William Fife's views on the outcome of the races? There is no known record, and it is unlikely that he would have been able to form a first-

Erin towing *Shamrock* I and *Shamrock II*. (Courtesy of Royal Northern & Clyde Yacht Club.)

hand opinion on the performance of the design, as he had to abandon the pre-race trials in New York due to illness. He must have been quite ill, since he had to be carried from the train on arriving at Fairlie. There is no record of what caused the problem, but by the end of the following month he had recovered.

Is it possible that if William Fife had been at the trials, and subsequently at the event in person, things might have been different? Or was *Shamrock I* just not good enough? The genius for design in wood may not have extended to a mainly metal composite boat. The results of this race must have been a great disappointment to both William and his father, who was now 78 years of age. William suffered a further disappointment when Lipton issued his second challenge in 1901 and invited G.L. Watson to design *Shamrock II*.

In trials with *Shamrock I* and *Sybarita*, *Shamrock II* had gear failure which resulted in a broken mast. Much was made of the incident, as King Edward VII had joined Thomas Lipton to watch the races and the media reported that the King had narrowly escaped death. Of course Lipton and the King were watching from the deck of *Erin* and neither of them were in danger. The races for the cup that year were good, and *Columbia* beat *Shamrock II* by a narrower margin than in the previous year.

Now really hooked on America's Cup racing, Sir Thomas, who was knighted in 1902, issued a further challenge in 1903. Although he did not win races, his popularity was soaring in America, where he also had many admirers among the large Irish immigrant population. The attendant publicity must have been good for business. Lipton decided to return to William Fife junior for the design of his next challenger, *Shamrock III,* which was built by Denny at Dumbarton. G.L. Watson corresponded with Fife and gave him the benefit of his experience with *Shamrock II.* He sent him sketches of part of the hull form and rigging. G.L. Watson was also asked to collaborate with Fife to tank test the hull in the new facility at Denny's shipbuilding yard. This test tank is still in existence today, maintained as part of the Scottish Maritime Museum.

Trials of this new challenger were held at Weymouth, and again the choice of trial horse was criticised. It was said that Fife had advised Lipton that *Shamrock I* was a faster boat than *Shamrock II,* and so she was chosen for this trial. It is interesting to note that at the time a journalist wrote, 'The man who counselled Sir Thomas Lipton to use *Shamrock I* as a testing machine was either an enthusiast, a lunatic or a fraud. The boat was outclassed years ago.' *Shamrock II* was subsequently broken up, which greatly pleased the Americans who thought that she was the superior boat and a more dangerous challenger.

It would seem that the third challenge was doomed from the start. *Shamrock III* lost her mast at Weymouth when one crewmember was knocked overboard and drowned and several others were seriously injured. In spite of improvements made on the boat, such as the roughness removed from her bottom plates, and wheel steering introduced for the first time in a British challenger, she was still beaten easily by *Reliance.* The American people were so taken with the plucky challenger that they proposed to raise a national tribute to Sir Thomas Lipton. This took the form of a silver service for his steam yacht *Erin.*

His popularity was immense. Praise ranged from that of the Mayor of Boston, who said 'nothing is too good for the best sportsman in the world' to that of an 11-year-old school boy who sent a donation with a note which said, 'I wish I was a big man and could build the fastest yacht in the world. I would give it to Sir Tommy as my Papa says he is the greatest, grandest and most gallant sportsman in the big world.' Little wonder that Sir Thomas went back for more!

At least the American government took the obstruction of challengers by spectator boats seriously and detailed the US Revenue cutters to enforce the regulations. Because there were too few official boats for the purpose, officials were to be placed on large steam yachts, such as *Erin,* which were allowed to be US vessels for the day.

William must have done some soul-searching to account for the failure of two of his designs. Whatever it was, he was not prepared to talk to anyone about his thoughts. In a letter to W.P. Stephens in September of that year he said, 'Regarding the races I am not inclined to say much, there are plenty of people to do the talking nowadays and I, for one, prefer to hold my tongue and have my own thoughts about matters.'

This third defeat made Lipton consider carefully the terms of the challenge before he returned with another *Shamrock*. The boats had to sail across the Atlantic and had deep keels with heavy ballast to balance the huge sail area on a restricted waterline. Once built, these 'freak' yachts were of no use for anything except the America's Cup races and owners were reluctant to spend a lot of money on a boat which would be scrapped after the challenge. In addition, with that size of boat and the rigging technology of the time, masts and spars were constantly being broken in strong winds.

Another factor which may have contributed to the defeat of British challengers was the casual British attitude to crewing. The Americans had professional crews, which were well trained for the event, while the British had only some professional crew members and numbers were made up with amateur yachtsmen. For example, Lipton's friend R.G. Sharman-Crawford crewed during the races on both *Shamrock I* and *Shamrock III*.

Five years passed before rumours began that another challenge was about to be issued. The press reported that Mr Fife had had consultations with 'a Glasgow gentleman' which gave rise to speculation that William Fife would design another boat for Sir Thomas. Immediately afterwards William Fife left for Canada, where he attended the races for the Canada's Cup. On arrival at New York on his way to Canada he was interviewed by the press. Accounts of this interview were cabled to Britain and created much surprise. Apparently he assured the press of a coming challenge and told them of his hopes and plans regarding the America's Cup contest.

Talking to the press and revealing such confidential details as new orders from clients was so out of character for the tight-lipped William Fife that the British yachting press suggested that the sea air had gone to his head or the person interviewed was not in fact Mr Fife! Was this press statement to the Americans pre-arranged with the client or was it perhaps that he too had been bitten by the bug which seemed to affect so many people associated with the cup? Was it that an overinflated sense of importance, and companionship of the rich and famous who wanted his designs, had led him to behave in this uncharacteristic fashion?

It was not until September that Sir Thomas announced yet another challenge under his conditions. These conditions were an attempt to eliminate the apparently unfair advantages the present system conferred. His challenge would be with a boat built to the current American rating rule. The Americans refused the challenge and held fast to the old rule, which

Launch of *Shamrock* 23-metre (1908). (Courtesy of *Yachting* World.)

had resulted in 'freak' boats with maximum sail area on an 85-foot waterline with minimum displacement. *Shamrock III* and *Reliance* had turned out to be the most extreme types built to this old rule.

Lipton then discussed this with Fife, who refused to design to the old condition. As a result Sir Thomas commissioned Fife to design and build a composite 23-metre whose frames would be prepared by Denny at Dumbarton. The boat would differ little from the design with which Sir Thomas had intended to challenge for the cup and was launched in April with little or no ceremony. Her owner was not present and she was called *Shamrock*. She was a large yacht and had to be launched with the new floating dock. The interior finish, as for all the Fairlie-built yachts, was superior. The saloon was panelled in rare hardwoods and tapestry, and electric lighting was installed for the first time in a Clyde-built yacht. She had accommodation for 22 crew.

Sir Thomas never gave up the struggle for the 'Auld Mug' and issued two more challenges, one in 1913 with *Shamrock IV* and one in 1930 with *Shamrock V*. These boats were both designed by Charles Nicholson. *Shamrock V* sailed eventually under new rules. The Universal Rule meant that a rating system was established so that standardised classes for racing yachts meant that handicapping would be unnecessary. This led to construction of a new type of boat, the enormous famous J Class with huge sail areas. Only ten of these boats were ever built.

Enterprise defeated *Shamrock V* in the last of Lipton's challenges. After 30 years of trying, Sir Thomas finally gave up at the age of 80 when the American people presented him with a gold cup after the final race. This cup was inscribed 'to the gamest loser in the world of sport'.

It is possible that, secretly, Sir Thomas was not averse to losing. He had always admired the American people and their way of life since his stay in America where he first came into contact with advertising. In his autobiography *Leaves from the Lipton Logs* he recounts that although hard work was a big factor in building up his business, if he had not been quick to recognise how great could be the power of advertising, he would never have had such an overwhelming success. His challenges for the America's Cup kept him and his business in the limelight. He had introduced tea drinking to America in 1890 and he never lost an opportunity to advertise. On her way back from a successful engagement against the Spanish in the Philippines, the battleship *Olympia* had called in at Ceylon and Lipton had instructed his manager to present every member of the crew with a packet of Lipton's tea. Later, while at anchor at Sandy Hook with *Shamrock I* and *Erin, Olympia* came into the bay and Sir Thomas Lipton was invited on board for breakfast with Admiral Dewey.

The fascination with 'The Cup' never left Sir Thomas: Even at 81 years of age, just before he died, he was still discussing a further challenge. It was a long time since the 11-year-old boy had sailed his home-made model yacht on a muddy pond, relic of an old brickworks in a field near his home. His model boat's name? *Shamrock* of course!

CHAPTER ELEVEN

Clyde Matters

From its earliest beginnings the Royal Clyde Yacht Club had concentrated on organised racing for smaller yachts. As a result there was a body of informed yachtsmen always ready to discuss and argue over measurements and handicapping. Although the club had been formed for owners of the smaller boats of the day, in the region of ten tons, increased wealth due to the Industrial Revolution gradually led to members owning larger yachts. Boats were individual designs, and fair competition was difficult to establish. Because there was much dissention among members about measurement, the club appointed an official body of measurers. The club had also been the prime mover in organising a regatta week on the Clyde when different clubs officiated at the races each day. At first the main participating clubs were the Royal Clyde Yacht Club, the Royal Northern Yacht Club and the Mudhook Yacht Club. This week, first proposed in 1896, became eventually the annual 'Clyde Fortnight'.

Meanwhile, in 1875, the Royal Yachting Association was formed in the south of England. The main objective was to attempt to set up standards of measurement and classification for yachts and to do away with local handicapping rules. The association hoped to achieve an arrangement that would be acceptable to those sailing in British waters. This sensible idea, which was eventually accepted, was at first vigorously opposed by the Royal Clyde Yacht Club, who felt that the rules were framed to suit conditions in southern waters. Feelings were so strong that one member went as far as to name his yacht *Noyra* ('no-RYA') in protest. Eventually, after a period of about 20 years, the Clyde renegades finally accepted the Linear Rating Rule.

During the period of discontent with the RYA the wealthy and influential Clyde yachtsmen instituted a regional approach to yachting and favoured designs which were suitable for use in northern waters. Thus a number of 'Clyde' classes evolved. The 17/19, the 19/24 and the 30 foot restricted classes were notable examples. A contributing factor in this development was the fact that three of the foremost names in international yacht designing of that period were members of the Royal Clyde Yacht Club, namely W. Fife, G.L. Watson and A. Mylne. These designers were also influencing the RYA and in due course a measurement rule evolved which gradually became acceptable to the members of the Royal Clyde Yacht Club. This club was

Helen, a 2½-rater (1895). (Courtesy of Royal Northern & Clyde Yacht Club.)

becoming increasingly popular and membership of owners with large yachts grew. These yachts were manned by fully professional crews and the younger members of the families were unable to participate in boat handling and racing. In consequence these young people took to smaller boats they could handle themselves and this gave rise to a group of proficient amateur yachtsmen between whom keen competition in racing and rivalry evolved.

One of the more popular class of these smaller boats whose prototype had been built in 1893 was the 19/24 class. A member of the Royal Clyde Yacht Club had suggested the idea for this class and it proved to be more seaworthy than the 17/19 class. A prototype, *Jeanette*, was built by McLean of Rosneath, but when it was finally decided to adopt it formally as a class in 1896, the Clyde Yacht Clubs' Conference asked Messrs G.L. Watson and W. Fife senior to finalise the design and work out the measurements. These little yachts had an overall length of 24 feet and a waterline length of 19 feet. They had gaff-rigged mainsails and the first boats cost about £200 to build. William Fife gave advice on the sagitta, which was the depth of concavity of the section at 0.6 of the length of the waterline from the bow. A normal sagitta was about 12 inches – anything over that was penalised in measurement. The sagitta was the prototype of the 'D' factor employed in the International Racing Rule.

Almeda II, a 5-rater (1895). (Courtesy of Royal Northern & Clyde Yacht Club.)

Professor Teacher, author of *Records of the 19/24 Class*, recounts how his second boat, *Tringa II,* built in 1902, was basically from the same design as *Ulidia* but considerably fuller up forward. On asking Mr Fife if he would guarantee that she would be a faster boat, Fife replied, 'Certainly not. I promise nothing, but if I were building a third from the same design I would make her fuller still.' Twenty-three years later when *Tringa* won the Tarbert No. 2 Cup, she, together with *Tresta* (26 years old) and *Sunbeam* (23 years old), were 'practically tight as bottles to this day'. The first eight boats to be built raced off Greenock in May 1897 and the class remained popular until the Second World War.

The enthusiasm for the class appears to have been confined to the Clyde. An American authority on yachting is reported as saying, 'They are a lot of ugly back numbers as to looks and design. Crude affairs . . . like those used by Galway fishermen. Not a progressive idea among them; judged by the outcome, they probably reflect the sentiments and brains of those who were instrumental in framing the rules governing them.' This scathing description of a design produced by two of the leading Clyde designers was perhaps a

19/24 Class *Tringa* (1899). (Courtesy of Royal Northern & Clyde Yacht Club.)

backlash from the unpleasantness with Lord Dunraven which surrounded the America's Cup races of that year. It is hardly a description of the design by two men who were among the foremost designers of their day.

The younger Fife was now travelling south to supervise building of his designs and to take part in racing on the Solent at Cowes. In 1895 he sailed the new 20-rater *Eucharis* he had designed for Lord Lonsdale and she romped home in her first race. Of double-skinned construction she had a first inner skin of diagonal planking covered by a coating of smeared canvas, followed by an outer skin of horizontal planking.

William junior had also attended the Gravesend regattas to assess the performance of his new 40-rater *Isolde,* built for Mr Peter Donaldson. She performed well and therefore he had good reason to feel pleased with himself. Back home on the Clyde a number of his designs, including all three of his boats named *Dragon*, were also doing very well.

The following year, 1896, he was just as busy with designs for abroad and new building in the yard. He was commissioned to provide designs for six Cork Harbour One Designs, which were built in Ireland. A 38-foot waterline cutter was laid down 'on spec' and a new 20-rater, *The Saint*, was built for Mr Frank Jameson, the Irish yachtsman. Double-skinned mahogany above the

20-raters *Senga* and *Eucharis*, later named *Hermia* (1895). (Courtesy of Royal Northern & Clyde Yacht Club.)

waterline and single-skinned elm below, she was a welcome addition to the 20-rater fleet.

To complement *The Saint,* Mr A.B. Walker ordered a 36-six linear rater *The Sinner.* His wife objected to the name, which he eventually changed to *Fern.* A local paper printed a story about a concerned individual who was speaking to an elderly Fairlie worthy and expressing an opinion on how unlucky it was to change a boat's name so soon after launching. The local replied, 'We don't care what ye ca' her, she's there and she cam' home "Sinner" than "Westra" the day, onyway!' (Play on words: sooner than *Westra*, the boat it had raced against.) He was referring to her wins at the Royal Largs and Royal Northern regattas.

William junior had to travel south again to supervise the alterations to the Earl of Lonsdale's *Eucharis* to make her an equal match for Mr Walker's *The Saint.* At the same time he was also busy with a design for a Canadian challenger for the Great Lakes Championship against the Lincoln Park Club of Chicago. These races were to be held at Toledo and the prize was to be $1,500 in gold and a $200 cup.

The Canadian challenger designed by Fife was a 45-foot fin keel yacht laid down in the yard at Fairlie beside *The Saint.* She was set up in frame and

Geisha (1897). (Courtesy of Royal Northern & Clyde Yacht Club.)

the parts carefully numbered and taken down. The ironwork spars and sails were all prepared and shipped to Canada, where she was put together and planked by James Andrews of Oakville, Ontario. Kit boats are not a new idea! The new boat, named *Canada,* won outright and the cup for the championship was thereafter named the Canada's Cup in her honour. While all this was going on the cutter laid down 'on spec' was not sold, so William junior launched her and raced her that year as *Cerigo.* After a successful season he had no trouble in selling her.

At the end of that summer, the equinoctial gales, which were unusually severe, wreaked havoc with those boats not already laid up for winter. At Dunoon, ten yachts were carried ashore, and what remained was only fit for firewood. The 1-rater *Era* was being towed round from the Kyles of Bute when the towrope broke and she went ashore. All that remained of her was matchwood. *Era* had belonged to Miss Charlotte Moir, the eldest daughter of Mr George Moir, who had purchased *Dragon II.* She was an enthusiastic and skilful helmswoman at a time when few women took an active part in the sport. Another casualty was a steam yacht which had been valued at £800 of which the only remaining parts were her engines and boilers, found buried in the shingle beach.

This eventful year ended with the famous court case of *Dunraven v. Clarke*. Lord Dunraven wanted to recover the full value of *Valkyrie II*, which had been sunk by *Satanita,* and sued for a sum of £7,500. Mr A.D. Clarke paid him the limited amount of £8 per ton under the Merchant Shipping Act rules, a total of £952. *Valkyrie*'s mast eventually became the flagpole of the Royal Clyde clubhouse at Hunters Quay.

During that year the longevity of Fairlie-built boats was to be noted once again. Two Fairlie old timers had appeared on the Clyde. *Siesta,* 120 tons, built in 1869, and *Hesperia,* 77 tons, built in 1873 for George Elder of Knock Castle. The longevity of Fairlie-built boats has always amazed people. Nearly 100 years before, the 20-ton cutter *Santry,* built in 1863, and altered by her builders in 1885, was purchased by a new owner in 1896. It was remarked at the time that few boats built in 1896 might be in such good shape in 36 years time. This reputation for solid lasting construction has remained with Fife-built yachts to this day.

In 1897 the Parker family reappeared as clients of the yard. Evelyn Parker, a member of the Liverpool branch of the family that had close associations with the yard in the time of the first William Fife, had the 30 linear rater *Forella* built at Fife's. Evelyn was a keen yachtsman, spent much of the summer in Fairlie, and took over the organisation of the 'Fairlie Roads Relief Regatta'. This regatta followed on from the traditional sailing matches at Fairlie held mainly for the local fishing skiffs. In 1889, Evelyn Parker organised the first official annual regatta at Fairlie, which took place the day before Largs regatta. Soon after the three lower Firth resorts of Largs, Fairlie and Millport combined to offer what came to be known as the 'Wee Fortnight', which provided excellent racing.

In 1898 William junior designed a 36-foot linear rater for an Irishman called Cummins which he called *Yum*. She was built at Carrigloe, near Crosshaven in Ireland, and was to have a fairy-tale existence all of her own. After racing with good results she changed hands and later passed to another owner, André Hachette, who took her to Le Havre and renamed her *Griselidis*. In all, she had five name changes under each new owner but nevertheless continued to win prizes. She was finally sold to Guy Tabarly in 1938 as *Pen Duick*.

The Tabarly family enjoyed her for two seasons before the outbreak of the Second World War. During the war she was laid up in a mud berth near Benodet. The war over, she was now in a state of neglect, and Guy Tabarly decided to sell her. His son Eric was horrified and did everything he could to dissuade prospective purchasers, and she remained in the family.

By 1952 Guy Tabarly decided to sell the hulk for the value of the lead keel. His son Eric again persuaded him not to sell and convinced him that he could refit the boat and she was passed into his ownership. In 1956 he finally had resources to restore her but regretfully a survey showed that she was out of shape and beyond redemption. All was not lost. Eric was so fond of the Fife hull that he took the original shape, and used it as a mould for a new fibreglass hull. The fibreglass replica was launched in 1959, and after various mishaps with broken masts was raced by Eric Tabarly in numerous cross-Channel races till 1960. She was then laid up when he began to compete in single-handed transatlantic races.

Pen Duick lay unused for 21 years, and when Eric finally returned to her the deck and superstructure had rotted. He arranged for Raymond Labbé, of St Malo, to restore her, and sailed her again in 1989. Today, with her distinctive black hull, *Pen Duick* evokes the memory of the graceful Fife designs of her day and reflects the unbending faith of Eric Tabarly in the immortality of Fife design. One hundred years after her launch, the spirit of *Yum* still sails on.

For William Fife junior, the beginning of the new century was satisfying, demoralising and tinged with sadness. In the year 1900 William Fife senior and William Fife junior had the satisfaction of finally buying the land on which the yard buildings stood. Up until that time the yard area had been rented from the Earl of Glasgow. Although great excitement greeted William junior's commission to design Sir Thomas Lipton's *Shamrock I,* he was extremely disappointed with her performance. Then in 1902 he suffered a personal loss when his father, William Fife senior, died in January. The 'grand old wizard of the North' passed away knowing that the gift for yacht designing had continued with his son.

Although in many ways a conservative man, William senior kept abreast of change in design, maintaining his reputation for sturdy sea boats which also looked graceful on the water. He had seen the yard develop from small beginnings when the first William and his brothers built boats on the open beach in all weathers to the establishment of a large yard employing 40 men and boys working under extensive covered facilities. Fame did not go to his head. He remained, as always, kind and considerate towards his employees, and had a good working relationship with his men, many of whom were related to him. A yarn told about an elderly Greenock yachtsman would have appealed to his pawky sense of humour. The man's wife had made him promise not to replace his yacht but just repair it when required. After a particularly bad storm the boat broke away from her mooring and was smashed on the shore. The unhappy owner, walking along the beach, spied the hatch cover with the boat's name on it. He promptly took it to his friend Fife in Fairlie and asked, 'Willie, will you mend that?'

William senior loved to sail a boat and attended most of the Clyde regattas. His fellow yachtsmen held him in great esteem and on two separate occasions presented him with a portrait in oils and a silver tea service. He cared about the village community and held various public posts. On William senior's death the yard was closed for a week as a mark of respect. A week before there had been another death in the family. William Jamieson, William senior's cousin, one of the oldest yachting skippers on the Clyde, had retired to Rhu on the Gareloch and died at the age of 75. Born in Fairlie, William Jamieson had left home at the age of 13 to serve on the yacht *Kite,* and throughout his career sailed many of his cousin's designs.

At the age of 45, the death of his father left William junior as head of the family, with responsibility for his mother and three unmarried sisters. He never married. Whether this was out of a sense of duty to his mother and sisters or because of the fact that his busy lifestyle of designing, supervising construction, travel abroad and sailing left him little time to meet the fair sex will never be known.

Life could not stand still. In 1903 Sir Thomas Lipton came to him for the design of *Shamrock III* and the same story of a disappointing performance was repeated. Nevertheless, this did not diminish the orders and workload for the yard. The order book was full; and in order to complete the work on time, more sheds were required and an extra piece of ground was bought adjoining the yard in 1904.

The yard was so busy that even with the added building facility, some boats, although designed by William Fife, had to be built elsewhere. For example, Myles B. Kennedy had the 141-foot yawl *White Heather* built by Fay & Co., Southampton. Her rig was later changed to that of a cutter. *Susanne,* a 154-foot schooner, was built by Inglis at Pointhouse for Oscar Huldschinsky. The photograph of her surging along under full sail by Beken of Cowes has captivated the attention of yachtsmen over the years. The sheer power, grace and majesty of this Fife creation have been caught for posterity by the camera.

Fife-built boats are survivors. *Rose* (1906), an 80-ton yawl built for J. Frame, was to survive for many years under different names. Re-named *Vida,* then *Thelma IV* while in the ownership of the Vicars family, she changed hands for a third time and was re-named *Griselda* by her owner J. Oswald Graham. *Griselda* was one of the larger boats remaining on the Clyde in the 1950s and a familiar sight at Sandbank. Sold again, she eventually entered charter work in the Carribean and was named *Double Cross.*

Another survivor, built in 1903, was *Moonbeam,* for Mr C. Johnstone. This

82-foot yawl was eventually sold to a French owner and after the Second World War, during which it was rumoured that she was involved with the French Resistance, was laid up in Cherbourg in 1956. *Moonbeam* then reappeared in the Mediterranean, where she had a fire on board and suffered some damage. By 1988 she was restored to her former glory and was up for auction at Southeby's for an estimated price of £2 million! Between being advertised for sale again in 1994 she made appearances at the Nioulargue regattas. *Moonbeam* is only one of the many Fife boats which have survived to a ripe old age. These survivors were built by craftsmen and were often beautifully finished with decorative wood panelling below decks. Many of these monuments to the Fife family are still afloat.

The popularity of yachting was growing worldwide and there was a need to standardise measurement. In 1906 an international conference was held in London attended by delegates from 11 countries. This was an attempt to devise an international rule of measurement for yachts which would be acceptable to all European yacht-racing countries. Agreement was reached and the new 'International Rule of 1906' was adopted. As a result the new metre classes were established. The 'big boat' era was coming to an end.

This new rule came into force on 1 January 1907. Myles B. Kennedy had already ordered *White Heather II,* a 23-metre composite cutter from Fife. She was 75½ feet long, requiring a crew of 22. These 23-metres were to be the 'big' racing yachts of the next few years.

In the following year, 1908, Sir Thomas Lipton commissioned William Fife to design and build his 23-metre *Shamrock* and challenged for the America's Cup under the new International Rule. The challenge was refused because the Americans had not participated in the 1906 conference. That year *White Heather II* and *Shamrock* sailed together and Sir Thomas Lipton's new boat was found to be the superior Fife boat.

After the death of his father, William junior modernised and expanded the yard further. A gas plant had been installed for power generation and acetylene lighting was introduced in all the sheds. During this period, when there was a growing demand for hollow spars the yard had an agency for an American manufacturer. Eventually the yard constructed the spars themselves using straight grained light pine. The inside was partially machined out then finished by hand before gluing together. Hollow mast technology was still in its infancy and A.K. Stothert of the RYA, being perturbed about the scantlings for hollow masts, had asked Fife's opinion. The reply was, 'Rule them out altogether and have solid masts which are quickly and cheaply replaced.'

Three separate foundries were also installed. In the 'big' shed where boats of up to 200 tons could be built, there was a brick furnace and a large tank with a specially designed tap underneath to allow molten lead to be run directly to the sandbox. There had always been controversy about whether a more homogeneous casting was obtained by 'running' the molten lead or ladling it into the mould. Fife's 'ran' the lead, whereas ladling was the favoured method on the south coast. The brass founder's furnace was in another shed and the blacksmith, Adam French, had his forge in yet another shed. Self-sufficient in boat and spar manufacture and with ample forging facilities, the yard was now well geared to cope with the explosion of work which was to follow as a result of the standardisation of yacht design in Europe.

CHAPTER TWELVE

The Metre Classes

When the International Rule came into force, Myles Kennedy commissioned William Fife to design and build the 23-metre *White Heather II*. The boat was delivered and no others were built that year; therefore he had few adversaries. The following year, 1908, Sir Thomas Lipton ordered another *Shamrock* from Fife, built to the new 23-metre rule in the hope that it might be accepted as a challenger for the America's Cup. The challenge was refused because the United States did not accept the International Rule and they went their own way to develop the Universal Rule. In spite of this rebuff, Sir Thomas enjoyed a year of fierce competition against *White Heather II*. Both these boats were designed and built by William Fife, evenly matched, and the yachting fraternity followed the progress of each race with great interest.

This battle between Sir Thomas Lipton's *Shamrock* and Myles Kennedy's *White Heather II* continued in 1909. Sir Thomas had been so pleased with the performance of this boat that as a mark of recognition to the family he presented each of William's sisters with *Shamrock* brooches. These were in the form of crossed enamelled flags, on one side the Royal Ulster Yacht Club and on the other *Shamrock*'s house flag. The coloured enamelled flags surmounted a bow in the shape of a shamrock studded with small emeralds.

During this period Myles Kennedy spent a considerable sum of money altering *White Heather II* in an attempt to get the better of *Shamrock*. One of his adjustments was to ask Fife to pad a section of the hull with solid mahogany screwed on to the planking forward and aft of amidships, tapering it to nothing at the ends. This resulted in a more buoyant hull, which required more lead on the keel to bring it back to the required waterline and carry more sail. The alterations were successful and the boats became even more closely matched. This is shown by *White Heather*'s 19 wins to *Shamrock*'s 22 in 41 matches. In one race the two boats sailed beam to beam, bows level for several miles. These two magnificent large yachts provided exciting matches throughout the year. They were both Fife designed, and were seldom more than a few yards apart in the thousand-odd miles they sailed against each other. The excitement of these contests must have compensated for Lipton's disappointment at the New York Yacht Club's refusal to accept his America's Cup challenge using *Shamrock*.

From the beginning the metre boats became very popular because they offered exciting competition on equal terms. Since not all yachtsmen could aspire to a 23-metre they turned to the more affordable smaller metre classes. In 1907, in addition to *White Heather II,* William Fife designed a ten-metre to be built in Norway, a 15-metre built at Robertson's of Sandbank, an eight-metre for a Spanish gentleman and one for the well-known Southsea yachtswoman Mrs R.G. Allen.

Mrs Allen, an exceptional helmswoman, may be regarded as the instigator of eight-metre racing on the Solent. She was a faithful client of the yard and had previously raced for several years in the 30-foot and 24-foot classes. Over a period of some years she had won 224 prizes in 286 matches. Her *Sorais II,* a 24-foot linear rater, was sold to Sir Archibald Orr-Ewing before Mrs Allen entered the eight-metre class with *Sorais III.* That season the performance of this eight-metre *Sorais* on the Solent was exceptional, 25 wins in 25 starts. Gaff rigged, she was canvassed to the limit of stability and in a fresh wind had to reef, especially when racing to windward.

The popularity and acceptance of the International Rule in Europe and the success of Fife metre boats in Britain led to a European demand from the master's drawing board.

The Spanish royal family had always been keen yachtsmen and owned a series of boats over the years. Fairfield had built the royal yacht *Geralda,* a 1,664-ton schooner. King Alphonso XIII also owned two small cutters, *Geraldilia* and *Maria,* both built in Spain. Another of his yachts, the 15-ton *Nenufar,* designed by Fife but built in Spain, had been named *Queen XXX* temporarily. It was rumoured at the time that one of Queen Victoria's daughters might be the future Queen of Spain and it was said that King Alphonso would have named the boat after her. He enthusiastically supported the new International Rule and ordered the six-metre *Osborne* from Fife. She was built at Fairlie alongside another six-metre for his friend the Duke of Medinacelli. *Osborne* and *Almoraima* were shipped out to Spain ready to sail in 1907.

Two years later keen competition between HM the King and his friend the Duke led them to order two 15-metres from Fife. This time the king's boat was built in Spain and named *Hispania.* William Fife visited the yard at Passages in northern Spain to check on the progress of building, and his cousin, Allan Fife, and another experienced yard worker went out to supervise the laying of the keel. The Duke, on the other hand, had his boat *Tuiga* built at Fairlie and it was sailed out to Santander by a British crew.

There was keen rivalry between the King and his friend, but when racing against each other the royal boat always just managed to come home ahead of *Tuiga.* The Fairlie yard's superlative workmanship has ensured that today *Tuiga* is still with us. Faithfully restored to her original design by Fairlie

Restorations at Hamble, *Tuiga* was re-launched in 1993 and joined other Fife survivors at La Nioulargue regatta. It is interesting to note that back in 1909 she sailed across the Bay of Biscay three times and not a single seam opened. *Tuiga* is now the club boat of the Yacht Club of Monaco. Recently, *Hispania,* which has spent 60 years as a houseboat on the mudflats of the Blackwater in Essex, has been taken to Fairlie Restorations on the Hamble to be given a new lease of life. It is hoped that HM the King of Spain may sail in his grandfather's yacht and perhaps *Tuiga* and *Hispania* will continue the battle for supremacy.

In 1911 King Alphonso commissioned yet another Fife design, the ten-metre *Tonino,* again to be built in Spain, but by a different yard, this time at Bilbao. *Tonino* was raced for two seasons then taken to Italy for the 1914–15 season. She remained there for the next 80 years to be discovered by Umberto Fabbiani in Genoa. He restored her to the original gaff-rigged design of 1911 and she raced in the 1995 La Nioulargue regatta.

In 1914 another two Fife designs followed *Tonino:* the seven-metre *Giralda IV* for the King and an eight-metre for his son, HRH Don Carlos. Both boats were built at Bilbao. William Fife visited the yard in Spain to ensure perfection for his prestigious clients. These two yachts were the last to be designed by William before the outbreak of the First World War.

In 1928 HM the King of Spain ordered the eight-metre *Osborne* for the Queen's birthday. The Spanish Embassy in London asked the yard for the plans of *Osborne* to be sent to Spain in the diplomatic bag. In addition the King requested a watercolour picture of the boat as a present for the Queen. The picture was painted by W.L. Wylie RA, who was supplied with the specifications for the boat. He had already been commissioned to paint a similar picture of *Calluna* for Mr Peter Donaldson. The watercolour sketch of *Osborne* cost £20 and 12 silk burgees were also provided. The Spanish monarchy was abolished in 1931 and the royal family had to leave Spain.

Although William Fife's designs were popular in Europe, where the new rule was widely accepted, elsewhere their performance left something to be desired.

In the Canada's Cup of 1907, both the Fife and Mylne designed boats were beaten in preliminary trials. A contemporary letter to the yachting press attempted to explain this by saying:

> Short sighted policy on the part of the Clyde clubs in establishing all sorts of purely local classes was bound to prove harmful in long term to the work of our

Crusader (1907), unsuccesful challenger for the Canada's Cup. (Courtesy of *Yachting and Boating Monthly.*)

designers. For years Fife and Mylne have been working inside the fence erected by the Clyde Conference and there were bound to be surprises when they came into open competition outside.

The writer of this article must have been completely unaware of the world-wide reputation of Fife designs and the current demand for metre boats for owners who did not sail on the Clyde.

Apart from the failure of his design to qualify for the Canada's Cup, William Fife had further upset the yachting fraternity by his previous uncharacteristic lack of discretion in his interview with the New York press on his way to Canada. He assured them that a new challenge for the America's Cup would be forthcoming and that he would be associated with the design. In fact, the challenge, when issued, was refused, but Sir Thomas did not cancel the design and the 23-metre *Shamrock* was still built by Fife.

Fortunately these events across the Atlantic did not detract from the excellent racing in the new metre boats, which resulted in a string of orders for the yard. Sir Thomas Lipton's 23-metre *Shamrock,* unacceptable to the New York Yacht Club, raced with *White Heather II. Mariska,* a 15-metre built for A.K. Stothert, had few boats her size to race against, and for her first season

Croftend House, home of William Fife II.

raced with the old 52-footers. George Coats, always ready to try something new, ordered the 12-metre *Alachie*.

It was a busy year for William. New designs for the metre classes, crossing the Atlantic for the Canada's Cup races, preparatory work on the design of a possible challenger for the America's Cup and great improvements in the working facilities at the yard itself meant that he had little time for leisure. There was upheaval in his private life too. In 1904 he acquired a plot of land on the hill above the village, and in 1907 the family moved to their new home. Till then two generations of Fifes had lived in Croftend House, just opposite the entrance to the yard, where, in the old days, the men had been accustomed to call for their wages at the end of the week.

The second William Fife was a superb craftsman with a genial personality, genuinely liked and respected in the village. The third William, on the other hand, although he had gained practical experience when he served an apprenticeship in the yard and managed the boatyard at Maidens, was a designer rather than a craftsman. With the passage of time, as his designs became well known, he mixed more and more with a higher level of society. He travelled first to Cowes as a young man with his father, and then frequently to America, Canada, Spain and Norway. In due course he became

The Place, home of William Fife III.

the sole proprietor of the yard at a time when its reputation had almost reached a peak. Compared with his father and grandfather he was materially much wealthier. When he moved to the new villa with his mother and unmarried sisters he called it 'The Place'. 'The Place' had been named after the large manor belonging to the Crawfords of Kilbirnie who owned the land where the original William Fife's father had farmed. William's new house on top of the hill in Fairlie was large, surrounded by a beautiful garden, and it had a separate garage with chauffeur's quarters above. This was a much more suitable residence for someone whose clients were the crowned heads of Europe, and millionaires. Later, in a letter to his friend W.P. Stephens in America, he told him how he had enjoyed planning the house and how happy they were in their new residence.

In spite of all this activity William still found time to spend on the water and enjoy sailing which, next to designing, was his favourite occupation. He frequently sailed boats which he built 'on spec' and were not sold when ready for launching. *Clio,* an 18-tonner, had been built 'on spec' the year before he moved to his new house. She had remained unsold, so he sailed her as his own. Although not built to the new metre rule she was not dissimilar to the newer boats. She had a full six feet of headroom and her mainsail was a novelty. It was crosscut, which was becoming universally popular, but the belly was cut from half a dozen canvas cloths much heavier than that of the rest of the sail. Sail-makers were already identifying the parts of a sail that begins to sag first with age.

Clio (1921) on route to Rothesay. William Fife, Robert Balderston on helm, James Balderston, standing, Archibald McMillan senior and John McMillan.

The year 1908 did not begin well for William. While supervising the construction of the 23-metre *Shamrock* he suffered a serious accident. The boat had not yet been decked and was temporarily spanned by planks. While walking across one of them, William slipped and fell into the boat. His head struck one of the steel angles and he was taken home unconscious. Fortunately, a doctor from Largs was in the village attending a patient and was therefore able to give prompt medical attention. For a 50-year-old man it must have been quite a shock to his system, but William suffered no more than concussion and a broken rib and was back at work within two weeks. The Fifes came from hardy stock!

The 1908 Olympic Games were the first to adopt the now fairer new metre rule and Blair Cochrane ordered the eight-metre *Cobweb* from Fife. The efficiency of the building capacity of the yard had improved greatly by this time. New working conditions and machinery had been introduced to the extent that *The Field* magazine was informing its readers that it was 'not too late to order an eight-metre in order to compete in the Olympics at the end

Horse drawn boat transport to railway station. (Courtesy of *Largs & Mill port Weekly News.*)

of July. Mr Fife can build an eight-metre in a month, fitted out and ready for sailing.' *Cobweb* did represent Britain at the Olympics and won her class.

That same year special efforts were made to have *Shamrock* ready for launching in April during high tide. The new floating dock had made launching easier, but a high spring tide was still required for larger boats like *Shamrock*. She was not just a racing machine; her interior was tastefully decorated as befitted a millionaire. The main saloon was panelled in tapestry and there were carvings representing Commerce and Navigation and even the sideboard was carved. In keeping with the colour of the boat, the upholstery was green. The crew's quarters were equally well finished in African mahogany and the passage and sail-lockers in Austrian oak. Like other 23-metres she carried a crew of about 22 paid hands. *Shamrock* was one of the few remaining boats with a large professional crew and the days of 'big boat' racing with completely paid crews were starting to disappear. More amateur sailors were now crewing and helming their own boats. The RYA decided in 1907 that when racing it was acceptable for a ten-metre to have only four paid hands, an eight-metre three, and a six metre one. This was an attempt to take into account the difficulty in obtaining in boat crews.

Of the metre boats William designed and built during this period, *Shamrock* 23-metre was fast to windward, and in that year's contests with *White Heather*

II was the better boat overall. *Mariska,* a 15-metre, was best in her class, but *Alachie,* the 12-metre for George Coats, was beached for a complete alteration when eight hundredweight of lead, which had been added as ballast after launching, was removed and added to the keel, which was recast. Occasionally the yard did not always get it right first time!

The six-metre class was slow to start in Britain. In 1908 there were only seven boats which raced, five in England and two in Scotland, although they were more numerous in Europe. On the other side of the world the Australians had shown interest in this class, which they eventually adopted after the First World War. In 1910, the fleet in Britain had grown to 20 boats, seven of which were based on the Clyde. They had not yet reached their peak of popularity, which followed after the war.

In 1910 the yard launched two six-metres designed by Fife. One of them, named *Clio,* was intended for himself but was soon sold and renamed *Ariel.* The other, *Cingalee,* for Mr Maudesley, was sent south by train. The boat was transported to the station at Fairlie by horse and cart! The yard built these six-metres as quickly as the eight-metres in a space of four weeks.

One country that was not going to allow the importation of foreign boats was the United States, which, in addition to refusing to recognise the International Rule, imposed an importation tax. At that time, also in America, there occurred the death of Captain Charles Barr, skipper of the *Minerva,* which had been built by William's father. Charles Barr had remained in America after racing *Minerva,* when he was chosen to skipper first *Columbia* then *Reliance,* in the America's Cup races. Before a race, when *Shamrock III* was berthed alongside *Reliance* he was asked his private opinion of Sir Thomas's boat. He replied that *Shamrock III* 'was a puir wee thing and was beaten before the start'.

As the yard grew William decided to design for himself a 61-foot twin screw motor yacht, yard number 590, which was equipped with two eight-cylinder paraffin Bergius engines. She was named *Clio,* as were most of his personal boats. This was the name of the first yacht he ever designed.

The 23-metre boats were already replacing the large racing yachts. At the same time few people could even afford to build and race at that size and level. Suggestion was made that the 19-metre class would be more suitable. William Fife's first two 19-metre designs were *Corona,* for Mr William Yates, and *Mariquita* for Mr A.K. Stothert. That year the yard also built the 65-foot auxillary schooner *Elise* for Mr W.A. Young of Paisley. After a long and chequered career in the Baltic and the Mediterranean she finally returned to the UK in 1980 to the harbour at Salcombe. When the owner died the new owners Ted and Brigit Meredith took on the mammoth task of restoration. In 1998 she graced the Fife regatta on the Clyde, taking her place alongside the other magnificent yachts of yesteryear.

CHAPTER THIRTEEN

The First World War and the Aftermath

After six years of exciting competition *White Heather II* was withdrawn from racing. This was the end of big cutter racing and the start of a trend to move to smaller racing classes. The largest racing class was now the smaller 19-metre and there was keen rivalry between British and German boats. The struggle for supremacy in yachting was to spill over into a much more serious confrontation between nations in the not too distant future.

Apart from two motor yachts and a small cruiser, all the boats built in 1913 at Fairlie were for the metre classes. Sir Archibald Orr-Ewing, who began in the metre classes with the eight-metre *Endrick*, moved down to a seven-metre *Strathendrick*. His brother was another proficient yachtsman who raced the eight-metre *Norman*. Major Sharman-Crawford, the Irish yachtsman and friend of Sir Thomas Lipton, continued to be a faithful client of Fife, and replaced his 12-metre *Ierne* with a smaller eight-metre, also named *Ierne*.

Keen racing in the 15-metre class led a Mr Stamp to order *Maudry*, a composite boat. Unfortunately, she, like *Waterwitch*, was a disappointment. She was undercanvassed and her design was no improvement on the *Lady Anne* of 1912. While racing from the Nore to Dover she was dismasted and lost her 'Marconi' mast. Marconi masts were so-called because they resembled the Marconi signalling apparatus, with struts and stays on the upper section of the mast. The other 15-metres, *The Lady Anne* and *Mariquita*, also suffered similar breakages. Bermudian rig was becoming more popular, but, with the materials of the day, the new elongated 'fishing rod' masts, often with hollow top sections, were difficult to stay efficiently in a narrow boat and dismasting was common.

In the month of June the Fairlie yard lost one of its faithful clients. Mr Peter Donaldson, 52 years old and Vice President of the RYA, had been seen leaving his house in Kilcreggan early in the morning and his body was found near the pier the following day. His firm of iron merchants had failed two weeks earlier. He had owned a number of Fife boats, among them *Yseult, Yvonne, Calluna* and the 40-rater *Isolde*.

To add to Fife's anxieties, there was another rising star in yacht design in the person of Charles Nicholson. Not only had he been chosen by Sir Thomas Lipton to design his next challenger for the America's Cup but he was also successful with all the yachts he designed that year.

Towards the end of 1913 the Americans repealed the tax law of 1909 which they had imposed on imported yachts on condition that they sailed to America. This did not affect yard orders, as all the new boats launched in 1914 were metre boats, mostly for European owners. The exception was the 90-ton yawl *Sumurun* for Lord Sackville. *Sumurun* is another Fife survivor. Her first skipper was Robert Wringe, who had been a skipper on *Shamrock*. He must have been losing his touch, because, while racing at Ramsgate, *Sumurun* collided with *Bloodhound* and almost lost her mizzen to *Bloodhound*'s bowsprit. It was a port-starboard incident and *Sumurun* was on port tack. Although *Sumurun* had the usual Fife touch of class in her hull, it was felt that she did not have enough sail for competitive windward work. Perhaps, like many Fife boats, she only gave her best performance in a good weight of wind. Could this poorer performance have been linked to the fact that below decks these boats frequently carried considerable extra weight?

The owners of many of these large yachts lived on board with a sizeable crew for a considerable part of the season. To ensure their comfort and the comfort of their guests the boats were fitted with a plethora of luxurious furnishings, which must have added considerably to the weight of the hull. Not everyone was content to race a boat like *Bloodhound*, where the Marquis of Ailsa only conceded to the provision of wooden benches below decks.

Sumurun passed from the ownership of the Sackville family in the 1940s and was converted from a gaff-rigged yawl to a Bermudian ketch. With a change of rig came a change of name to *Erna* and she spent some time in the Mediterranean and the Caribbean. In 1983 she was purchased by an American millionaire who restored her nearer to her original design and renamed her *Sumurun*. She won the Atlantic Cup in Newport's Classic Yacht Regatta in 1984 and was named the best performing yacht in the cruising class fleet of the Antigua Race Week that same year. In 1986 she returned to the Clyde 72 years after she had been built to take part in a race organised during the Viking Festival at Largs. *Sumurun* dwarfed all the other contestants. In her younger days she would certainly have been smaller than most of the other boats.

In 1914 the season opened with no apparent awareness that all was not well in Europe. The popularity of the 15-metre class was growing and had done much to enhance the reputation of the designer Charles Nicholson. Fife was acknowledged to be the best designer in the eight-metre class but his 15-metre *Maudry* had been a failure. Based on Nicholson's success in designing these larger boats and the reluctance of Fife to build to the America's Cup rules, Sir Thomas Lipton chose Nicholson to design his next new challenger for the America's Cup. This challenger, *Shamrock IV*, was launched on 26 May, the Queen's birthday, and during the launch HMS

Victory fired a royal salute. For the occasion Sir Thomas had chartered a special train to bring his numerous guests from London. Mr P. Burton, an invited guest to the launch, had been racing the previous day at Harwich in Sir Thomas's 23-metre *Shamrock*. The boat was in the prize list, and Mr Burton missed the special train. In order not to miss the launch he chartered another special train, which left 30 minutes after the first one. This must have been the last few months when such extravagant behaviour would be possible, as the country was soon to be at war. Not long after this launch, yachtsmen mourned the passing of Myles Kennedy, who died in June, and *White Heather II* did not race that season.

The Fife yard was building a new eight-metre for Major Sharman-Crawford, and a new six-metre for Norman Clark-Neill, who was making his debut in the class with *Marmi*. After the war Clark-Neill was to become a member of the British Seawanhaka Cup team sailing *Reg,* another Fife six-metre.

At the Royal Mersey Regatta in June 1914 *Hispania,* which had been bought from the King of Spain by J.R. Payne, beat *Istria* and won the King's Cup. Later that summer, in July, Clyde Fortnight was overshadowed by the growing uncertainties which resulted in the outbreak of war. The racing fleet was notably smaller because a number of owners had been recalled to regimental headquarters, and the King's yacht *Britannia* was withdrawn from the last few races. Elsewhere it seemed to be 'business as usual'. *Shamrock IV* was sailing with *Shamrock I* at Cowes before leaving for her journey across the Atlantic.

The yachting press, apparently oblivious of the state of international affairs, was looking forward to Cowes Week towards the end of the season, where numerous German, Norwegian and English yachtsmen were expected to compete. The press even hinted that the King would have a new racing cutter for the following season, as *Britannia* now had no sizeable opposition and had to sail in the handicap class. This was not to be. War was declared and Cowes Week was cancelled. This was the first time that there had been no Cowes Week since its inception in 1834, during the reign of William IV. Yacht clubs all round the country followed this example and cancelled all remaining regattas. Patriotically, some donated the remainder of their prize money to the war effort.

Many of the yacht crews were naval reservists, who enlisted immediately. Yachts were now laid up; steam yachts deemed suitable for war service were converted to hospital ships, mine sweepers, or used as patrol boats. Norman Clark-Neill actually bought the SY *Adventuress* and loaned her to the Admiralty. He was a sub-lieutenant in the RNVR and served on her as a member of the crew. His uncle, Kenneth M. Clark, also loaned his SY *Zoraide* to the war effort.

What happened to *Shamrock IV,* now in America? Sir Thomas Lipton had received a cable from New York regretting that Britain was at war, and Sir Thomas requested that the challenge be postponed for one month. If war continued the match should be postponed for one year. It is obvious that certain levels of society were completely unaware of the gravity of the situation.

Shamrock IV and *Erin* were already halfway across the Atlantic when war broke out. They picked up the news by wireless from a German cruiser and the Royal Navy instructed them to proceed to Bermuda. From there they went to New York, where *Shamrock IV* was laid up and *Erin* returned to Britain to join the war effort as a Red Cross ship. She ferried doctors to France and to Salonika. Unfortunately, she was eventually torpedoed, with the loss of six lives.

The authorities immediately seized all German yachts in British ports. The 366-ton *Germany,* owned by Dr Krupp von Bohlen, was detained, but her crew were allowed to return to Germany. Not so lucky were two British yachtsmen, William Thompson and Frank Randall, who were in Keil to make arrangements for six-metre races. They were interned, but word was eventually received that they were being treated reasonably.

It was not enough that the yachting fraternity should serve in the Navy and lend boats for the war effort. Appeals were made first of all for blankets, which would no longer be needed by crews of yachts which were laid up. This was followed by a request for the donation of binoculars and spyglasses not only from yachtsmen but from all sportsmen. Finally, in December, when the full impact of winter hit the troops in France and their tented encampments turned to quagmires, an appeal was made for the donation of gum boots, fishermen's waders, khaki and black waterproofs, and oilskins from former yachtsmen. The country had been ill prepared for this war and there would be no more pleasure sailing till it was all over.

A review of the number of yachts afloat was made just before the start of the First Word War. It was estimated that there were 3,889 compared with 2,000 in 1880. This was a considerable increase from the 50 yachts recorded in 1800. At that time William Fife was still considered to be the foremost British designer and builder, credited with more than 300 boats designed by him.

The International Rule had been a great success and 800 yachts had been built in the course of eight years since its introduction.

The Fairlie yard did not close at the outbreak of war. In fact, it became extremely busy with work for a new client, the Admiralty. Some of the younger members of the workforce went to fight for King and Country but the rest had a protected employment, which was directed to the war effort. William Fife himself, aged 57, was too old to enlist, but his nephew, Robert

Flying-boat hull. (Courtesy of Scottish Martitime Museum.)

Balderston, joined the Argyll and Sutherland Highlanders as a captain. Robert Balderston was the eldest of four children, the son of William's only married sister Janet. William himself had never married, and treated his eldest nephew Robert almost as a son. Young Robert left school at the age of 16 and was taken into the yard to train as a draughtsman.

Just before the war, in 1914, at the age of 28, he changed his name to Balderston Fife, and his ageing uncle made him a partner in the business. When war broke out and Robert enlisted, William was again in sole charge of the yard. Situated as it was, far from the Channel and any possible threat of invasion, the yard was ideally located and became totally committed to the war effort.

The yard first of all built a series of centre board cutters for Admiralty stations followed by a series of motor boats, as well as gigs and whalers which were still carried as ships' boats by the Navy and used in training. In addition four 50-foot pinnaces were produced. The following year, in 1915, a 90-foot cutter was laid down for Charles Johnston, but because of pressure of war work it was to remain unfinished till after the war. During 1916 and 1917 another series of motor boats and water boats were built with engines supplied by the Bergius Launch and Engine Company – again War Office work.

The craftsmen in the yard also turned their skills to the construction of hulls for seaplanes. These were called J and F flying-boats. The flying-boats

Fife's yard, 1914. (From *Fairlie Past and Present*.)

had their engines installed by the Dick, Kerr Works at Preston, later to become the English Electric Company. The hulls were made by capable yachtbuilders round the country, fitted out by the Phoenix Dynamo Company and then sent to Dick, Kerr to have the engines fitted. Later, after the war, the aircraft department at Preston was re-established at the Dick, Kerr Works. John Alexander, who had previously worked at William Fife & Son, supervised the hull builders. Riggers were also pressed into service in the construction of portable aeroplane hangars, made from wire rope and canvas and intended for use in Mesopotamia.

While all this was going on, pleasure boating on the Clyde was limited to the upper reaches of the Firth, but excluding Loch Long and Loch Goil. There was to be no sailing between sunset and sunrise and a permit was required. Permission had to be obtained from the Navy if a regatta was to be held.

By 1915 the country realised that war was indeed here to stay and the Admiralty actually issued a ban on the reporting of yacht and steamer movements in the yachting press. Until now the press had been giving a full account of which boats were being refitted for mine sweeping or hospital work! Meantime Sir Thomas Lipton still hoped to compete in the America's Cup and in 1916 wrote to New York to this effect. *Shamrock IV* was still laid up in Brooklyn and many thought it inappropriate to think of these matters in such a time of strife. The war years saw the loss of many yachtsmen, both at home, from old age, and young men on the battlefield. The sailmaker Tom Ratsey lost his two sons, both of whom had followed him into the business. In Scotland, Robert Duncan, who had been skipper to the late James Coats for 40 years, died at Gourock. He had been 'loaned' to Sir James Bell to sail *Thistle* in the America's Cup and had also been skipper to the Kaiser when he bought her and changed her name to *Meteor*. The deaths of people like Myles Kennedy and Sir Maurice Fitzgerald meant that yachting would never be the same again after the war.

In the midst of all the tragedy of war and the necessity of having to produce motor boats instead of sailing boats, William Fife was to suffer a much greater personal tragedy. Mary Fife, his second youngest sister, who had acted as his secretary for many years, committed suicide with a shotgun on 2 September 1915. There was no newspaper report and she was buried quietly two days later. The explanation given by the family was that she was suffering from menopausal depression. She was 51 years of age. By all accounts Mary must have been an accomplished young woman in her earlier years. Apart from acting as William's secretary, she was an excellent pianist, played duets with her sister Jean, and accompanied singers at local soirées and social gatherings. In 1896, when she was 32, William built her an 18-foot linear rater called *The Sulky,* so she evidently shared her brother's love of sailing. Why she should take the decision to end her life at this particular time is a mystery. Perhaps she had become aware of the full horror of the slaughter in France, perhaps someone close to her had been reported missing? Whatever the reason, her family must have been totally devastated, as they were all devoted to one another.

At the end of the First World War, yachting received a setback. The state of the economy was such that few people could afford the large yachts of pre-war years. Many sailors had disappeared, and so had professional skippers, many of whom had served in the Royal or Merchant Navies. Boats had either been requisitioned for war service and sunk, or had lain in disrepair for four years.

The International Rule of 1906 should have been revised in 1917, but for obvious reasons this was delayed until 1919. The International Conference in London in November discussed whether the old International Rule should be adopted with changes, laying down restrictions and limits within which a design could work, or alternatively, whether it should adopt the American Rule and change it with restrictions. William Fife told the conference that a good boat could be built by either of these methods, and so a revised version of the International Rule was devised and adopted. The chairman of the RYA observed: 'I am greatly indebted to the senior British yacht designer Mr

William Fife OBE.

William Fife of Fairlie for his kind assistance in supplying me with the necessary data used in compiling the new propositions.' The new restrictions meant that the displacement of the boat depended upon the waterline length, a fixed minimum displacement for a given length and a maximum draught. Long overhangs were no longer allowed. There were restrictions on sail plan, mast and boom construction. The mainmast had to be solid, but the upper third could be hollow.

William was recognised for his services to shipbuilding during the war, and received an OBE. He was also presented with a certificate (No. 69) from the National Scheme for Disabled Men acknowledging his employment of men disabled in the First World War. The certificate was signed by the Minister of Labour, Ernest Brown, and the President of the Scheme, Lord Allenby.

One favourable outcome of the war was development in the aircraft industry of the manufacture of laminated structures. This development was extended to using the technology to manufacture hollow wooden spars in the boat industry. The early high Bermudian masts failed frequently, and the boats were top heavy and could not be readily pressed in stronger winds. The manufacture of hollow spars or parts of spars, allowed under the new rule, was a great improvement.

At the beginning of 1919 there were strenuous efforts to renew racing. On the Clyde, the Royal Northern YC and the Royal Clyde YC asked their members how many would be prepared to turn out in the new season. There was an encouraging response from owners of 'smaller' yachts such as the six-metre, the Clyde 19/24 class, the old 1.75-raters and the Holy Loch Pleiad class. For the smaller number of larger yachts there would be a handicap class.

Finding crews for the boats was another problem. Fishermen were less inclined to leave fishing for crewing. Wages in the fishing industry had improved due to food shortages during the war, and yacht crews demanded the same rate of pay as crews on steamers. Seamen on steamers had their rate of pay settled by the Seaman's Union. Before the war yacht crews earned between £1 6s and £1 7s per week; clothes were provided, and the men supplied their own food. If the crew worked on a racing yacht there was a bonus of £1 for a win, 10s for a second place and 5/- for starting. There was also a 2/- allowance for food. The rate of pay agreed by the Seaman's Union was between £3 10s and £4.

Owners of the few large yachts were determined not to pay the rates which crews were now demanding. One of their arguments was that although these men wanted equality with steam crews they did not all have 'tickets'. Popular boat sizes were getting smaller and the need for paid crews was not so great.

In an attempt to revive yachting, the King proposed to refit *Britannia* so that she could support the regattas round the coast. Sadly there were no boats her size to race against and so the refit was postponed till the following year. The Royal Clyde YC sent a telegram to the King from the first cruise dinner since 1914. It congratulated His Majesty on the cessation of war and assured him that they were doing their best to resuscitate the spirit of yachting. To encourage the sport, the King presented two cups for competition on the Clyde. One went to the Royal Northern YC and the other to the Royal Gourock YC to be sailed for by small boats, especially 'those in which industrial workers might compete'. In fact it was now being recommended that prizes should be in the form of money and not cups. Yachting was becoming more organised and sail numbering was introduced.

In spite of the willingness of yachtsmen to continue where they left off before the war, fitting out was considerably delayed. There was a shortage of materials and labour and all costs had risen considerably.

Sir Thomas Lipton lost no time in preparing for the confrontation with his American rival. The new Nicholson *Shamrock IV* sailed in trials against his own Fife 23-metre *Shamrock* which had crossed the Atlantic in April. The Olympic Games were to be held in 1920 at Antwerp, and an increase in international competition with boats built to the new improved International Rule was about to take place. William Fife was about to reach another peak of achievement.

CHAPTER FOURTEEN

The Six-Metre Class

After the First World War, for economic reasons, yachts were becoming smaller and the new metre classes built to the International Rule began to come into their own. They provided exciting competition, were closely matched and the skill of the helmsmen and crew counted towards winning a race as much as the actual design of the boat.

Although American yachtsmen still tended to favour their own Universal Rule, they adopted the International Rule for boats of twelve, eight and six metres. This led them to discuss team racing with British yachtsmen and resulted in team matches in six-metres, with four boats representing each team. These matches were organised to be held alternatively in the United Kingdom and America. The trophy jointly presented by the Royal Yacht Squadron and other leading clubs became known as the British-American Cup.

The *Field* magazine, published in Britain, stated 'the small boat of the future round the coast should be the new international six metre'. These boats were about 20 feet on the waterline, six-and-a-half feet to seven feet beam, and had a draught of about five feet. Displacement was about two-and-a-half tons, and in the early years, before the introduction of a genoa and a spinnaker, they had a sail area of 500 square feet.

The first races were to take place on the Solent, and nine British boats were built, from which a team of four was chosen. Each boat cost between £900 and £1,200. Six-metres, built to the new improved International Rule, had less canvas and were more stable than the six-metres built to the 1907 International Rule. It was agreed that the owners of these old sixes could compete in the class if they measured to the new rule and had a solid mast. Up to this time the mast was fitted with only a single set of crosstrees.

Unlike the America's Cup, where the challengers had to cross the Atlantic under sail, it was allowed to ship the challengers across. The four American boats arrived in Britain on the steamship *Francesca* and the races were held on the Solent at the end of July. Two of the British boats were Fife designs: *Polly,* owned by Mr Basil Gould, and *Flya,* owned by Evelyn Parker. They were successful in winning the cup. *Polly* was recognised as the best six-metre that year. Her owner was a civil servant, home on leave from Persia. He had hardly ever sailed a boat before but nevertheless ordered a six-metre from

Madrigal II, Fife Classic Regatta 1998.
(copyright Marc Turner)

Moombeam III, Fife Classic Regatta 1998.
(copyright Marc Turner)

Belle Aventure, Ex-Eileen.
(copyright Marc Turner)

Magda IV in foreground, *Solway Maid* astern, Fife Classic Regatta 1998.
(copyright Marc Turner)

Altair (1930), on the occasion of her visit to the Clyde to celebrate her 60th Birthday.
(copyright John McFie)

Kentra (1923, Gaff Ketch, Wm Fife 3rd) at the fourth Fife Regatta in 2013.
The William Fife-designed yachts return to their birthplace on the Clyde.
(Copyright Marc Turner PFM Pictures www.pfmpictures.co.uk)

Astor, ex-*Ada* (1923), built for Sir Alexander McCormick Sydney.
(courtesy Richard Straman)

Viola (1908, Gaff Cutter) and *Rosemary* (1925, Bermudan Sloop).
The Fife Yachts are one of the world's most prestigious group of Classic yachts.
(Copyright Marc Turner PFM Pictures www.pfmpictures.co.uk)

Fife. It was helmed by a friend and he himself, along with the paid hand, constituted the crew. This race was instrumental in standardising the rules for the number of crew permitted on board. A crew of four was specified, plus a lady, who would not count as a crewmember. This prompted one of the American helmsmen to ask the sailing committee to define 'a lady'. After deliberations it was decided that there could be a maximum of five crewmembers on board a six-metre!

In spite of the recovery of small-boat sailing, there was no improvement in the economy. In 1921 naval ships were no longer required and as there had been a temporary cessation of yachting during war years, yacht building was at a low ebb. It was reported that there was considerable unemployment on the Isle of Wight and the south coast. Most yacht-building yards were quiet, but one of them in Scotland still had some work for its employees.

That year the Fife yard built four six-metres – *Polly, Flya, Caryl* and *Freesia* – and a 30-foot restricted class, *Clio. Clio*, which had been laid down 'on spec' just after the war in 1919 was only finished in 1921. William sailed her himself during the first Clyde Fortnight after her launch and won five flags. Not only was he a gifted designer but he was also a superb helmsman. At the same time, because of the previous success of *Polly* in the British-American Cup on the Solent, it is little wonder that Fife was asked to design more six-metres for the event in Oyster Sound the following year. This also helped to keep the yard busy. He was asked to design five new six-metres: *Reg, Gairney, Suzette, Ayesha* and *Vanity*. William attended Cowes personally to take charge of tuning *Gairney*, which had not been doing too well. The poor performance was put down to the mainsail not setting properly. During a race, William had the sail lowered, hoisted and reset according to his judgement while the boat continued to sail to windward. In spite of this they lost hardly any time and came in third behind *Freesia* and *Suzette*, another two Fife designs. This feat was accomplished during strong windy conditions and proved that the new Bermudian rig was easier to handle than the old gaff rig.

The team for the British-American Cup to race in Oyster Sound was finally chosen. It was made up of *Reg* (Fife), helmed by Capt. R.T. Dixon, *Caryl* (Fife), helmed by Frank Robertson, *Coila III* (Fred J. Stephen of Linthouse) and helmed by his son John, and *Jean* (Nicholson) helmed by Sir Ralph Gore. After six days' racing the Americans won the cup. Winds were light and did not suit the British boats. There was some compensation later when *Coila III* won the Seawanhaka Cup.

The races for the Seawanhaka Cup trophy were first held in America and the first challenge was in 1895 by the British yachtsman Arthur Brand. The cup is the oldest international trophy for small yachts. The challenger and defender have to be of equal rating and the winner is the best after five races. In its first 30 years of existence the cup had never left the other side of the

Atlantic till won by *Coila III* in 1922. This meant that for the first time it would have to be defended the following year on the Clyde.

Coila III had been designed by Fred Stephen who, as a young man of 23, had previously designed his first *Coila,* a three-tonner built in 1886. This boat had a successful racing career and was top of her class in 1888. In 1908 he designed the six-metre *Coila II,* which in ten years of racing won 192 prizes, of which 110 were firsts. He subsequently designed his most successful yacht in 1922, the six-metre *Coila III.* After a good performance in the British-American Cup she was chosen to represent Britain in the Seawanhaka Cup, which she won. In 1923 she successfully defended it against the American boat *Lea.* The owner was the helmsman and two of his sons were members of the crew. In 1924 she was again successful against the Norwegian boat *Unni.* The sequence was broken when the Americans won back the cup with the six-metre *Lanai.*

Three of the four-boat team chosen for the British-American Cup in both 1921 and 1922 were built on the Clyde. In addition *Coila III,* which was part of the team, had also won the Seawanhaka Cup in 1922. This led to suggestions that the team races should be held on the Clyde in 1923 and not on the Solent. An argument ensued. Barbara Hughes, a well-known south coast yachtswoman, wrote an indignant letter to the yachting press stating that she was outraged that the races should not be held on the Solent. Her reason? The Solent was better for racing than the Clyde, and the visitors would be entertained at the Royal Yacht Squadron, 'the most exclusive yacht club in the world'. More important was the fact that the King would not be able to spectate at the races if they were not held on the Solent! It is questionable if the Clyde yachtsmen would have agreed with her, nor would the Americans, a nation of republicans who are noted for their lack of formality and who had thrown off the yolk of sovereignty more than 100 years before. There were letters to the press which criticised the lack of preparation of the British team. There had been no formal training together as a team and no thought had been given to the expected conditions and the type of courses expected at Oyster Bay.

Although this criticism was made in the press, there was at least one person who had attempted to look ahead and had made the effort to ascertain local conditions in Oyster Bay. William Fife was not only a designer and a builder but an accomplished helm and could appreciate that local conditions could well affect the outcome of the races. He had written to his friend W.P. Stephens, requesting a chart of the area and tide tables. His friend complied and sent an old chart used by the man who had laid out the courses. His letter also contained detailed descriptions of tide conditions and a summary of conditions in the 1895 races. He stated that winds were usually light and in fact rarely reached a 'reefing' breeze. He also remarked that the boats would have to be fast in very light to moderate winds. The press criticism was therefore not justified in so far as the team did not know about local conditions beforehand.

The following year *Coila III* again successfully defended the Seawanhaka Cup on the Clyde and the British team was successful on the Solent. In 1924, the following year, the British won at Oyster Bay.

Soon a revolutionary idea was going to change six-metre racing. Up until this period the class was growing all the time. A Scandinavian Gold Cup had been established, and in 1927 a race for this cup was held in Long Island Sound. Sven Salen's *Maybe* carried an entirely new type of jib, the genoa, that he had tried out with success at Genoa. Because only 85 per cent of the fore triangle was counted in the calculation of sail area, the extra area was free. In addition, he used a double-sided parachute spinnaker which was easier to gybe and so completely revolutionised sailing in six-metres.

While all these developments were going on, the arguments as to where the British-American Cup races were to be held in Britain continued. Sir Thomas Dunlop and Sir Charles MacIver, Commodore of the Royal Clyde YC, had been co-opted onto the committee which arranged the matches for 1928, and they urged that the races should be held on the Clyde. In 1928 the argument 'Clyde versus Solent' was settled, and the event was held for the first time on the Clyde.

When the time came for the races, the gale force winds, which had devastated Clyde Fortnight earlier in July, had fortunately abated. This year's match was unusual in that all the American boats were designed by Crane, and all the British boats by Fife. The home team was E.A. Richards' *Thelma,* E.S. Parker's *Fintra,* Ronald Teacher's *Finvola* and the Nawab of Bhopal's *Naushabah,* helmed by Sir Ralph Gore. It was a decisive victory for the British team and another triumph for the Fairlie yard.

Meantime the rising popularity of the eight-metres gradually led to a decline in the ownership of six-metres. By 1934 only the Clyde could produce a team to represent Britain in the British-American Cup races. Two of the boats were new Fife designs of that year, R.M. Teacher's *Melita* and Arthur Young's *Saskia II.* Unfortunately the cup went to America. In 1937 Fife received a letter from the Honorary Secretary of the Solent Division of six-metres to say that they had managed to start racing again. It listed the best performing sixes that year and three of the five are on record as Fife designs.

Originally the rigging plans of the six-metres had been fairly simple, with one set of crosstrees. There is a report that in 1910 five boats had been dismasted, following which it was suggested that designers might have to adopt outriggers for the shrouds, and that hollow masts should be prohibited. The American boats had in addition a small separate cockpit for the helmsman, which became more popular after the introduction of the genoa.

Fintra, six-metre (1927). (Courtesy John McFie.)

By 1932 the IYRU reduced the size of spinnakers and the midship girth measurements. The beam was now increased to about six-and-three-quarters feet and the waterline to 23 feet. Rigging plans were also changed to accommodate both the genoa and spinnaker. Understanding of rigging technology improved, and although most boats changed to three sets of crosstrees and jumper struts, Fife continued to provide two sets of crosstrees.

Evelyn Parker's Fife-designed *Fintra,* which had been top in the class in the years 1928 to 1931 was sold to Arthur S.L. Young in 1933. In 1935 Fife received a letter from the designer, Mylne, saying that Arthur Young had asked him to re-rig *Sabrina*, as she was now called, 'in the style of the American sixes with three sets of crosstrees'. Respect between designers of the time led Mylne to add the interesting comment: 'I shall only act with your permission . . .' The views of Fife on a boat of his design obviously came before the wishes of the client!

During his life William Fife designed 62 six-metres and was regarded as the 'father' of the class.

CHAPTER FIFTEEN

Balderston Fife

Mention has already been made of William's nephew, Robert Balderston, who had joined the yard when he left school at the age of 16. He served with the Argyll and Sutherland Highlanders during the First World War and rejoined his uncle at the yard after the war as business manager of the establishment. Many designs are attributed to Robert Balderston, working in conjunction with his uncle. Truth be told he was not a designer, although he had trained as a draughtsman and was knowledgeable about the materials used in boat construction.

In 1924, when William was 67 years of age, he wrote to his long-standing journalist friend W.P. Stephens, 'It is better to wear out than to rust out. I get lots of work but my nephew takes all the drudgery and I am left free to my designing which is a joy to me rather than work.'

The impression that Robert Balderston was a designer may have arisen through misrepresentation in the press or because of his own tendency to exaggerate in order to cultivate people who could help further his career. His training as a draughtsman may have enabled him to execute final drawings of his uncle's designs, and he may therefore have appended his signature. He is credited with the design of *Gweneth* in 1911 just after attending Glasgow University.

The Field reported in 1922 that five new six-metres from the yard had been jointly designed by Mr William Fife and his nephew, Captain R.B. Fife. It also suggested that 'the latter is considered on the Clyde to have a wonderful eye for a boat and we should not be surprised if in the future he should prove himself able to carry on the traditions of Fairlie as successfully as his uncle has done'. This would never come to pass; Robert Balderston lacked the spark of genius that had passed from father to son for three generations.

William treated his nephew as the son he never had. From the age of 17 he had been virtually adopted by his uncle and was started as an apprentice in the drawing office. He attended only two classes in naval architecture at Glasgow University, but never graduated. He was probably a competent draughtsman but lacked the capacity for original design.

In 1939, when the Admiralty had taken over the yard for the duration of the war, Balderston Fife was looking for employment. His curriculum vitae states that he 'had training with special reference to selecting, buying and converting home and foreign timber for the construction of wood and

Robert Balderston Fife (1886–1953). (Courtesy of *Largs & Millport Weekly News*.)

composite yachts'. There is no mention of design ability or design work. As a young man he had a bachelor flat above the garage at 'The Place' in order not to disturb his elderly uncle and aunts when returning home late from evenings out. When war broke out in 1914 he was gazetted as a second-lieutenant and served with the 51st Division Argyll and Sutherland Highlanders in France from 1915 to 1917.

Invalided home in 1917 the forces employed him for light duties at the Record Office in Woolwich. He was later appointed acting staff captain while his own staff captain was on sick leave. With his knowledge of timbers and boat building, he became a production manager and an inspector of flying-boat hulls. His apprenticeship in the Fairlie yard made him eminently suitable for this post. After the war he was demobilised with the rank of captain. He returned to Fairlie describing himself in his curriculum vitae as a partner in William Fife & Son, responsible for 'the construction of yachts and selecting all timber used in that construction'. Again he does not mention that he is a designer. He married Alice Donaldson, who had already been married twice and had two daughters. They set up home in 1929 in a large house called 'Trigoni' which lies on the outskirts of Largs only three miles from Fairlie.

Surviving correspondence would suggest that Robert Balderston was a fairly self-centred man, eager to please those in a position who might be able to further his interests in business or his position in society, but with little time for people from whom he would gain nothing. In this respect he was not like his uncle or his uncle's father.

Invitations to local yacht clubs' annual dinners and requests to attend the Armistice Day ceremony at Morrison's Academy, Crieff, as a former soldier and pupil, were refused. Yet he did not hesitate to accept an invitation to the annual dinner of the Royal Thames Yacht Club and on numerous occasions was present for the racing at Cowes and Torbay. Largs Sailing Club invited him to give a lecture to members before the start of the sailing season. His reply? 'It is entirely out of my line and I could not spare the time for the preparation.' It is difficult to see why a short talk to the local sailing club would require much in the way of preparation from someone who was so intimately involved in the day-to-day management of a yard, and it certainly would not be 'entirely out of his line'.

Even more astonishing is his reply to a request from *Burke's Landed Gentry* for an entry under his name as Balderston Fife. He could not have appreciated the impact that three generations of Fifes had made in the sphere of yacht design. He actually wrote: 'I doubt if in fact that during the past 150 years my forebearers have made a name as yachtbuilders and naval architects that is known all over the world that entitles the family history to appear in *Landed Gentry*. The history of the male side of my family is of Balderston of Paisley.'

Robert was happy to change his name to Fife and be taken into the firm as a partner with all that it entailed, but he did not want the lowly origins of the family to become public. He obviously had no understanding of the important contribution to yacht design made by the previous generations. He preferred to revert to his Balderston antecedents for *Burke's Landed Gentry*.

His desire to advance in society may be judged from the fact that he went as far as to apply to the Lord Lyon King at Arms in Edinburgh for a Balderston coat of arms. This was granted in 1922. Ironically this was the same year in which he changed his name to Fife! In the declaration provided by him, his father is described as a thread manufacturer. He was in fact a manager in one of Clark's cotton mills in Paisley.

In 1919 Robert was made a partner in the yard. He dealt with correspondence, but the main decisions were always deferred to William Fife. Robert Balderston was younger and therefore more able to travel around the yachting centres where a personal follow-up service was expected by Fife clients. He had been trained in the selection of wood for building and had become familiar with the types of paint and varnish available to give a good finish to a boat. Clients would write to the yard asking for 'special' paints used on their boats; even Baron de Rothschild had asked him to send some paint to Bordeaux for his six-metre *Prudence*.

His advice was also sought on polishing hulls to increase speed. For example, Arthur Connell, the shipbuilder, was not happy with his new 12-

metre *Zoraida*. He felt that she was slow, and wrote to Balderston Fife asking his opinion on polishing with Ronuk. Frank Ratsey had suggested this when she had been slipped at Cowes. Balderston's reply was:' I do not like Ronuk and do not believe in it.' He suggested 'a mixture of fine rottenstone powder and linseed oil removed after polishing by washing in turpentine or methylated spirit'.

Fife boats were well finished. One of Balderston's responsibilities was to ensure that the hulls received their customary five coats of paint and their final one of 'first class enamel'. The spars and decks received four coats of varnish.

Balderston Fife was always short of money. He complained about the increased assessment of 'Trigoni' rates. Bills for household items such as electric irons, coffee machines, electric torches, a trouser press and replacement of his kitchen floor covering were all passed through the firm. He had married a woman who by all accounts was very extravagant. Unlike the older members of the family, who walked to the yard, he always arrived in style in his car when cars were a rare sight in the village. Lacking the natural talent of previous generations of Fifes, he tried to impress with his lifestyle, made possible by his partnership in the firm. He was not above currying favour with those whom he thought would be able to help him.

At the outbreak of the Second World War, when the yard was taken over by the Admiralty, he had to look for alternative employment and he wrote to Hunter-Weston of Hunterston asking if there was any position he could obtain. He was now without income from the yard to help finance his extravagant lifestyle. He also wrote to the Secretary of State, the War Office, the Ministry of Supplies for timber and to the Brigadier of the 51st Light Anti-Aircraft Brigade. He even wrote to the Ministry of Labour in 1939 with his own suggestions for an unemployment scheme. The Ministry replied that his suggestions were completely unacceptable as they were contrary to legal arrangements and would result in the unemployed having less money!

Robert Balderston spent the war years at a desk in Edinburgh Castle. His wife was able to keep a maid, something which was unusual in wartime, since most people were engaged in some form of war work. Their dinner parties were also remarkable in that they seemed to have more than the sparse rations allocated to the general public.

When his uncle died in 1944 the war had not yet ended. The yard passed back into his hands in 1947 and he promptly sold it to Ian Parker and his brother. The Parker brothers were descendants of the same family which had been one of the first clients of the first William Fife, and the family had continued to order boats from the yard throughout the period of ownership of three generations of Fife.

The new firm, now owned by the Parker family, changed name and became the Fairlie Yacht Slip Company. A local man, Archibald McMillan junior, was appointed manager. When the Admiralty returned the yard to private hands it compensated for loss of continuity of orders by commissioning the building of Admiralty-designed craft. Some demand for wooden fishing boats also ensured continued employment of the now smaller workforce for a short period. In 1951 the yard built the first yacht since 1939. This was *Madrigal II,* which was built from the original Fife design to replace the yacht *Madrigal* which had to be destroyed when the yard re-opened because she had developed dry rot while laid up during the war. By now the yard had lost all original connections with the Fife dynasty; there only remained a few old craftsmen on the point of retiral.

CHAPTER SIXTEEN

Cruising and Racing

During the period when William was having success with his six-metre designs, he did not stop creating larger yachts for clients who wanted comfortable cruising boats or boats which could take part in ocean racing and at the same time be a home for the owner.

Mention has already been made of *Clio* built 'on spec' in 1919 but not launched till 1921 on account of the slump in the yacht-building industry. As a buyer was not readily found William decided to use her as his own boat and gave her the same name as all his personal craft in the past. *Clio* was the goddess of history in Greek mythology.

Clio was well sailed by William, and her stunning performance guaranteed her sale. Between her launch and the present day she has been cherished by her various owners. In 1983, Jeff Law and Don Constanzo found her sitting on the hard tarmac at the port of Cannes under a new name – *Sheevra*. They purchased her from her ailing owner and restored her over two years of hard work. Mercifully her previous owners had kept to her original specification and the resurrected 30-foot National Restricted Class reappeared at classic boat regattas, winning prizes wherever she sailed.

Another restored survivor, built in 1923, was *Kentra,* originally built for Kenneth Clark of Acharacle. She was a cruising boat, and only one in the long line of racing and cruising yachts owned by this Scottish millionaire. Sixty feet on the waterline and 100 feet overall, including bowsprit, *Kentra* was of solid construction, as befitted a gentleman's cruising yacht, able to cross oceans if required. The family had owned cotton thread mills in Paisley, and after the business was sold Kenneth Clark became one of the 'idle rich'.

In her first year *Kentra* spent time cruising on the west coast of Scotland, and she was sold the following year to Charles Livingston, whose family owned the Cunard Shipping Line. She was sold again in 1936, and after passing through the hands of several owners she carried on with charter work in the Caribbean before returning to Britain. She was originally rigged as a ketch and converted to Bermudian rig in 1953 when the old bow was cut away and the bowsprit removed. Subsequently, after more charter work in the Mediterranean, she returned to the West Indies, was refitted in Antigua, and then returned to Britain in 1983. She lay idle for seven years and was then brought to McGruer's yard on the Clyde for restoration. Don

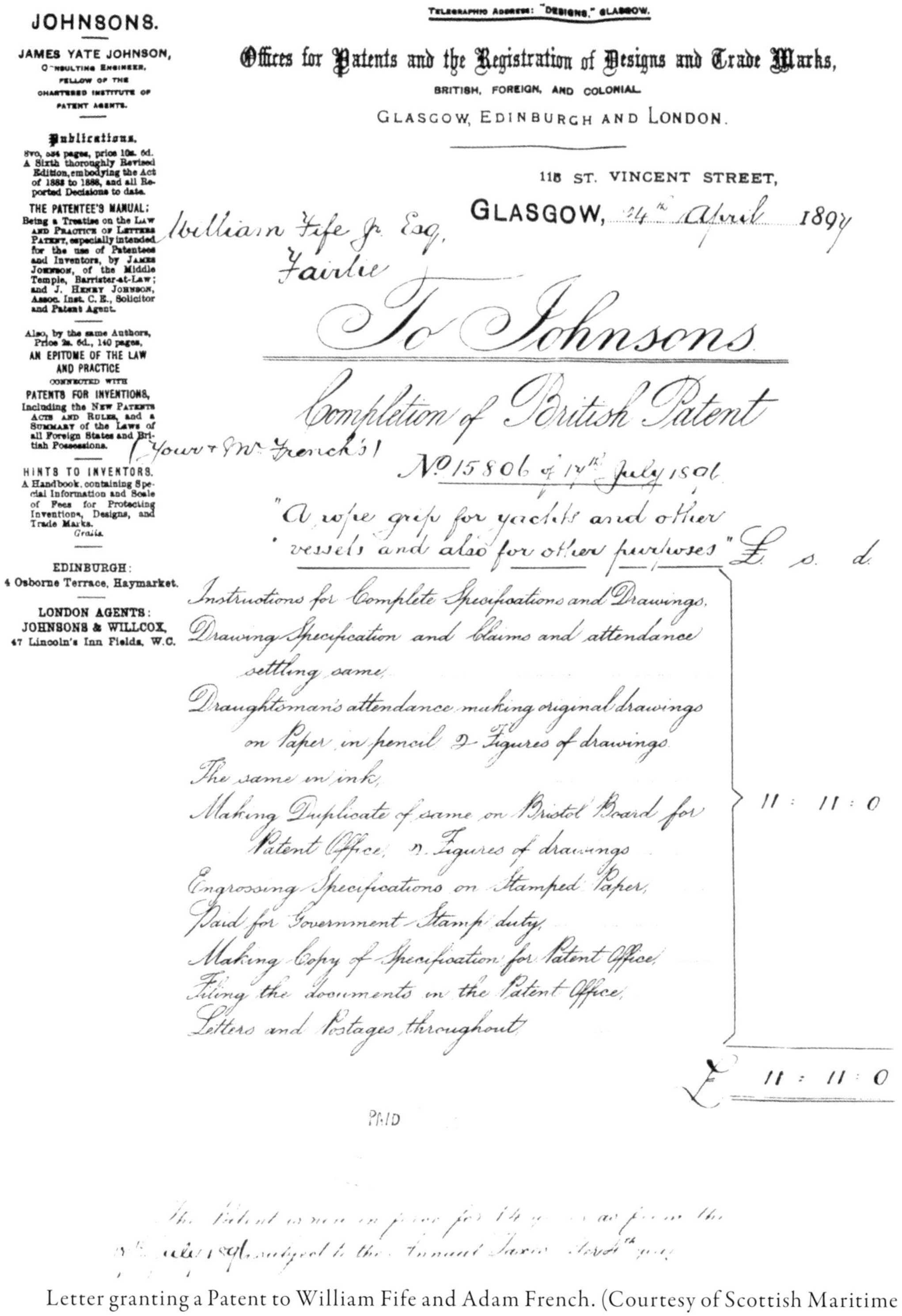

TELEGRAPHIC ADDRESS: "DESIGNS," GLASGOW.

JOHNSONS.

JAMES YATE JOHNSON,
CONSULTING ENGINEER,
FELLOW OF THE
CHARTERED INSTITUTE OF
PATENT AGENTS.

Publications.

8vo, 584 pages, price 10s. 6d.
A Sixth thoroughly Revised Edition, embodying the Act of 1883 to 1888, and all Reported Decisions to date.

THE PATENTEE'S MANUAL;
Being a Treatise on the Law and Practice of Letters Patent, especially intended for the use of Patentees and Inventors, by James Johnson, of the Middle Temple, Barrister-at-Law; and J. Henry Johnson, Assoc. Inst. C. E., Solicitor and Patent Agent.

Also, by the same Authors, Price 2s. 6d., 140 pages,
AN EPITOME OF THE LAW AND PRACTICE CONNECTED WITH PATENTS FOR INVENTIONS,
Including the New Patents Acts and Rules, and a Summary of the Laws of all Foreign States and British Possessions.

HINTS TO INVENTORS.
A Handbook, containing Special Information and Scale of Fees for Protecting Inventions, Designs, and Trade Marks.
Gratis.

EDINBURGH:
4 Osborne Terrace, Haymarket.

LONDON AGENTS:
JOHNSONS & WILLCOX,
47 Lincoln's Inn Fields, W.C.

Offices for Patents and the Registration of Designs and Trade Marks,
BRITISH, FOREIGN, AND COLONIAL.
GLASGOW, EDINBURGH AND LONDON.

115 ST. VINCENT STREET,
GLASGOW, 24th April 1897

William Fife Jr. Esq.
Fairlie

To Johnsons

Completion of British Patent
(Your & Mr. French's)
No. 15806 of 17th July 1896
"A rope grip for yachts and other vessels and also for other purposes"

	£	s.	d.
Instructions for Complete Specifications and Drawings. Drawing Specification and claims and attendance settling same. Draughtsman's attendance making original drawings on Paper in pencil 2 Figures of drawings. The same in ink. Making Duplicate of same on Bristol Board for Patent Office, 2 Figures of drawings. Engrossing Specifications on Stamped Paper. Paid for Government Stamp duty. Making Copy of Specification for Patent Office. Filing the documents in the Patent Office. Letters and Postages throughout.	11	11	0
	£ 11	11	0

PAID

The Patent is now in force for 14 years as from the … July 1896, subject to the Annual Taxes …

Letter granting a Patent to William Fife and Adam French. (Courtesy of Scottish Maritime Museum.)

Constanzo, former owner of *Sheevra*, was asked to take part in the initial restoration stages. Unfortunately, money ran out and she had to be sold. She was then transferred to Fairlie Restorations on the Hamble, where the job was completed.

Fife boats were built to last, and *The Lady Anne* was no exception. Constructed in 1912 as a 15-metre racing gaff-rigged cutter for George Coats, she underwent extensive alterations in 1926 when she was re-rigged as a Bermudian ketch to a new sail plan by William Fife. She retained her original mast, with a short section added. The bowsprit was shortened and bulwarks were added, as this was considered much safer for the men who had to work on deck. The inside was completely refitted and furnished with electric light. Unlike *Britannia,* the alteration of *The Lady Anne*'s sail plan did nothing to hamper her performance and she won many prizes that season.

During the period when *Clio, Kentra* and *The Lady Anne* were built, the Fife yard was also building mainly 'small' boats, six-, eight- and twelve-metres, William considered himself lucky to have so much work. He wrote in 1925, 'I suppose we must be thankful', when he compared his yard's workload to that of others. 'There is very little doing in the country. Nicholson has two cruisers and a twelve but as far as I know there is only one other racing boat, a six by Mylne.'

That year also saw the death of one of the yard's best craftsmen. Adam French was a blacksmith who worked independently but whose association with the yard lasted over 50 years. He supplied most of the ironwork for the boats and invented many devices, which added to the success of the Fairlie yachts. The Patent Office in Glasgow granted a patent (No. 15806) to 'William Fife Jnr. Esq.(and your Mr French)' for 'A rope grip for yachts and other vessels and also for other purposes', on 17 July 1896.

Perhaps to cheer himself up, William went to the south of France for a few days in the company of his old friend Tom Ratsey. His six-metre *Zenith,* built in 1924, was 'still too good for the French and Spanish boats when there is a good breeze', as was *Caryl* (another six). This was a consistent trait of Fife boats. They sailed well in a good breeze. Built to last, they were probably heavier than their opponents were.

The country had not fully recovered from the First World War, fewer people were able to afford large yachts, materials had become more expensive and workmen were seeking higher wages. William was now 68 years of age and at the end of the year was confined to the house for six weeks with a carbuncle on his leg – probably a varicose ulcer brought on by poor circulation.

The British economy started to slow down nationwide. Yachtsmen in the south of England were beginning to complain about the lack of new larger boats being built on the Clyde, especially the 12-metre class. They also felt that the larger Scottish-based boats were not making the effort to travel south and enter the races at Cowes and Torbay. The reason probably lay in the much slower recovery from the aftermath of war in Scotland compared to the south of England.

In fact the economy was worsening, unemployment was growing, and in 1926 this culminated in the General Strike. The yard did not escape from the consequences of this situation and orders dropped dramatically. It was a year when fewer boats were built or sold. For example *Rosemary IV,* a cruising boat started 'on spec', was not sold till two years later. Only three six-metres and three 12-metres were built and in addition one other boat, *Hallowe'en,* a Bermudian cutter for Colonel Baxendale – a most notable boat in the years to follow.

In 1925 the Fastnet Race was inaugurated, and Colonel Baxendale took part but did not win. Determined to do better he came to Fife and ordered a new yacht for the next race in 1926. *Hallowe'en* was 47 feet on the water line and 60 feet between perpendiculars. She was another of the yard's successful boats and has had a long and distinguished career. She fulfilled the ambition of Colonel Baxendale, finishing the Fastnet Race in the fastest time, which has never been bettered on the original course. A few years later she was sold to the Royal Norwegian Yacht Club and renamed *Magda XII.* Before the Second World War broke out she was shipped to the United States, where she was renamed *Cotton Blossom IV.* In 1986 her owner, Walter Wheeler, donated her to the Classic Boat Museum at Newport, Rhode Island. The museum was fortunate in that a Fife admirer bought her and over a period of five years the museum's staff restored her. By this time the owner could no longer afford her, and in 1991 she was again looking for a new owner. One was found, and in 1993 he decided to restore her to the original rigging plan and remove the mizzen. Yet another Fife survivor is still giving pleasure, as she must have done when she was first launched all those years ago.

One of the three 12-metres launched that year was *Moyana,* designed and built at Fairlie for Wilfred Leuchars, who lived in Natal, and who was a partner in the firm of London solicitors Hunt, Leuchars and Hepburn. William was asked to go to London to meet Leuchars and discuss requirements for his new boat. Notes of extras discussed and requested were made on the Piccadilly Hotel notepaper. The covering for the cushions had to be 'something like the tapestry in the Piccadilly Hotel'! Mr Leuchars was obviously a creature of habit. He kept the boat for two years, and then in 1928 he ordered another, *Moyana II.* The original *Moyana* ended her sailing days as *Amity* in a mud berth on the Isle de Noirmoutier just off the coast of

Conway One Design. (Courtesy of Sandy Neilands.)

South Brittany. After lying there for some years, a Fife enthusiast decided to restore her. Unfortunately it was decided to lift her out of the mud with a crane, and she promptly disintegrated. All that remains is the lead keel and a beam from the boat bearing the Lloyds specification number.

The larger racing classes were becoming less affordable, making smaller one-design classes popular. The emergence of the new smaller classes was a reflection on the state of the economy and the desire to race in equally matched boats where the skill of the helmsman determined the winner rather than the amount of money spent on the boat. One such class was the Conway One Design Class in North Wales.

Just before the First World War, a group of sailing enthusiasts from the Conway estuary decided to promote small-boat sailing in a local design, the Conway Restricted Class. In 1925 William Fife was approached and asked to design a class suitable for racing and day cruising in local waters. The only specifications were that it had to be a waterline of 16 feet, length overall 24 feet 6 inches,

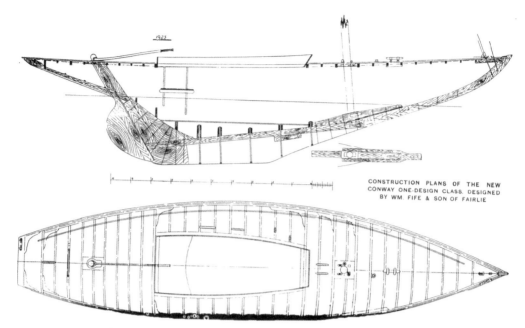

CONSTRUCTION PLANS OF THE NEW
CONWAY ONE-DESIGN CLASS, DESIGNED
BY WM. FIFE & SON OF FAIRLIE

Fife Association Conway One Design. (Courtesy *Yachting World.*)

and a draught of 3 feet 3 inches suited to the depth of water available in the river Conway. The rig was optional, but the first two boats built were Bermudian rigged. The original Conway restricted class also had a waterline of 16 feet, but the draft was 3 feet and the length overall was 20 feet. The new class was called the Fife Association Conway One Design.

Altogether William designed 15 boats for the class and A.M. Dickie & Sons of Bangor, North Wales, built them all. Mr Dickie had an earlier association with the yard at Fairlie. Archibald Dickie, founder of the yard 'Dickies of Tarbert', had originally been an employee of Fife. He and two other men had built a most successful yacht called *Trio,* and he then moved to Tarbert to start his own business. One of his sons, Peter Dickie, had been sent to Fairlie to serve his apprenticeship with Mr Fife before returning to Tarbert. He moved to North Wales, and in 1924 he took over the premises of the former Rowland Dockyard and founded the firm of A.M. Dickie & Sons at Bangor. His grandson, also Peter Dickie, has carried on the tradition of building Conway One Designs and they are now being built in fibreglass. In one club race Peter Dickie sailed his aunt's old wooden boat and beat all the fibreglass hulls. On another occasion the weather was extremely rough and only the older wooden boats were out on the water, the others returning to shore.

This design work was welcome during the lean period at Fairlie, and by the end of 1926 business started to improve to the capacity of the yard.

William's friendship with W.P. Stephens in America continued over the years, and, although they never met again, they were in regular correspondence. At this time William wrote to his friend saying 'We are very busy here, our yard is very full up till the end of July next year.' He put it down to the fact that people were getting tired of motoring as a sport and were coming back to the sea: 'There is no difficulty in getting boats to build; trained men to build them is our difficulty.' The war had taken its toll; there were fewer experienced craftsmen available and they were demanding a more realistic living wage.

At the same time attempts to standardise rating rules to achieve fairer sailing were continuing. An International Conference of European Nations had been arranged at the end of 1924 in an attempt to have the same rating rule for both Europe and America. The Americans were building a new 18-foot rating class under an American or Universal Rule which was very similar to the six-metre class under the European International Rule. By the end of 1926, after much deliberation, the Americans were prepared to adopt the International Rule for all classes of small racing yachts. Soon different countries would be able to compete on more equal terms with American boats.

In Britain, to encourage the sport to recover from the recession, King George V decided to alter the royal yacht *Britannia* in order to match the new generation of boats and bring her out for the sailing season. William Fife was put in charge of the alterations. In 1893 the height of the original mast had been 125 feet and the main boom had been 91 feet. The mast height was increased to 140 feet by fitting a socketed topmast and the boom length reduced to 84 feet. The overall sail area did not alter much, but the sail plan changed to a higher aspect ratio. Alterations were also made to the keel.

In February 1926, William travelled to Marven's yard at Cowes to inspect the King's boat *Britannia* and was very pleased with the progress made. Later, in June, he was on board to supervise final tuning on the Solent, and it was reported that he was pleased with her performance. By August, however, it was obvious that all was not well with *Britannia,* and she was to be laid up before the end of the racing season. The alterations to *Britannia* had not been successful. In a stiff breeze she performed poorly; in fact it was with the greatest difficulty that she sailed at all. In her original rig she would have handled well under these conditions. It was the general opinion that it was fortunate that she had not already had an accident, and it was admitted officially that the alterations, which had been carried out after expert advice, were unsatisfactory. A blow to the reputation of William Fife – especially as it involved the King's yacht.

Age was beginning to affect William. He was depressed by the news of the death of many of his contemporaries in yachting circles. He still had a full

Shamrock following *Britannia*. (Courtesy of *Yachting World*.)

order book and could have had more commissions if he wished, but he 'did not care for a lot of work now'. His popularity as a designer was declining.

The yachting editor of *The Field* posed the question 'Which designer would a prospective owner of a new twelve-metre choose?' Only three designers had produced twelve-metres – Fife, Mylne and Johan Anker – but in his opinion he advised that Alfred Mylne was 'one of the cleverest and most beautiful designers and most able engineer in draughtsmanship and of rigging'. At 69 years of age William had reached his peak of achievement and his monopoly of metre designs was now being challenged.

However, all was not doom and gloom. His six-metre designs continued to be successful. Captain Leslie Richardson, who lived in France, chose him to design his six-metre *Velella,* which was built in Italy in order to avoid extra expense in having it shipped out to the Mediterranean. She had a good racing season, and 'like all Fife boats she seemed a witch at eating her way out to windward'. The top Mediterranean boats that year were all sold at the end of the season. *Velella* was purchased by an American yachtswoman, Miss A. Anthoney, who renamed her *Mowgli II.*

In spite of the advice of the editor of *The Field* to chose Mylne as a designer for a 12-metre, William's new *Moyana* for Wilfred Leuchars was a winner.

Nor did it stop Arthur C. Connell of the Scotstoun Shipbuilding Company from ordering a Fife-designed twelve to be built at Fairlie. Another 12-metre built that year for Leon Becker of Antwerp was still sailing in Scottish waters in the 1950s. She belonged to Andrew Tindal and had no auxiliary engine. As a result, she had to be towed through the Crinan Canal when making a passage to or from the west coast.

Alexander Thom, a relative of the Tindals, sailed *Cerigo* from Brixham to the Clyde, taking seven days for the passage. Professor Thom was an engineer and archeo-astronomer, best known for his study of megalithic stone circles. He put forward a theory that Stone Age people were able to use Pythagorean geometry and that they had devised a unit of measurement which he called 'the Megalithic Yard'. Many of his observations were made when sailing round the islands of the west coast of Scotland.

The year 1926 saw the disappearance of some notable yachtsmen of the old school, some of them clients of the yard. In April, Andrew Bain, member of most of the Clyde yacht clubs and a long-term sailing man, died at the age of 82. He had owned the Fife 17/19 *Hatasoo,* built in 1892, creating a record with her and winning 100 prizes within four years of her launching. His nephew, John Downes, was often on board as crew and was himself a well-known yachtsman. In July, one of the Aspin brothers, Herbert, passed away. He had been secretary of the Royal Northern Yacht Club.

In September, on the Isle of Wight, Herbert Maudesley died. It is interesting that the word 'spinnaker' is a derivation of the name of his yacht *Sphinx.* He raced her on the Thames against *Niobe,* owned by a Mr Gordon. Mr Gordon was the first to set this type of sail on a boat in 1865, and it was called 'a Ni-ob'. The following year Mr Maudesley used a similar sail. The local Itchen Ferry men called it a 'Sphinxer' or 'spinker', being a corruption of the name of the boat. Dixon Kemp introduced it into yachting vocabulary as the term 'spinniker' when he was describing a race on board *Sphinx.* The spelling 'spinnaker' was not in use until 1869. Mr Maudesley's son, Algernon, was the founder and promoter of the British-American Cup races for six-metres and owned the Fife six-metre *Cingalee.*

In October, the death occurred of William Coats, of the Ferguslie cotton mills in Paisley. Although he did not race, he owned the steam yacht *Queen of Scots,* and a cruising boat. His family was a client of the Fifes. George Coats, later Lord Glentanner, had owned the 15-metre *The Lady Anne,* the 12-metre *Alachie* and the six-metre *Gairney.* Other members of the family owned the 12-metre *Cintra* and Clyde 23/30 lug classes.

Another Fife client, Mr William Wylie, had a rather nasty accident at Cove when assisting with the mooring of his yacht *Vida IV.* His foot caught in the anchor chain and was almost severed. Keeping his wits about him, he instructed the skipper to tie a tourniquet, and *Vida* headed for the infirmary at Greenock, where his foot was amputated. This remarkable man was 72 years of age and had been active in yachting for 50 years. Mr Wylie's firm, Wylie and Lochead, over the years was responsible for the furnishing of many of the interiors of the more luxurious yachts built at Fife's.

The stock boat *Rosemary IV,* built in 1926, with no prospective buyer and not launched until 1928, became the cause of friction between the yard and the yachting press in 1934. Laurent Giles wrote an article in *Yachting Monthly* entitled 'Rosemary IV and Her Kind'. He deplored the design of a yacht for ocean racing, which was in fact a cruiser hybrid, as a result of the International Rule, and he welcomed the introduction of the Ocean Racing Rule Measurement. *Rosemary IV* was, according to him, a perfect example of a boat exhibiting features which were not desirable in ocean racing. He did concede that she was 'a fine example of a fine type of yacht for those who enjoy sailing for sailing's sake and who want to get where they are bound quickly'. *Rosemary's* lines had been reproduced in the article. Just after this, *Yachting Monthly* wrote to the yard for permission to publish plans of the eight-metre *Fulmar.* Balderston Fife refused, and objected to the article written by Laurent Giles. He said that permission would not have been given to publish *Rosemary's* lines if he had known that the article was to criticise her. *Yachting Monthly* replied that the article had been written to stimulate discussion and that Balderston could have answered the criticism in the letter column.

Naval architecture was now based on scientific design principles. Ship and boat building were expanding, there was a demand for more designers, competition between them was becoming fierce, achievement became high, and Fife was no longer the only good yacht designer around. Some, like Laurent Giles, frequently criticised his designs, yet others, like the young designer Uffa Fox, were lifelong admirers.

Uffa Fox, author of many books on sailing and famous for his revolutionary dinghy designs, began his apprenticeship working on flying-boat hulls and hydroplanes. The young designer visited the Fairlie yard on numerous occasions and usually managed to persuade William Fife to allow him to publish the lines of some of his boats in his books. He was greatly impressed by the workmanship and construction of Fairlie-built boats. Writing of *Latifa* he remarked that strength is a feature of Fife boats, and no matter how hard they were driven. In a letter to William he said he would write about her construction 'as an illustration of the excellent way in which your yachts are built, as it is such things as this that lifts them high above the ordinary level'. Uffa Fox continued to praise Fife yachts and publicise them right up until the yard closed on the outbreak of war.

CHAPTER SEVENTEEN

Twilight

During the period from the end of the First World War until 1927, William only built three eight-metre yachts. The demand during that time had been for six and 12-metres. This was in great contrast to the numbers of eight-metres he had built before the war. The change in the International Rule, in 1924, had resulted in a preference for Bermudian rigs and the eight-metres were beginning to become popular again.

In 1926 he had orders for four eight-metres. Two were for owners on the Clyde, one for Southampton and one for Belgium. *Caryl* for Mr W. Robertson and *Cluaran* for W. Betts Donaldson were the home-based boats, and *Finola,* for Herbert Johnston, was to be delivered to Southampton by steamer, with a rigger in attendance. As the yard was busy and William could not promise delivery before the beginning of July, which was into the racing season, he offered that either himself or his nephew would go to Southampton to supervise the final fitting out and tuning. At the same time the yard was building *Zinita,* a 12-metre for Arthur C. Connell, a shipowner and faithful client of Mr Fife. When Connell decided to sell her in 1930, he complained bitterly about 'the WC which always filled up, overflowed and stained the carpet'! He was fond enough of her to keep her sail number for his next 12-metre after a Norwegian purchased *Zinita.*

The Connell family had built many famous tea clippers, and the two brothers, William Connell and Arthur Connell, were well-known yachtsmen. The Fife yard had built four boats all named *Zinita* for the family. The first, built in 1893, and designed by William Fife (then junior) was a 20-linear rater. After a successful racing career she was purchased and taken to America. In 1905 she was sold to a breakers' yard and the hull was eventually sold to a film company who used her in *The Perils of Pauline,* starring Pearl White. After a chequered career in salvage and towing she eventually sank. This was not the end; Fife boats are made of sterner stuff. She was raised in 1931 and restored as a sailing yacht.

The second *Zinita* was a 30-linear rater and the third *Zinita,* built in 1904, was a 65-linear rater. The fourth *Zinita* was the 12-metre with the leaking WC. The Connell boats mirror the fashion and fortunes of the yachting fraternity of the times over 24 years. Rich families gradually increased the size of their yachts till before the First World War. After the war the new International Rule was in force and the metre boats became popular.

Cambria launch in 1928. (Courtesy of *Yachting World*.)

The only cruising boat launched from the yard in 1927 was *Dodo IV,* for William Bergius, the manufacturer of Bergius marine engines. During the First World War, between 1915 and 1918, the yard had built 12 motor boats for the Bergius Launch and Engine Company as part of a War Office contract.

Although in 1928 the yard built only four boats, William was busy producing designs for six- and eight-metres and in addition a clutch of Conway One Designs, all of which were built elsewhere. One of the four boats was *Cariad,* which went out to Australia on the SS *Mongolia*. The hull arrived safely, and the owner, Mr McBeath, had her finished by a local yard, Morrison and Sinclair. It is perhaps an indication of how easy it was to travel and dispatch goods by sea at that time when Mr McBeath wrote to Mr Fife, asking the yard to dispatch a large piece of teak to repair his counter which had been damaged in a collision. Despatching boats may have been easy but they were not cheap. Due to high shipping costs and taxes, many people abroad were ordering designs and having them built by their local yards. This was to be the pattern for the next few years, as William's designs for six- and eight-metre were still in demand overseas.

Fife boats were showing their superiority abroad. In the French regattas, even Mr J.R. Payne's six-year-old 12-metre *Vanity,* the oldest boat in the fleet, came away with three firsts and three thirds.

Perhaps the small number of boats built by the yard in 1928 was due to the fact that it was also building a 23-metre, *Cambria,* for Sir William Berry. *Cambria* appears to have been the first large Bermudian racer built in Britain. She turned out not to be a top-class racing boat, as she was frequently beaten by the older, gaff-rigged, Fife 23-metre *Shamrock*.

In September of that same year, 1928, another large boat was commissioned by Luis Fulton of Greenock. This was *Eileen,* an 85-foot auxiliary ketch. Fulton tried to offer his *Rosemary* in part payment for the new boat, but William refused. By May the following year he could not have been satisfied with the progress on her, as he wrote to Robert Balderston, asking him to 'get a move on with my boat'. An indication perhaps that production was not as efficient under the appointed manager (Balderston Fife) as when the Fifes themselves managed the yard.

Meanwhile, an old friend of William, Charles Prince, now living in Paris with a holiday home on the Isle de Noirmoutier in Brittany, contacted the yard about a possible order. In previous years he had written to Fife asking for quotations for an eight-metre, but Fife had replied that it would be much cheaper to build in France, and that he would be happy to supply the design at £125. He even offered to make two inspection visits if it were built in Le Havre. Charles replied it would be cheaper but 'then it is not a winner and consequently not your work'. Once he had accepted the idea of having the boat designed by Fife and built in France, Charles Prince asked William to design an 8.5-metre for his boys. William refused, saying he would not be happy about designing one, as he had never designed for this class. Prince eventually settled for an eight-metre, *Vim*, built in France after enquiries about costs of building at Fairlie and shipping to France.

Charles Prince's lifestyle in Paris, together with his new holiday home in Isle de Noirmoutier was a drain on his pocket. He had to install pumps and dig wells to provide water for his wife's lily pond. At one point he even considered sharing an eight-metre with a friend, but subsequently rejected the idea. He frequently invited William to visit him in Paris and assured him that he made better cocktails than they had sampled at Le Havre.

The quiet hard working William obviously had a more sociable side to his character, which only a few chosen people saw. Outwardly he was a typical dour Scotsman, almost uncommunicative when questioned by the yachting press about possible orders received by the yard. He was not particularly close to his workforce, who referred to him as 'The Boss'. However, he must have inherited something of his genial father's character. He obviously joined in the social scene when visiting away from his native village and he came alive when out in a sailing boat. Living as he did with his sisters, who obviously idolised him, and who had a strong sense of duty to the church, he behaved with complete decorum at home.

The following year, in 1929, there was a boom in yacht building. The Fairlie yard turned out five six-metres, and designs were sent to Australia for *Toogooloowoo II* to be the first of an Australian class of six-metres. Five eight-metres were built, and a design for *Sogdalina* was sent to Bilbao for Count de Zubira to be built in Spain. The Count had previously owned a ten-metre, designed by Fife, which was built at Bilbao. *Sogdalina* was built under the supervision of skipper Oliver Burdon, who later wrote to Fife telling him that she had won six races and that she sailed particularly well in strong winds. The Spanish builder had wanted to remove 500 pounds of lead from the keel, but William advised against this.

Eight-metre under construction (1930). (Courtesy of *Yachting World.*)

The rush by clients to build new sixes was in an effort to be chosen for the team for the next British-American Cup races. Unfortunately, the four boats chosen to represent Britain lost, and this result was repeated in the contest the following year. The British boats did not have large genoas or spinnakers; they probably had ignored the previous comments on the lack of sailing practice as a team, and were overconfident as a result of previous victories. These two defeats, the economic crisis in the following years and the rising popularity of the eight-metres, reduced the demand for six-metres. In fact the yard was only to build six more in the next nine years before it closed.

There was another reason to hurry with the launch of racing boats in 1929, as the yard had secured an order for a large 160-ton schooner which had to be launched in the spring of the following year. Space was required to lay down the keel of this large boat at the beginning of June.

After the tremendous workload of the year and the prospect of building a really large schooner, William, at the age of 72, decided to take a holiday after the keel of the large boat was laid in June. Sir Alexander McCormick, who had retired and was living in Jersey, still corresponded regularly with William. He was having alterations carried out on his boat, *My Lady of Aros,* and he wrote to William. In his letter he wished him an enjoyable cruise to the Northern capitals, the Norwegian fjords and the Arctic Circle. William and his sister Jean went on holiday for about three weeks at the end of July. When the cruise ship called at Oslo (or Christiana, as it was then known) King Olav sent his royal pinnace to bring William ashore, as he was a great admirer of his work.

A busy winter of work on the new schooner followed. This schooner was later launched as *Altair*. A yachting correspondent visited the yard on one of his regular tours to report new building activities in the spring of 1930. As a result of the visit he wrote an article extolling the excellent craftsmanship of the men who worked there. He compared a Fife boat to a Chippendale chair – 'almost too beautiful to use'. He gave the workforce the praise it was due when he stated that craftsmanship was a vital element in the yard of the 'wizard' of Fairlie. 'You will find it in every shed and shop.' Fife designs were beautiful and practical, but it was the workmanship of the men that ensured that the boats performed well under stress, and that same workmanship is responsible for the fact that so many are still sailing today.

Nineteen thirty was a lean year for big yacht building in yards. It was fortunate that the order for *Altair* had come when it did. Apart from *Altair* Fife had only one 12-metre and two eight-metres building. *Altair* was for Captain Guy McCaw, who wanted to cruise in the South Pacific. It had been many years since a large schooner had been launched at Fairlie. Length overall of 109 feet, she was launched in May. A draught of 13 feet 6 inches required the floating dock for launching. Her interior was panelled in walnut, and the chairs and settees upholstered in pale blue Morocco leather. When she was launched from the dock, to William Fife's consternation she was not horizontal in the water, but floating with her bow well down. Mr Archibald McMillan senior, the yard foreman rigger, sailed her to determine where it would be best to add extra lead to correct the trim. There were other problems. When Mr McMillan and his son Duncan were fitting the topmast it was discovered that the diameter was too great for it to fit into the mast band. Duncan had to shave quite a bit of wood from the base to make it fit. William Fife was not at all pleased and was 'jumping up and down on his bunnet, saying "this will ruin me".'

In 1986 *Altair* underwent complete restoration at Southampton. The dedicated team ensured that she was authentically restored to her original specification, including hand-stitched sails (in modern Dacron) but no pale blue leather upholstery. After her refit she proved her sailing abilities had not deteriorated by winning at the Nioulargue Classic Yacht Regatta.

Today *Altair* is still sailing and is a delight to behold, bringing back a touch of the old days when yachting was a gentleman's pastime. Captain McCaw only kept her for two years and sold her to Sir Walter Runciman, who sailed her in British waters up until the outbreak of war. Like all privately owned

Altair (1931) sailing on the Clyde in 1991. (Courtesy of John McFie.)

Mr Archibald McMillan senior at the helm of *Altair*. (Courtesy of Miss K. McMillan.)

craft she was taken over by the Admiralty and after the war ended up in Portugal, and finally in Spain.

In 1991, after her second restoration, *Altair* came back to Fairlie on the Clyde for her 60th birthday. A special reception was held at Kelburn Castle for visiting guests, and they were taken for a sail on the Firth. Although not part of the official event, the author and her family were privileged to spend a day on *Altair* while she was being photographed under different aspects of sail. The feeling of immense power under one's feet and the ease with which she responded to the slightest movement of the helm is something which can never be forgotten. Long may she continue to give pleasure to those who love the sea.

As a result of *Altair*'s successful restoration, a new company, Fairlie Restorations, was formed at Hamble. Their aim was to restore some of Fife's better yachts. *Tuiga, Fulmar* and *Kentra* are now sailing again. Other yachts by Fife were waiting to be transformed back to their original state by this fairy godmother.

The 12-metre *Zoraida* was built at the same time as *Altair* for Arthur Connell. As already stated, he owned several Fife boats over the years and was quite fussy about details. One of his instructions to Fife when *Zoraida* was being built was: 'Please ensure that the cabin soles are made of well seasoned timber and do not warp or creak.' He was fairly conservative, and requested that the cabin panelling and upholstery be the same as on his

Zoraida before launch (1931) and the floating dock. (Courtesy of John McFie.)

previous twelve, *Zinita*. He also wished to retain her sail number, K8. Instructions were also given as to the lockers required for crockery and glasses, and a special locker 'fitted for bottles'!

Unfortunately *Zoraida* did not perform as well as her predecessors. William Fife went to Cowes to deal with complaints about the boat, but just missed Connell, who had already left for Weymouth. At Weymouth, Sherman Hoyt, the American six-metre helmsman, sailed her and said she was slow. Her owner was therefore convinced there was definitely something wrong. The next regatta was at Torquay, and he missed getting advice from Balderston Fife who had been there with his wife but had left Torquay before *Zoraida* arrived. Connell then wrote to the yard, asking for advice on polishing the hull to improve performance. Perhaps he should have continued to call her *Zinita*? There is a great deal of superstition about changing a boat's name.

Of the two eight-metres built that same year, one did not fare too well. This eight-metre was the one built for George Gooderham of the Royal Canadian Yacht Club, who said he wanted a boat to meet the challenge for the Canada's Cup. She was called *Invader II,* and was taken out to Toronto on the *Athenia.* Unfortunately she was not successful in winning the cup.

It was left to the other eight-metre, *Saskia,* to save the honour of the yard. Built for A.S.L. Young she was chosen to defend the Seawanhaka Cup for

Zoraida (1931), rigger at work. (Courtesy John McFie.)

Britain. Her crew consisted of the owner, Mr J.G. Stephen (helm of the *Coilas*, designed by his father), Major C.J. MacAndrew, and two paid hands. Sailing against the American eight *Priscilla III*, *Saskia* retained the cup for Britain. The New York Yacht Club subsequently requested line drawings and a model of *Saskia*, which were provided by the yard.

In 1935 *Saskia* was owned by Mr R. Steele and Mr Preston. That year she won the Royal Yacht Squadron Jubilee Cup and the owners commissioned a silver model to be made. Her performance led the Olympic committee to ask her owners to take her to Keil for the 1937 Olympic Games.

The slowing down of the economy was again matched by the disappearance from the yachting scene of some notable yachtsmen. Sir Thomas Lipton died at the end of the year. In spite of the fortune he had spent on yachts and on his challenges for the America's Cup he had never actually sailed any of his own boats. He always used professional crews, and his friend and adviser, Colonel Duncan Neil, handled the sailing arrangements.

Andrew Coats, admiral of the Mudhook Yacht Club, passed away. Owner of two Fife boats, 12-metre *Cintra* and the 52-footer *Camellia*, he was a member of the thread manufacturing family in Paisley who all owned sailing craft. It was said that at one regatta after the First World War, no fewer than 20 boats, racing yachts and supporting steam yachts were flying either the Coat's or Clark's house flags.

Tom Ratsey, an old friend of William Fife, and of W.P. Stephens, the American journalist, was celebrating his 80th birthday. To mark this occasion his sailing club presented him with a painting of his yacht *Dolly Varden*. W.P. Stephens was now 77 and about to retire from his post as recorder of yachts for Lloyds in America. William Fife, a mere 74 years of age, had just designed the beautiful cruising schooner *Altair*, 'worthy of Fife at his best'.

CHAPTER EIGHTEEN
Sunset

The years 1931, 1932 and 1933 were very lean for the yard. Only five boats were built in each of these years, and in 1933 one of them was a motor boat 'for stock'. The Fifes always tried to keep the workforce employed, and whereas in the past they had built fishing skiffs in hard times they now built boats 'for stock' or 'on spec'. However sailmakers around the country were still busy, and in a letter to Ratsey, in April of 1932, William said, 'We only wish we had orders enough to cause a push as in 14 days we shall be idle.' Normally at this time of the year clients were clamouring to have their boats launched in May for the opening of the sailing season. The stock boat was slow to move, an order was cancelled in 1933 and only a 12-metre, a 16-foot centreboard boat and an 18-foot YRA rating were built. To keep the workforce employed, the yard undertook to supplement output with other types of projects. This included construction of bathing platforms for Millport on the Greater Cumbrae and supplying wood to the Fairlie Bowling Green and the Fairlie Gun Club for repairs to their premises. Moorings were also laid for a local boat hirer.

The following year, 1934, the British-American Cup was to be held in America. This helped create a small boost to yacht building on the Clyde, and Fife built two six-metres, both of which were chosen for the team. They were *Melita* for R.M. Teacher, and *Saskia II* for A.S.L. Young.

Unfortunately the Clyde team were unsuccessful in their challenge in America. Elsewhere, however, the Fife 12-metre *Miquette,* built that same year, was making her mark. The 12-metre class had fewer adherents now and good racing was scarce. The success of *Miquette* at the beginning of the season prompted the Commodore of the Kiel regatta to write to William to congratulate him on the success of his recently launched 12-metre. He also asked if he could persuade the owner, Major Ralph Grigg, to bring his new 12-metre to the Kiel regatta and perhaps to the Scandinavian races. The Commodore also asked Fife to use his influence to bring more British boats to race at Kiel.

That year the yard also had an order for a cruising boat. It was from an old friend of William's. The keel for the 64-foot auxiliary ketch *Frea* was laid for Sir Alexander McCormick, who was now living in Jersey in retirement.

Enquiries had also been received from the Commodore of the Kenya Yacht Club, who wanted a design for a class which could be sailed in Kenya but also built and sailed at the Royal Corinthian Yacht Club in England. The idea was that expatriates on leave in England could enjoy sailing in the same class of boat that they sailed in Kenya. William's solution was to offer them the Conway One Design, saying that he was building one for Mr Wilfred Leuchars. She was named *Intombi* and was to be shipped out to Natal.

The previous year William had offered to design six-metres for the Chantier Naval du Petit Lac at Corsier on Lake Geneva. These plans were to cost £90. The owner, G. Gangloff, requested information on how to alter the six-metre *Caryl* and also a drawing for a new mast.

Construction costs and wages were rising. Mr H.W.G. Lewis, owner of *Kismit,* built in 1895 by Fife, had brought her over to Liverpool from Ireland and had written to the yard asking for a sail plan. William charged him ten shillings, which Mr Lewis thought 'excessive'. In reply, William said that it cost a draughtsman's wages each year to supply copies of drawings, as the yard had built so many yachts. It is interesting to note that even after 35 years *Kismit* was 'still the fastest boat of her size around here, has beautiful lines and is much admired'.

Although the cost of building was rising and orders were few and far between, the yard was still selective when it came to building boats. A request from Buenos Aires for a design for a 14-foot international sailing dinghy was met with the brusque reply from Balderston Fife: 'We do not build or design dinghies.' The rush of work in 1934 must have inspired false confidence in the business, only to have it destroyed by the lack of orders in 1935. Apart from a Mylne-designed ketch launched that year, only three other boats were built: the six-metre *Fiona* for E.S. Parker, an indefatigable yachtsman and faithful client; *Carron II,* an eight-metre for J. Lauriston Lewis; and *Eilean,* a 60-foot cutter for brothers Robert and James Fulton.

Sadly, Evelyn Parker was not to enjoy *Fiona,* his latest new six-metre, for long. He only sailed her for one summer and died in February of the following year at the age of 65. He was a leading light in the six-metre class, treasurer of the RYA, rear admiral of the Mudhook Yacht Club and Commodore of the Cumbraes Yacht Club. This old Etonian had all his boats painted white with an Eton-blue boot top. He had been an active man and thought nothing of spending four nights on the sleeper train from Liverpool to attend two races every week on the Clyde. Summers were spent on the island of Little Cumbrae, where he had a house. The island had long been a favourite visiting place of the Parker family since George Parker visited it in the 1830s in his proa.

On one occasion Evelyn Parker sailed one of his six-metres, *Fintra,* single-handed, because his crew had missed the steamer and did not arrive in time for the start of a race. In spite of this he was still first round the windward mark. In his entire racing career he only missed one start because his launch had broken down. Like other Parkers, he was a faithful patron of the Fifes, and all his six-metres and launches were built and designed at the Fairlie yard. He was usually chosen as a member of the British-American Cup team in one of his Fife-designed and Fairlie-built sixes.

It is perhaps unthinkable to us today, but the date of the 1934 British-American Cup races was specifically changed in order that Mr Parker could have two days shooting partridge before setting off for New York! In the event, it turned out that this change of date was unnecessary, as *Fintra* was finally not chosen for the team that year. He was the treasurer of the RYA, and perhaps this helped him arrange events to suit his social commitments.

At this time William lost yet another old friend. Both he and his American friend W.P. Stephens were saddened by the death of Tom Ratsey. William wrote, 'I will miss Tom Ratsey – he was a man – we used to go together to the South of France in the early Spring and I enjoyed his company and his old yarns. He had a wonderful memory.' In spite of being 78 years of age William assured W.P. Stephens, 'I am glad to hear you are well and still active. I am glad to say I am the same and still enjoy designing boats.' William also made comment on the lack of building orders for boats, except for low priced motor boats: '. . . this kind of work does not interest me'.

In spite of his age and lack of orders, the old 'wizard' had not lost his touch. The eight-metre *Carron II* sailed well, and J. Lauriston Lewis sent William a Christmas card with a photograph of her leading other eight-metres. William also requested photographs of her from Beken of Cowes, in order to send them to the *Glasgow Herald* for publication in a special trade review.

By this time 'quality, not quantity' might have been the motto of the yard. The following year, apart from a launch for Ian Parker of the Little Cumbrae, the yard built only four boats. One of them 'for stock' was not sold till 1938. Cagey as always, William wrote to W.P. Stephens saying 'things are not so bad in this country and we have a fair amount of work on hand'.

Of the boats built that year, one of them became well known and admired but another did not race successfully. The 12-metre *Vanity V,* built for John Payne, was a disappointment, but this was not William's fault. The owner did not like the accommodation normally found on racing 12-metres, saying that 'they are glorified day boats and the saloon is used as a sail locker'. Afterwards, when he complained about her racing performance, Fife replied in a letter that he thought there was too much weight in her, which slowed her down in light weather.

Complaints followed about the mast, accompanied by photographs showing a bad bend between the lower crosstrees and the deck, which only occurred on port tack in a fresh breeze. William was now 79 years of age.

Some of Mr Payne's complaints may seem petty. He wrote, 'I thought you were going to put down plain blue linoleum same as you did in the old *Vanity*. I don't know what sort of stuff has been put down but it is blue and white with black streaks and it looks cheap and nasty and spoils the look of the boat when anyone goes down the companion way.' Mr Payne wanted the best of both worlds – a good racing 12-metre, but a boat with comfortable and tasteful accommodation. The two seldom go together. In fact *Yachting World* wrote to the yard for an accommodation plan to show readers that the 12-metre could be made habitable for cruising.

In the winter of 1935 William was approached by Michael Mason, who wanted a change from eight-metre class racing for a while in order to try his hand at ocean racing. He wanted a gaff-rigged schooner of about 50 tons built to the new ocean racing rules. Quite adamant, he specified 'no machinery', and did not want any engine at all; he was determined to have lighting by oil lamps. Mr Mason intended to cruise through the Magellan Straits and back round the Horn; he also wanted to sail round the North Cape. William responded by saying that he didn't think a boat designed for ocean racing would make a suitable cruising boat. Mason acceded, but insisted on having her built to the ocean racing rules, and expressly desired that the accommodation be comfortable for cruising. He wanted a schooner rig, which he felt must be good if the Newfoundland Banks fishermen had used it consistently for so long.

Once again, as usual, William got his own way, and sent him plans for a 69-foot 9-inch Bermudian cutter built to the new RORC rules. She would have an Oregon pine main mast, which was good for ocean work, and a spruce topmast. She cost £7,250 and was to be called *Latifa*. Her construction was composite, steel frames, teak planking and a teak deck. Unusual for the Fairlie yard she had a canoe stern. The yachting press felt that it was fitting that the first design to the new rule should come from the Clyde yard, and when finished they remarked that 'it did not matter what the yard builds, it is inevitably beautiful'. The following year *Latifa* was altered to yawl rig and it is in this form that she can be seen as a reminder of the genius of the last William Fife who regarded her as one of his finest designs. After William died she was chosen by his sisters as a memorial to their brother, and a gilded scale model of *Latifa* still sails, head to wind, as the weather vane on the spire of Fairlie Parish Church. Not only was she beautiful but, in keeping with all yachts built at Fairlie, she was strong. Uffa Fox observed that she was absolutely watertight when he saw her laid up for the winter after her first year of strenuous sailing, including a voyage to Madeira and back in gale-force winds. In fact he so admired her that in later years Uffa climbed up the outside of the church spire to touch the gilded *Latifa* 'for luck'!

Latifa (1936) wind vane model on top of Fairlie Parish Church spire.

Another yacht launched that year was *Peregrine*. She was designed by Captain O.H. Watts for Mr H. Sharpe, a company director from Dundee, and after restoration by naval architect David Loomas is still afloat.

There were signs that it was not going too well for the business at this time. One yacht, started 'on spec' in 1936, was not sold till 1938. Although there was no lack of enquiries for quotations for building boats or for supplying plans, it looks as if the yard was pricing itself out of the market. For example, the yard was asked for a quotation for a 22-ton auxiliary ketch by a firm of naval architects in Southampton. It was priced at £5,620, which prompted the reply that this was 'by far the highest we have received'.

Lieutenant-Commander John Illingworth had visited the yard, and, after admiring *Latifa,* asked for a price for a yacht. He also said it was 'too much and regret this' as he had been very pleased with all the boats he had seen at Fairlie. Other clients, like A.R. Richardson, said, 'I regret I cannot afford to ask you to build for me', after receiving a quotation. Perhaps the most telling reply was from a firm of yacht brokers in London who had given their client Fife's quotation of £15,500 for a new 102-ton auxiliary schooner. 'Our client nearly had heart failure and told me Nicholsons offered to build him what he wanted for £ 10,000.' Another letter from yacht brokers Shepherd in 1938 said that the quotation for a 55-tonner was 'prohibitive'.

What was the reason for this increase in price when a 'special' reduction might have secured the orders and ensured continuing work? William was nearly 80 and, although he turned out *Latifa,* and would design a few more quality yachts before he died, his output had slowed down. His nephew was not a designer and perhaps did not have the confidence to accept such work, which he might have to finish for his uncle.

There are certain inconsistencies in the way in which Balderston Fife replied to prospective clients. To a client asking for a quotation for a 16-foot centreboard dinghy, he replied that the yard would build one for £130. One month previously he had replied to a similar request saying that the yard was unable to quote for a sailing dinghy as 'we only build highly finished yacht's boats'. If work was scarce and quotations for yachts not accepted, one would think that it would have at least given some work to the men to build a few dinghies.

Balderston was married to an extravagant wife. His uncle was slowing down and not designing as many yachts as before. This, combined with rising costs of materials and wages, may have led to Robert Balderston trying to squeeze more money out of the business. This was to have the effect of driving old clients to other yards.

In 1937 William designed only four boats, and the yard built only three of them. Two were eight-metres, one a design only, for Carl Wikstrom of Stockholm, and the other, *Felma*, for F.A. Richards. *Felma* failed to win the Coupe de France, but *Evenlode,* built to RORC rule for Chris Ratsey, was much admired and Uffa Fox said he would 'dearly love to own such a lovely little ship'. The other remaining build that year was *Eilean*, a 56-ton auxiliary ketch for the brothers James and Robert Fulton of Greenock. There was not much work in the yard.

Fife began to slow down at about 80 years of age. Given that the yard had a much greater capacity than the two eight-metres and the *Evenlode* they were building, complaints were still coming from prospective clients that quotations were too high. Mr K. Neale declined to have a design plan at £75, and said 'I am afraid you may have retired from business before I can get a boat. I have always admired your boats and designs more than any others – the name Fife to me means the best in both design and build.' This man's father had owned three Fife boats, the six-metre *Flya, Dodo III* which had belonged to Mr Bergius and *Amity* (ex *Moyana)*, built for Wilfred Leuchars. Another client lost!

Still the requests came in. G.L. Watson wrote asking for the specification for an auxiliary schooner for Colonel Clark. The peculiarities of some clients did not stop at choice of linoleum as for *Vanity*. Its specification was to include cheaper upholstery because 'when a lady comes along to select, something more expensive might be decided upon'! Another surprising fact is that these large yachts were sometimes fitted with Aga cookers. The specification was to quote for normal cooking utensils 'as utensils for the Aga cooker are expensive'. *Altair* was originally fitted with an Aga, which weighed between 10 and 11 hundredweight.

With so little building going on it would be reasonable to expect the yard to take any form of suitable work, which might bring in money. Not so. John Barbour, who had ordered a 24-foot Sportsman model from Chris-Craft, which was arriving in Greenock from America, requested storage of the boat for two months. It was turned down because 'we have no facilities for storing boats here'. A 24-foot boat would not have been noticed in the corner of one of the big sheds, which must have been virtually empty by this time.

The following year the same pattern of building only three boats at Fairlie was repeated. Though few in number, the boats were as good as ever and some of them are still sailing today. The largest was *Mariella,* a 78-foot auxiliary Bermudian yawl for James Paterson, whose firm had provided 'Camp' coffee to soldiers in India. She was designed by Alfred Mylne and he too wrote to Balderston Fife saying he hoped the original cost of £11,275 could be reduced.

Of composite construction, steel frames and teak planking, *Mariella* was a beautiful boat and greatly admired on the Clyde. James Paterson kept her for only one season and then sold her to Ronald Teacher, no stranger to Fife-built boats as he had sailed his Fife six-metres in the British-American Cup races. Mr Teacher was elected Commodore of the Royal Clyde Yacht Club in 1938 and retained this office until 1970. *Mariella* had been requisitioned for war work by the Admiralty during the Second World War. Returned to Teacher after the war, she became a familiar sight at all the Royal Clyde regattas. She was also to the fore on 30 June 1956 when the Royal Clyde Yacht Club celebrated its centenary with a regatta at Rothesay.

There had been no royal personage racing on the Clyde since King George V had attended Clyde Fortnight in 1920. The Duke of Edinburgh, Patron of the club, arrived in the Royal Yacht *Britannia* for the centenary celebrations and took part as helmsman on his International Dragon Class *Bluebottle*. The regatta was a magnificent sight and included over 200 yachts. Many of them had come from Europe to compete in this class. The event was followed the next day by a cruise in company, led by the Commodore in *Mariella* and the Duke of Edinburgh, accompanied by Uffa Fox, sailing *Bluebottle*.

Throughout his ownership of *Mariella* Mr Teacher kept her in immaculate condition. In post-war years she was one of the few large yachts afloat on the Clyde. At a Royal Clyde Yacht Club gathering, a conversation with Mrs Teacher about the family boats brought forth the remark that 'we always went to Mr. Fife for our yachts'.

After Mr Teacher's death *Mariella* had a succession of owners. She travelled round the world, sometimes in private hands, sometimes on charter. An unusual coincidence occurred when she was visiting Australia to take part in the Sydney to Hobart race in 1990. Forced to seek shelter from a cyclone at Hamilton Island off the Queensland coast, the skipper discovered that the local postmaster's father had been born in Fairlie and that he had worked in the yard on *Mariella* and had crewed on her when she was owned by James Paterson. She returned to the Caribbean in 1993 and was bought by Carlo Falcone, who raced her regularly. *Mariella* won the 1994 and the 1995 Antigua Classic Yacht Regatta both in her class and overall. Although fairly young by comparison with some of the other Fife survivors, it is likely that she will still be sailing into the next century.

Apart from *Mariella* there was little else building that year. William was asked to design a 35-foot waterline auxiliary yawl for Major Bengtson in Sweden, to be built in Sweden. To keep the men occupied a 40-foot motor launch and a 43-foot Bermudian cutter were started 'for stock'. The motor launch was sold to a Largs man but the yacht was not sold until 1940.

In December 1938 the yard received an unusual request from a firm of architects, James Houston of Kilbirnie. Mr Houston was designing a new cinema to be built in Largs on the site of the former Millburn House. The cinema was to be called 'The Viking', a name to recall the Battle of Largs in 1263 when the invading Vikings were defeated. The cinema was a really avant-garde design and its frontage was to feature the prow of a Viking galley apparently floating on a pond and lit from beneath the water. The yard was asked to quote for 'the supply and fitting up of a complete forepart of a galley as shown on the accompanying drawing. It should be an exact replica of a Viking galley.' The plans for the ship were to be provided by a Glasgow firm, Gutherie and Wells. Balderston Fife, effectively manager of the yard, replied, 'We could not take in hand with this work except possibly when we are slack in the middle of summer and therefore beg to be excused from quoting.' The work was finally undertaken by a firm of boat builders, McLean of Greenock.

The yard at that time was virtually at a standstill. Why was the work turned down? There were only two boats building in the yard, and both were 'for stock'; only two more boats were to be built before it closed.

Enquiries were still coming in for quotations. In May 1939 the Royal Hong Kong Yacht Club requested designs for a racing keelboat and a racing cruiser. Another quotation sent to Burma was judged to be 'too dear'. Yet another client who wrote in January suggested that the international situation seemed more acute and he would postpone getting a quotation till he had sold his old boat. His letter to the yard concluded: 'No doubt everything will be settled by spring'! Approaching war clouds did not seem to worry some members of the yachting fraternity.

Several requests for designing and building six-metres were still being given favourable replies. Was this because the plans were already available? Alexander Stephen, shipbuilders in Glasgow, were also favoured with quotations for 12-, 13-, and 14-foot rowing dinghies to be built of Honduras cedar. A far cry from the previous year's response that 'we only build highly finished yacht's boats'.

There were only three boats in the yard in 1939. *Solway Maid* had been started the previous year 'for stock', and two others were started and completed that year: *Madrigal,* a 48-foot auxiliary Bermudian cutter for Campbell Paterson, brother of James Paterson, who had briefly owned *Mariella*, and *Flica II,* a 12-metre designed by Laurent Giles for Hugh Goodson.

The outbreak of the Second World War in September 1939 put a stop to all commercial and pleasure-boat building. The yard was closed, never to open again as William Fife & Son. *Madrigal* was not launched, and remained in the yard for the duration of the war. Eventually, after the war, it was discovered that extensive dry rot had developed and she had to be burnt.

Solway Maid had better luck. Built 'on spec', she had been offered for sale for some time. Finally, in 1940, still lying in the yard, Ivan Carr acquired her at a very reasonable price. Ivan ran the Carr Flour Mills at Silloth, and in addition to yachting he enjoyed driving fast cars. He must have had an eye on the boat because, on a previous visit to the Clyde in his then current yacht *Carita,* he had already enquired about the 'fast cruising yacht' for sale. In common with other would-be purchasers at the time he felt the price was too steep.

The Admiralty had requisitioned the yard and, in order to clear the space of boats, the last remaining stock boat was considerably discounted, and Mr Carr took this opportunity to buy her. *Solway Maid* was destined to spend her war years in a mud berth on the Solway Firth. Ivan Carr worked tirelessly to fit her out, as this had to be abandoned when the Admiralty took over the yard. There had been no time to have the Fife

Mardigal II (1952), skipper Peter Currie.

dragon trademark carved on her bow, but she was Mr Carr's pride and joy, and he always kept her in immaculate condition.

After the war, *Solway Maid* returned to a mooring in Fairlie Bay. Mr Carr would arrive in his sports car on Friday evenings, have his dinghy brought to the jetty by one of the local children and then depart with his wife for a weekend of cruising on the Firth of Clyde. When he died in 1974, his second wife could not bear to part with the boat. Finally, in 1987, she was sold to Roger Sandiford. David Spy carried out restoration in 1989–90, and she is still sailing, mainly in the Mediterranean. *Solway Maid* was the last boat launched from the yard.

The destruction of *Madrigal* after the war was not the end of that story. In 1950 Campbell Paterson had a replacement built by the Fairlie Yacht Slip Company, using the original Fife plan for *Madrigal*. Anchored in Fairlie Bay, near *Solway Maid,* these two Fife creations were now the 'big boats' of the day, yet they were only between 40 and 50 feet in length overall – mere midgets compared with some of the pre-war yachts.

Madrigal II continued to grace the Clyde scene till her ageing owner decided to turn to motor cruising. She was sold in 1968 and went across the Atlantic. In 1990 she returned to the Clyde for a brief spell under the ownership of James Miller and was a familiar sight off the Royal Northern and Clyde Yacht Club. In 1996 the present owners had her refurbished by Fairlie Restorations, changing the interior layout to a more practical one.

The last boat to be given a yard number, 829, was *Flica II,* a 12-metre. She too is a survivor. She sailed in America's Cup challenge trials against *Sceptre,* which was designed by David Boyd. She also appeared at Clyde Week (by this time the event had been reduced to a week from a fortnight) racing against *Sceptre.* It was a magnificent sight to see the two large yachts at close quarters, but somewhat unnerving if you happened to be in close proximity to the two 'giants' in a much smaller boat.

When the yard closed in 1939 that was effectively the end of William Fife & Son. William died on 11 August 1944 at the age of 87 years. The family had run the yard for over 140 years, since the beginning of the 19th century. Nearly 1,000 boats had been built in that period.

When the premises were taken over by the Admiralty for the duration of the war, they were occupied by an underwater research establishment, moved from Portland to Fairlie to be further away from possible German invasion. After the war ended in 1947, the Admiralty left Fairlie. Some local men were still employed to carry out repairs to wooden Admiralty boats, launches and lifeboats or warships of the Allies that came to Greenock for refuelling and stores.

By now Robert Balderston Fife was 61 years old. The yard was sold to Ian Parker and his brother, the same family whose ancestors had been clients of the first William Fife in the early 1800s. The wheel had turned its full circle. The new owners re-named the yard Fairlie Yacht Slip Company. In 1985 it was sold to a housing development company and demolished. Where the sheds stood that saw the birth of great yachts such as the 'terrible' *Fiona, Shamrock* and *Cambria,* there is now a row of modern houses.

The yard itself may be no more, but there are still many of its beautiful creations afloat, a testimony to the genius of the Fifes and the superb quality of craftsmanship of the Fairlie men.

CHAPTER NINETEEN
The Craftsmen

Fife designs gave rise to beautiful boats with a very high standard of workmanship, and their finish was such that they stood out above all others. Built to last, of the finest woods, they were put together by dedicated craftsmen. No wonder their owners cherished them and returned to Fife and the yard again and again for new designs.

In the beginning, when the first William Fife started to build boats, there were no yard buildings. Construction took place, even in winter, in the open, on the foreshore, with no shelter at all from the bitter east wind which has always plagued Fairlie.

This was a family business, and at first the only boat-builders were William and at least two of his brothers. Later, when William married and had a family of his own, all his sons were apprenticed to the yard as shipwrights. The Customs and Excise records of 1833 state that the yard employed nine working shipwrights. Records show that five of them were his sons. The same number of shipwrights is listed as being employed in 1851. The sawyer and blacksmith who lived in the village may have carried out work for the yard but were independent tradesmen.

In the early years, the village was not easily accessible except by sea and most of the timber was obtained from the Kelburn Estate or from Kilbirnie, and was mainly oak. Work could only take place during the hours of daylight or if there was a full moon. The second William Fife is said to have described *Pearl,* built in 1873, as being built 'ahint the shed' by his brother, Alex, in his spare time 'by the licht o' the mune'.

In the old days it was not unknown for wood to be smuggled or thrown overboard by incoming ships in Fairlie Roads for collection on shore. In 1821 Customs recovered a log of American pine 'found at sea'. Later, in 1825 and in 1845, logs of black birch were recovered locally, for which no tax had been paid. When the Customs officer offered the wood for sale the highest offer he could get was from William Fife & Son. Tidewaiters at Fairlie and Largs were advised by the Customs officer to 'look out for timber on the beaches'.

The opening of the Forth and Clyde Canal in 1790 gave Clyde shipbuilding yards direct access to timber from the Baltic, shipped through the Eastern end of the canal. The development of transatlantic trade also brought access to the timber of North America and Canada. This timber usually arrived as 'green' wood and could not be used immediately for boat building. It therefore had to be seasoned, either by steeping in water or lying outside to be weathered.

An example of the variety of wood used in the construction of one of Fife's boats is shown by the types supplied for the building of *Mariella*. (Appendix 1.) Ships' carpenters employed on the hull used teak, Oregon pine, Pacific spruce and American elm. The ships' joiners worked with teak, Oregon pine, Pacific spruce, plywood, Australian oak, birch, mahogany and cypress. The spars were made from Oregon pine and Pacific spruce, and the crosstrees from American elm.

Mahogany, spruce, cedar, Oregon larch, American elm, teak, oak, cypress, yellow pine, plywood and ash were used for the construction of a racing eight-metre, *Invader II*. Every part of a boat had a particular wood, which was best suited for its construction.

The cost in man-hours to produce *Mariella* is shown in Appendix 2. The bulk of the cost lay in the wages paid to the carpenters and joiners. Apart from woodwork, the carpenters had to fit brass bollards, rowlock plates on dinghies, make and mount spars, clean chain and 'keep up steam' for the bending of planks. Joiners were employed mainly on the interior finishes, fitting drawers and cupboards, but they also had to fit the compass, flag staff, deck hatches, rails for soda siphons (!), footholds on deck, and make folding chairs. They were also required to fit linoleum, unpack and check silver, and fit upholstery. Sometimes the firm of Wylie and Lochhead installed the upholstery. Mr Wylie was a good client of the yard.

Riggers were not only responsible for the actual rigging; they also made canvas covers for winches, capstans, deckhouses and sail covers. Other trades involved were plumbers, painters, blacksmiths, polishers, framesetters and draughtsmen. The carver applied the final touch when he put the dragon's head on the bow. For this intricate piece of craftsmanship on both sides of the hull he was paid the princely sum of £1 10s!

The men worked hard and were not overpaid by today's standards. In the days of the first William Fife they had to work out of doors in all weathers, using hand tools, and only during the hours of daylight, which were very short in winter. There were no mechanical saws. Logs were cut in the sawpit, where, as has been mentioned already, contraband was sometimes hidden.

The villagers lived in rented houses feued to the Kelburn Estate. In 1876 the Fifes bought a portion of land from the Earl of Glasgow, opposite the site of the yard, on which stood the two-storey house, 'Croftend'. When they moved up the hill to their new residence 'The Place', two of the more senior employees occupied the top and bottom storeys of 'Croftend' and paid rent to the Fifes. These new tenants were Mr McNeur, the draughtsman, and Mr William Fife, carpenter, cousin of the third William Fife. Later they were

Forge in the blacksmith's shop.

followed by Mr Stuart McAuley, foreman carpenter, and Mr Archibald McMillan, foreman rigger. The second William Fife was a man who was interested in the welfare of his workforce. In 1877, 1878, 1892 and 1899 he made loans to yard employees, enabling them to purchase their homes. This was a period when the yard was busy and making money. It was also a means of keeping the workforce in the village.

The Fifes were businesslike in everything they did. Although they formed a limited company in 1856, it was not until 1900 that they acquired the land on which the yard stood. This may have been because the Earl of Glasgow was unwilling to sell the ground, or perhaps the second William Fife was so taken up with designing that he did not have time to consider other matters. The third William introduced many improvements to the yard, including a

Craftsmen of the 1920s. (Courtesy of *Largs & Millport Weekly News*.)

degree of mechanisation; and it may have been his idea to purchase the land. Certainly by that time the business could well afford to acquire the site and expand.

In 1903 an additional adjoining plot to the north of the yard was purchased from the Kelburn Estate. A blacksmith's shop and another building shed were erected on this new site. This successful steady expansion had started in 1851, with a workforce of nine men, and over a period of 50 years, up to 1902, the workforce had increased nearly five fold to 40 men and boys.

The third William Fife modernised the yard after his father died. Acetylene gas lighting had been introduced by 1907, and saws and other tools had been mechanised. Hand tools were still used in finishing work and were owned by each individual craftsman. When starting an apprenticeship, young men were supplied with tools, for which they paid the yard over the period of their apprenticeship. When the yard was taken over by HM Anti-Submarine Experimental Establishment at the beginning of the Second World War, electric power had to be installed for the lathes and machine tools. Power was generated by a diesel engine.

The time taken to build a boat depended upon size and how busy the yard was at the time. An eight-metre could be finished in weeks, but some larger cruising yachts would take up to nine months. If built 'on spec', the boat might lie on the stocks till sold, sometimes two or three years later. This stock-building provided employment when orders were thin on the ground.

When the yard first started, in addition to building new ones, boats were repaired and laid up for the winter. Others might be taken in part exchange

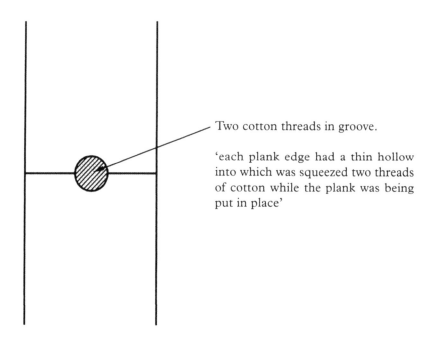

Two cotton threads in groove.

'each plank edge had a thin hollow into which was squeezed two threads of cotton while the plank was being put in place'

Special method of caulking frequently used by the yard to give a smooth finish to the hull.

for a new one and later sold. Once the business became established and well known, the yard was so busy with new build and design that there was no time for maintenance and repair work.

A client wishing to order a boat would initially discuss it with the Fifes, and a specification would be drawn up. This might incorporate special requirements made by the client and, occasionally, even included the size of the shed in which the boat was to be built. Payment arrangements were by instalment. An initial payment, followed by one when the keel was laid, and thereafter at certain stages till completion.

It has been said many times that two of the main features of Fife boats were sturdiness and seaworthiness. They seldom leaked, and many have survived to the present day. This is due to the superb craftsmanship, but also perhaps to the special methods of construction and caulking, which gave a smooth finish to the hull, and which usually remained, even after the boat had been exposed to heavy weather. A hollow groove was formed along the whole edge of each plank into which was squeezed two threads of cotton. The Fifes also developed certain other ideas of their own.

The third William Fife designed a cleat for the America's Cup challenger *Shamrock III* in 1903. The metal castings which held the wooden bar were given a lip on the underside, and this took the wear off the wood and prevented

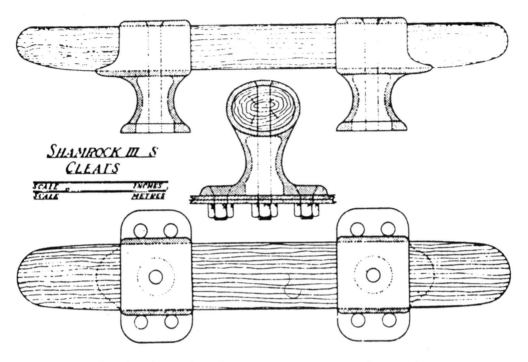

SHAMROCK III S
CLEATS
SCALE   INCHES
SCALE   METRES

Cleat for *Shamrock III*. (From *Racing, Cruising and Design*.)

chafing of the sheet or rope. A bolt running down through the centre of the casting and the teak bar strengthened the whole fitting.

Another Fife invention, which intrigued Uffa Fox when he visited the yard, was a special frame-bending machine. In a letter to William Fife he says, 'I am sorry that I have not taken a photograph of the machine which bends up floors and thickens angle but will write about it in my book on design as an illustration of the excellent way in which your yachts are built, as it is such things as this that lift them high above the ordinary level.' In 1936 *Yachting World* published plans for *Piccolo,* a 35-foot racing cruiser by Fife. The description reads: 'Fife bends steel floors round without cutting them and because of this they are thicker and stronger in the angle at the heel. Far better than the usual floors which are built up and cut at this point.' Yet another reason why Fife boats were sturdier than others!

The yard was the main source of employment for the village. The same families were associated with it over three generations of Fifes. There were

Lofting floor.

Spar making, 1930. (Courtesy *Yachting World*.)

The big shed.

the Fifes themselves, their brothers, uncles, cousins and nephews. Other families employed as carpenters included members of the Boyd, Crawford, Dickie, Sheddon, McFie and Boag families. The members of the McMillan family were riggers and carpenters. The French family, who were independent blacksmiths, and not directly employed by the yard, made fittings for the boats. As the yard expanded, more people were employed from outwith the existing small village community.

Both William senior and William junior were sticklers for detail. A tale was recounted by the late Professor Alexander Thom, engineer and archaeo-astronomer, which illustrates this. When hinges were mounted, the slots in the screws had to be parallel to the hinge. A tradesman had driven in the screws with a hammer instead of a screwdriver and was admonished for not having the slots in the correct position. When asked by the angry Fife: 'What do you think the slots are for?' The man replied 'for taking the screw nails out'!

The one drawback about employment in the yacht-building industry was its seasonal nature. Building finished about the end of May, and normally

Frame bending machine. (From *Sail and Power*.)

there was no work in the yard till the end of the sailing season, when new orders were commissioned. Usually men were paid off in spring and many found temporary work as paid hands on racing yachts. Unlike paid hands, racing skippers tended to be employed for the full year. Skippers were responsible for fitting out in spring, overseeing maintenance during the winter, hiring crews, and generally running the boat. Some owners, like Sir Thomas Lipton, had little to do with actually racing or sailing the yacht.

Sailmakers and riggers readily found summer berths. The sons of the senior McMillan, rigger in the yard, crewed on various yachts. Willie and Archie McMillan were part of the crew of Evelyn Parker's six-metre *Fintra*, which sailed to victory in the British-American Cup races of 1928.

The yard had put the village of Fairlie on the map. All over the world its name had become synonymous with superb craft. These boats were built entirely by local men over a period of three generations. There was not a villager who did not feel proud of 'their' yard. They turned out in numbers to watch launches, and they eagerly followed the fortunes of the racing yachts. There was always pride and satisfaction when they performed well, and the outcome of racing was always a topic of conversation with current and ex-employees of the yard.

Now, 60 years after the yard closed on the outbreak of the Second World War, many of these yachts are still afloat, the golden dragon on the bow proudly cutting through the waves and proclaiming their origin from the yard of William Fife & Son.

CHAPTER TWENTY
The Fife Regatta

In 1996, while sailing with Alastair Houston aboard the Fife eight-metre *Fulmar*, Duncan Walker asked, 'When are we going to have a Fife Regatta in Scotland?' Alasdair replied, 'If you bring the yachts, I will organise it.' Alistair and his sister Fiona, who brought her organisational skills to the project, were responsible for the first Fife Regatta held in 1998. It was attended by ten yachts.

That summer the regatta week commenced from Largs Marina, with a race round the island of Greater Cumbrae. This was followed by a race from Largs up the firth to the Royal Northern and Clyde Yacht Club at Rhu, where a dinner was held. The following day there was a passage race to Rothesay and a visit to Mount Stuart, the former home of the Marquis of Bute. The final passage race involved sailing through the Kyles of Bute down the Firth of Clyde through the Tan, a channel between Greater and Little Cumbrae islands, past Fairlie, the birthplace of the yachts, and finishing at Largs Marina. Social highlights included a dinner for owners with Lord Glasgow at Kelburn Castle. The prizegiving was held on the final day at the castle. Everyone declared the event to have been a resounding success.

Five years later, by popular demand, a second Fife Regatta was arranged for 2003. The format was the same as the 1998 regatta. This time 22 Fife yachts attended along with three invited guest boats, *Adix*, *Sara Moraea* and *Shannandoh*. *Kentra*, who has attended all of the Fife regattas, celebrated her 80th birthday on board. There were so many guests that the waterline was considerably lowered!

Another five years would pass before the next regatta, which was held in 2008. Nineteen Fife and two guest boats, *Peggy Bawn* and *Mariette*, attended. *Hatasoo*, the oldest boat in the fleet, had to retire from the round Cumbrae race as she was leaking. The McGrouther brothers decided to abandon the regatta and sail her back to their yard at Kilcreggan. That year was particularly auspicious for *Viola*, who was celebrating her 100th birthday. It was marked in style with bottles of champagne roped round the hull cooling in the marina water. There were so many people on the pontoon drinking her health that they ended up ankle deep in water, as it succumbed to the extra weight. The racing and event formula for the week was as in previous years, with the addition of a race on the King's Course in mid firth.

In 2013, another regatta was arranged, again with 18 Fife boats and two guest boats, *Rainbow* and *St. Patrick*, attending. This time the programme changed. The first race was held in windy conditions from Largs to a mark at the Cloch lighthouse, and then proceeded to Rothesay. The next day was a sail through the Kyles of Bute to Tighnabruaich, where a race to Portavadie started. This was followed by an overnight stop at Portavadie and a day of rest. *Kentra* celebrated her birthday and this time it was her 90th. That year the winds were very strong and some of the smaller boats retired from the race to Rothesay. As before, the event was a resounding success.

Five years later there was no Fife Regatta on the Clyde, but a regatta was held in the Mediterranean by Les Voiles de St Tropez to celebrate 150 years of the classic William Fife designs.

When the regatta is held on the Clyde, it must not be forgotten that in some cases these yachts have to sail hundreds of miles to participate and enjoy sailing at their birthplace. This is not without its dangers. In 1998 the event was overshadowed by the untimely loss of Eric Tabarly, a lifelong admirer of Fife. He had set sail from Benodet after hosting a gathering of classic yachts to celebrate the 100th birthday of his beloved *Pen Duick* and was lost overboard on his way to the Clyde. *Pen Duick* was present for the duration of the regatta, with the French ensign flown at half-mast, but she did not take part in the races. Madame Tabarly knew Eric would have wanted his boat to share the event with other Fife designs at their birthplace. On his way to the 2013 regatta, Mario Piri, owner of *Latifa*, was unfortunate to break his leg while sailing single-handed on his way to the Clyde across a stormy Bay of Biscay. *Latifa* was sent to the regatta with a replacement crew.

All was not doom and gloom. The 2008 Fife Regatta was filmed as a background to *Fast and Bonnie*, a documentary on the history of William Fife III made for BBC TV by producers Denis Cosgrove and Brian Barr, who are sadly no longer with us. The cameraman caught some magnificent shots of Fife designs doing what they do best: performing in their natural habitat.

The year 2020 had been designated by the Scottish government as 'The Year of Scotland's Coasts and Waters' and the fifth Fife Regatta was to be part of special events marking the year. With a heavy heart the organisers cancelled it due to the Covid-19 pandemic. The fifth Fife Regatta will now take place in June 2022 and a new race to Hunters Quay will visit another famous Clyde yachting venue.

YACHTS ATTENDING THE FIFE REGATTAS

1998	2003	2008	2013
Magda IV	Belle Adventure	Altair	Astor
Moonbeam III	Clio	Ayrshire Lass	Ayrshire lass
Madrigal	Hatasoo	Fintra	Corralie
Mignon	Jap	Fyne	Ellad
Hallow'een	Kentra	Hatasoo	Fintra
Elise	Kookaburra	Halloweeen	Fiona
Kentra	Lotus	Ierne	Kentra
Solway Maid	Mignion	Lucky Girl	Latifa
Starlight	Mikado	Mariquita	Mignion
Pen Duick	Moonbeam IV	Mignion	Mikado
	Pierette	Mikado	Oblio
	Rosemary	Moonbeam III	Saskia
	Seabird	Oblio	Seabird
	Sian II	Rosemary	Solway Maid
	Siglen	Soloway Maid	Sonata
	Soloway Maid	Truant	Tringa
	Sonata	The Lady Anne	Truant
	Sunshine	Sonata	Viola
	Tern	Viola	
	The Lady Anne		
	Thelma III		
	Viola		

	Guest boats	Guest boats	Guest boats
	Adix	Peggy Bawn	Rainbow
	Sara Moraea	Mariette	St. Patrick
	Shannondoh		

Epilogue

The passion for Fife yachts continues. They shine at classic regattas – and some of them are more than 100 years old. Throughout this book mention has been made of the many restorations; some of them are second or third restorations. There has also been the building of a number of replicas to original Fife designs using modern materials.

Since the last edition of *Fast and Bonnie, Eileen*, built in 1928 for the Fulton brothers of Greenock, was rescued for restoration. After several changes of ownership and a change of name to *Aquarius* in the 1960s, she was converted from a cutter to a yawl. She took part in the 1964 China Seas race from Hong Kong to Manila. During a typhoon she lost her stern and mizzen mast and did not finish. She took part in the race again under the name of *Green Beret* and came second in her class. Discovered by Jean Claude Joffre, she was transported to a yard in Antwerp, where he hoped to restore her. Unfortunately, he passed away before restoration was possible. She lay in the yard for a few years and was finally restored for a French owner. Her sister ship, *Maryk*, is at present in Serbia.

Eva, built in 1906, was found languishing in the port of Alicante. The owner who rescued her found that restoration was too costly and so she was taken on by the owner of Astilleros Marítimeo del Mediterráneo yard. The mahogany hull was rotting, the stern had been chopped off and the interior needed stripping. The hull was re-planked and controversially lined with a single diagonal layer of 4mm thick wood to increase stiffness. *Eva* went on to win several top prizes at regattas and was crewed by her owner, Juan Carlos Eguiagaray, and his family.

The eight-metre *Severn* was found without a keel by Fred Meyer. She was restored by David Viera of the yard Absolute in Portugal. The problem of finding a suitable keel was solved when a drawing was found at the Scottish Maritime Museum of a keel for another Fife eight-metre with the note 'also for yard number 787'. Fred was also involved in the restoration of *Rita IV*, a Fife-designed ten-metre, built in Copenhagen for King Christian of Denmark. *Rita IV* was also restored by David Viera at his Portuguese yard, and Fred has written a book about her restoration.

Saskia, built in 1931, returned to Scotland from Australia to participate in the eight-metre International World Cup Centenary regatta held at the Royal Northern and Clyde Yacht Club. At the end of the regatta her owners put her up for sale before returning to Australia. The new owner, Murdo McKillop, had her refitted to top-class condition. She attended the 2013 Fife Regatta and was leading the fleet overall till she had to leave early to compete at Cowes Week, where she carried off two prizes

One of the most extensive restorations must be that of *Eilean*, built in 1936 for the Fulton brothers. The brothers' previous yacht had been named *Eileen*, as had their father's. Change of spelling may have been to avoid confusion with other yachts. She was discovered lying in a mangrove swamp in the Caribbean by Angelo Bonati of the Italian watch company Panerai. After crossing the Atlantic she was taken to the yard of Francesco del Carlo in Viareggio. The extensive restoration was supervised by naval architect Enrico Zaccagni. *Eilean* is now the flagship of Panerai. For many years the company sponsored classic regattas round the world, and although they no longer sponsor regattas, *Eilean* appears regularly on the classic circuit. She has just returned to the del Carlo yard for a refit after three years of hard sailing, including three more crossings of the Atlantic.

The 15-metre *Tuiga* is now the club boat of the Yacht Club de Monaco and is crewed by club members. Guest helms have included Prince Albert of Monaco and the late Eric Taberly. *Rosemary*, built in 1924, attended the 2008 Fife Regatta and was sold to Patricia and Rob Dunn. Patricia, daughter of the author, wanted to preserve another Fife yacht. After restoration by Ashley Butler she was sold two years later to a Canadian owner. Naval commitments had prevented extensive sailing and it was felt the hull would not benefit from lying ashore for extended periods.

The grand old lady *Viola*, based for many years in La Rochelle with her guardian Yves Rautureau, is now in Monaco with her new guardian Kostia Belkin. Completely refitted to perfection by the Candela boatyard in La Rochelle, Kostia commissioned a book describing the restoration. This has been written by Bruno Barbara of the yard. *Viola* may not be the largest Fife built but at 111 years old is still a winner. In 2017 she won the overall trophy for Monaco Classic week and appeared on a Monaco postage stamp. In 2018 she carried off the Fife Memorial trophy at the Voiles de St Tropez in addition to being voted boat of the year in 2017 and 2018 by *Yachting Classic* magazine. Her placings at six classic regattas in 2019 were either first or second. It is no wonder that her owner was voted Sailor of the Year by Yacht Club de Monaco.

In Australia there are several Fife designs still afloat, the six-metres *Toogooloowoo II*, *Sjo Ro*, *Judith Phil* and *Georgina*. Others include *Vanessa* (eight-metre), *Sayonara*, *Fairlie II*, *Awanui* (*Eunamara*) and *Awanui IV*. Concern had been expressed about the state of *Morna*, as she was slowly deteriorating at her mooring. The good news is that she has been bought by a yard and will be restored. Built originally for Sydney surgeon Sir Alexander McCormack, she was mainly used for cruising but under various succeeding owners was raced successfully in the Sydney to Hobart races.

Tonino, a ten-metre design commissioned by the King of Spain in 1911 and built in Spain, has been in the Tecnomar yard of Emiliano Paronti in Fiunicone for some time. Restoration was started but is presently on hold. There are two eight-metres in Naples: *Finola*, to have a new mast, and *Peggy*, for restoration at the Nino Apnea yard.

Mariquita had a major restoration at Fairlie Restorations on Hamble in 2004. She is now for sale. *Intombi*, built for Wilfred Leuchars in 1934, is still sailing and won the small Bermudian class and overall prize at Cowes spring regatta in 2019. *Sumurun*, owned for 40 years by Bob Towbin, is now under guardianship of Alain Moati, who is having her history recorded in a book by Jacques Taglang. The Scottish Maritime Museum received the gift of *Powerful* from Tim Morton in Canada. She was built in 1920 for A.C. Connell, one of three brothers of the Connell family of shipbuilders. Her identical sister ships *Majestic* and *Terrible* enabled the brothers to race against each other on equal terms. Fife yachts such as *Vagrant*, *Powerful* and *Fricka* will hopefully be preserved in museums for much longer than those still afloat.

Last but not least is *Latifa*, for many years owned by Mario Piri, who completed two circumnavigations. Said to be one of William Fife III's favourite designs, she is now under the guardianship of Kent and Carmel Lowry, who, after a winter in the Caribbean, will take her through the Panama Canal to the Galapagos Islands and finally New Zealand.

The fascination with Fife design has not only led to restorations but also to the building of replicas from original plans. Chantier Stagnol in Brittany built seven copies of *Seabird*, originally designed and built in 1889. The yard also built Fyne a copy of another 1889 design. Both replicas have attended Fife Regattas. Wooden Boat Yard in Maine built a replica of *Invader II*, originally designed to compete for the Canada Cup. The owner has had a sister ship, *Defender*, built at the same yard to compete with the new *Invader II*.

Other Fife design are still afloat whose owners are just happy to sail without competing in regattas. Only a selection of the survivors have been mentioned.

The previous editor of *Classic Boat* magazine has suggested that the obsession with Fife and Herreshoff designs is excessive and tends to overshadow designs of other equally good designers. People have a love affair with their Fife designs. They have withstood the test of time, sail well and look good. Good designers are always recognised. It is the individual's decision which designer is chosen. The craftsmanship of Fairlie-built yachts has ensured their survival and the fact that they are still admired today.

In 1998, Rhani Koc spotted a derelict yacht in a marina in Turkey. Impressed by her lines, he bought her and took her to his shipyard. She turned out to be the 12M *The Lady Edith*, built by Fife in 1924. Her tender is another Fife. Richard Matthews Oyster Marine donated the hull of a motorboat built for the Admiralty by Fife during the First World War. Another 8M, *Fulmar*, found lying in a yard in Hamble Yacht Services, has come back to the Clyde for restoration.

Types of Wood Used in the Construction of *Mariella*

Carpenters	Teak
	Oregon pine
	Pacific spruce
	American elm
Joiners	Teak
	Oregon pine
	Pacific spruce
	Plywood
	Austrian oak
	Birch
	Mahogany
	Cypress
Spars	Oregon pine
	Pacific spruce
	American elm (crosstrees)

Labour Costs for Building *Mariella,* Yard No. 824 (1938)

Wages: Totals

Carpenters	£2,054	4s	1¼d
Joiners	1,338	2	1
Smiths	351	16	4 ½
Riggers	80	3	3
Painters Including spars	196	5	11½
Draughtsmen	144	3	1
Plumber	41	19	2
Polisher	58	3	4
Carver	1	10	0
Frame setters	82	0	0
Paid Crew	10	0	0
	£4,358	7s	4¼d

Breakdown of wages for Carpenters, Joiners and Painters:

Carpenters	£1,937	19.s	4 d
At spars	61	3	1¾
Mounting spars	55	1	7½
	£2,054	4s	1¼d

Joiners	£1171	9.s	2½d
At spars	166	12	10½
	£1,338	2s	1 d

Painters	£191	7s	8d
At spars	4	18	3½
	£196	5s	11½d

Yard List

The Yard List is a list of boats known to be designed or built by members of the Fife family. Some of the designs were allocated yard numbers but were built in groups in other yards and named later.

Key to Symbols:

cb	Centre Board
DRGT	Draught
LWL	Load Water Line – water length line
LBP	Length Between Perpendiculars
LOA	Length Overall
NAME	Boat Name known at launch
NUMBER	Known Yard Number
R	Rater
OD	One Design
SC	Screw
YRA	Yacht Racing Association
TM	(Tonnage) Thames Measurement
REG	(Tonnage) Registered Under Deck

Unless otherwise stated, the units of measurement used throughout the Yard List are in feet (decimalised).

BOAT NAME	Yard NUMBER	YEAR	DESIGNER	BUILDER	TYPE	FIRST OWNER	Tonnage TM/Reg	LWL·ft	LBP·ft	LOA·ft	Beam·ft	Draft·ft
HEROINE						Mr Hutcheson, Fairlie						
COMET		1807	William Fyfe I	William Fyfe I	Cutter	James Smith of Jordanhill	7					
CATHERINE		1809	William Fyfe I	William Fyfe I	Sloop	James Lamont, Greenock	26					
JENNY		1811	William Fyfe I	William Fyfe I	Smack	Archibald Taylor, Lochgilphead	12					
LAMLASH		1812	William Fyfe I	William Fyfe I	Yawl	John Hamilton, Holmhead & Captain Oswald, Scotsonhill	50					
SHARK		1814	William Fyfe I	William Fyfe I	Smack	John Mitchell, Lochgilphead	14					
INDUSTRY		1814	William Fyfe I		Paddle Luggage Steamer	Clyde Shipping Company, Glasgow	69		68		17	8
KIRKMAN FINLAY		1816										
MARGARET		1820	William Fyfe I	William Fyfe I	Trader	John & Thomas Anderson, Greenock	32					
GLEAM		1832	William Fyfe I	William Fyfe I	Cutter	H. Gore-Booth	30					
PHANTOM		1833	John Fyfe	John Fyfe	Fishing boat	George Parker	10					
DORIA		1840	George Parker	William Fyfe I	3 mast Schooner	George Parker	16		58		8	
MIDGE		1844	William Fife II	William Fife II	Cutter	R.G. Lawrie	8					
OITHONA		1846	William Fife II	William Fife II	Yawl	J.M. Rowan	84					
CHRISTINA		1848	William Fife II	William Fife II	Cutter		8					
STELLA		1848	William Fife II	William Fife II	Cutter	Dr Hugh Morris Lang	8					
LEDA		1850	William Fife II	William Fife II	Cutter	Messrs Finlay	6					
CORALIE		1850	William Fife II	William Fife II	Cutter	A. Sanders	37		52.7		13.3	7.9
AQUILA		1851	William Fife II	William Fife II	Cutter	J.M. Rowan, Glasgow	43	55			14.1	
ONDA		1852	William Fife II	William Fife II	Cutter		21		45.5		10.7	5.9
CYMBA		1852	William Fife II	William Fife II	Cutter	J.M. Rowan, Glasgow	53		59			
SATELLITE		1852	William Fife II	William Fife II	Yawl	Com. J.N. Bainbridge RN Sligo	69			68	15.7	8
SHADOW		1853	William Fife II	William Fife II	Cutter	Hon H. White (1976)	46		58		14.1	7.9
SUNBEAM		1856	William Fife II	William Fife & Son	Cutter		16					
CRUSADER		1856	William Fife II	William Fife & Son	Yawl	W. Fife & J. Duncan	29		49		12.2	6.6
OITHONA		1856	William Fife II	William Fife & Son	Cutter	J.M. Rowan, Glasgow	79		70.7		16.6	8.4
LOTIS		1857	William Fife II	William Fife & Son	Schooner	Lord Hamilton	89		84.3		15.6	7.9
QUERIDA		1857	William Fife II	William Fife & Son	Cutter	Adolphus Fowler Cork	38		54.2		13.4	7.1
FAIRY QUEEN		1857	William Fife II	William Fife & Son	Cutter	James Grant jun., Glasgow & Millport	8					
VIDETTE		1858	William Fife II	William Fife & Son	Cutter		8		37		8	7
MOONBEAM		1858	William Fife II	William Fife & Son	Cutter	H.S. Holford (1876)	25		45.9		11.7	7.3
WAYWARD		1858	William Fife II	William Fife & Son	Cutter		9					
SURGE		1858	William Fife II	William Fife & Son	Yawl	C.T. Couper	55		63.2		16.6	8
AMY		1859	William Fife II	William Fife & Son	Schooner	H. Heys (1976)	72		73.7	93.7	15.2	8.7
GEORGINA		1859	William Fife II	William Fife & Son	Yawl	Captain Hay	7					
EMILY		1859	William Fife II	William Fife & Son	Cutter		11					
MIDGE		1859	William Fife II	William Fife & Son	Cutter		5					
STORM		1859	William Fife II	William Fife & Son	Yawl		37		54.1		19.9	8.7
AZALEA		1860	William Fife II	William Fife & Son	Cutter	Mr Campbell	8					
CHRISTABEL		1860	William Fife II	William Fife & Son	Cutter	Mr Kennard, Falkirk	14					
CORSAIR		1860	William Fife II	William Fife & Son	Cutter		15					
WILD FLOWER		1860	William Fife II	William Fife & Son	Schooner	Lord Muskerry, Wexford (1876)	48			63.6	13.4	7.6
ZEPHYR		1860	William Fife II	William Fife & Son	Cutter		7		28.2		8.2	5
CAPRICE		1860	William Fife II	William Fife & Son	Cutter		14					

Name	Year	Designer	Builder	Type	First Owner	Tonnage TM / Reg	LWL ft	LBP ft	LOA ft	Beam ft	Draft ft
EDITH	1861	William Fife II	William Fife & Son	Schooner		6					
IERNE	1861	William Fife II	William Fife & Son	Schooner	I. Groves, Liverpool	62		71.5		14.2	8.2
ROWENA	1861	William Fife II	William Fife & Son	Schooner	W. Walshe	62		71.5		14.2	8.2
AUX	1862	William Fife II	William Fife & Son	Cutter		90					
CHLORA	1862	William Fife II	William Fife & Son	Cutter		7					
CINDERELLA	1862	William Fife II	William Fife & Son	Cutter	D.W. and A. Finlay	15					
CLUTHA	1862	William Fife II	William Fife & Son	Yawl	C.J. Turner	91		73.7		17.2	9.2
EVADNE	1862	William Fife I?	William Fife & Son	Cutter	A.P. Lyle	10					
HARRIET	1862	William Fife II	William Fife & Son	Cutter	J.M. Forrester	16					
RIPPLE	1862	William Fife II	William Fife & Son	Cutter		5					
SILVIA	1862	William Fife II	William Fife & Son	Cutter	J. Eadie jun.	8		32		8.5	
BEDOUIN	1862	William Fife II	William Fife & Son	Schooner	D. McInnes	44		57.5	13.8	8	
FIERY CROSS	1863	William Fife II	William Fife & Son	Schooner	J. Stirling, Dunbartonshire	51		65.4		13.6	7.8
SANTRY	1863	William Fife II	William Fife & Son	Cutter	R. Bartholomew	25		47.2		11.4	7.8
SURF	1863/4	William Fife II	William Fife & Son	Yawl	C.T. Couper	54		65.4		14.1	8.2
GLEE	1864	William Fife II	William Fife & Son	Yawl	D. McInnes	10					
FAIR GERALDINE	1864	William Fife II	William Fife & Son	Cutter	F. Fitzgerald	31					
FLORA	1864	William Fife II	Possibly- Rothesay Fyfe	Cutter	J. Turnly	16					
LUNA	1864	William Fife I	William Fife & Son	Yawl	W.B. Walker	26		49.7			7.7
KILMENY	1864	William Fife I?	William Fife & Son	Cutter	A. Finlay	30		54.9		11.4	7.4
TORCH	1864	William Fife II	William Fife & Son	Cutter	D.W. and A. Finlay. Glasgow	15		44.3	48	6.9	6.2
XEMA	1864	William Fife II	William Fife & Son	Cutter	H. Dudgeon	35		54.2		12.5	8.7
LELIA	1865	William Fife II	William Fife & Son	Cutter		35					
ADELINE	1865	William Fife II	William Fife & Son	Screw lug	Alexander Parker	20					
MAYFLOWER	1865	William Fife II	William Fife & Son	Schooner	H.H. Hamilton	55		65.8		14.2	8.1
FIONA	1865	William Fife II	William Fife & Son	Cutter	H. Lafone Liverpool	80					
LELIA	1865	William Fife II	William Fife & Son	Cutter	R. Ferguson	35		43.2			
RIVAL	1866	William Fife II	William Fife & Son	Cutter	R. Tennant	15		54.5			
AVON	1866	William Fife II	William Fife & Son	Cutter	John & James Steven	30		54.5		11.4	7.5
AVOSET	1866	William Fife II	William Fife & Son	Yawl		17					
DENBURN	1866	William Fife II	William Fife & Son	Cutter	S. King	31		54.4		11.6	7.5
HILDA	1866	William Fife II	William Fife & Son	Yawl	D. Logan jun.	11		35.2		8.8	
PETREL	1866	William Fife II	William Fife & Son	Sloop		20					
CICADA	1867	William Fife II	William Fife & Son	SC Steam		20					
LENA	1867	William Fife II	William Fife & Son	Yawl	J. Forrester, Glasgow	45		61.4		13.2	8.6
MARIA	1867	William Fife II	William Fife & Son	Cutter	N.B. Stewart	35		58		11.9	7.6
MORA	1867	William Fife II	William Fife & Son	Cutter	E. Greer	14					
PERSIS	1867	William Fife II	William Fife & Son	Schooner	Mr T. Stevens	71		74.7		14.9	9.7
SEAWARD	1867	William Fife II	William Fife & Son	Cutter		15					
DEER	1868	William Fife II	William Fife & Son	Steam		12					
EAGER	1868	William Fife II	William Fife & Son	Cutter		27					
FAIRLIE	1868	William Fife II	William Fife & Son	Cutter	S.G. Sinclair	14		41.8		0.9	7.1
FAY	1868	William Fife II	William Fife & Son	Schooner	G. Elder Knock Castle	65		73		14.5	8.8
JUBHAR	1868	William Fife II	William Fife & Son	Schooner	R.J. Walker	65					
CORAL	1868	William Fife II	William Fife & Son	Cutter	Miss J. Johnston	10		36		8.2	6
DINORAH	1869	William Fife II	William Fife & Son	Yawl	J.B. Atkinson	39		60		12.5	9.6

BOAT NAME	Yard NUMBER	YEAR	DESIGNER	BUILDER	TYPE	FIRST OWNER	Tonnage TM / Reg	LWL - ft	LBP - ft	LOA - ft	Beam - ft	Draft - ft
IDA		1869	William Fife II	William Fife & Son	Cutter	J.J. MacFarchan	14					
SIESTA		1869	William Fife II	William Fife & Son	Schooner	Mr E. Bagley	127		93		17.8	10
SNOWFLAKE		1869	William Fife II	William Fife & Son	Cutter	Lord Middleton	60		64.2		15.2	8.8
WANDERER		1870	William Fife II	William Fife & Son	Cutter		12					
AMADINE		1870	William Fife II	William Fife & Son	Schooner	John S. Mills Liverpool	92		83.7		16	
EVELEEN		1870	William Fife II	William Fife & Son	Cutter		39		60.6		12.3	9
FOXHOUND		1870	William Fife II	William Fife & Son	Yawl 40R	Marquess of Ailsa	36					
GAZELLE		1870	William Fife II	William Fife & Son	Cutter	Alexander Sim	4					
LADY EVELYN		1870	William Fife II	William Fife & Son	Schooner	Marquess of Ailsa	141		94.5		18.6	1.06
RAMBLER		1870	William Fife II	William Fife & Son	Cutter		14					
REINDEER		1870	William Fife II	William Fife & Son	Schooner	Marquis of Cholmondely (1876)	106		84		17.3	9.9
AYRSHIRE LASS		1871	William Fife II	William Fife & Son	Cutter	Thomas Reid Paisley	4		22		7	3.9
FAIRY		1871	William Fife II	William Fife & Son	Cutter		3		23		6	5
ROSA		1872	William Fife II	William Fife & Son	Cutter			10	36.1		8.2	
ALCESTE		1872	William Fife II	William Fife & Son	Cutter	Hugh Walker Greenock	39	59.3			12.5	8.2
SPINDRIFT		1872	William Fife II	William Fife & Son	Cutter		20					
TRIUMPH		1872	William Fife II	William Fife & Son	Cutter		5					
WIZARD		1872	William Fife II	William Fife & Son	Cutter		17					
CLYMENE		1873	William Fife II	William Fife & Son	Cutter	Francis Powell Dunoon	26	40	59.8		12.6	8.5
CUCKOO		1873	William Fife II	William Fife & Son	Cutter	Lord Lennox (then Mr H. Hall)		93	79.2		16.7	11.4
HESPERIA		1873	William Fife II	William Fife & Son	Schooner	George Elder Knock Castle		77	77.2		15.2	8.9
LANCER		1873	William Fife II	William Fife & Son	Cutter			10	38		7.9	7
OENONE		1873	William Fife II	William Fife & Son	Cutter	Ebenezer Oliphant Ascog & James Paterson, Lamlash		20	45.4		10.4	6.2
PEARL		1873	William Fife II	William Fife & Son	Cutter	A. Buchanan	5					
BLOODHOUND		1874	William Fife II	William Fife & Son	Cutter	Marquis of Ailsa		40	62		12.3	7.8
CYNTHIA		1874	William Fife II	William Fife & Son	Cutter	J. Henry	5					
CYTHERA		1874	William Fife II	William Fife & Son	Cutter	D. Richardson		117	85.4		17.7	11.4
EXCELSIOR		1874	William Fife II	William Fife & Son	Cutter		7					
LADY GODIVA		1874	William Fife II	William Fife & Son	Cutter		10					
NEVA		1874	William Fife II	William Fife & Son	Cutter	R. Holmes Kerr, Largs		62	70		14.5	9.7
CLIO		1875	William Fife II	William Fife & Son	Cutter	W. Fife	5		28		6.6	
JOHN-AU-GAUNT		1875	William Fife II	William Fife & Son	Cutter							
BEE		1875	William Fife II	William Fife & Son	Smack	W. Fife, W. Jamieson, John Ferguson	46					
COMARAICH		1875	William Fife II	William Fife & Son	Yawl	Lord Middleton Yorkshire		115	84.5		18	11.1
LATONA		1875	William Fife II	J. S. White Cowes	Yawl	A.H. Rowley		165	95.7		20.3	12.5
NEPTUNE		1875	William Fife II	William Fife & Son	Yawl	Mr Ninian B. Stewart	50		64.8		13.5	8.9
SAXON		1875	William Fife II	William Fife & Son	Yawl	Edward Collins, Glasgow		117	86		18	11.1
STORMFINCH		1875	William Fife II	William Fife & Son	Cutter		9					
THYRA		1875	William Fife II	William Fife & Son	Cutter	Mr.J. Millburn	20					
AVOCET		1876	William Fife II	William Fife & Son	Yawl	A.F. Penraven	17		39.7		10.5	6.8
CAMELIA		1876	William Fife III	William Fife & Son	Cutter	Mr T. Lawson	5		28		6.6	
LADY MARGARET		1876	William Fife II	William Fife & Son	Trader	W. Kerr Millport						
FAIRY		1876	William Fife II	William Fife & Son	Cutter							
MELITA		1876	William Fife II	William Fife & Son	Schooner	D. Tod	5	161	99.1		19.5	11.1

Name	Year	Designer	Builder	TYPE	Tonnage TM/Reg	LWL-ft	LBP-ft	LOA-ft	Beam-ft	Draft-ft	FIRST OWNER
BEAGLE	1877	William Fife III	Culzean Shipbuilding Co.								Marquis of Ailsa
THANE	1876	William Fife II	William Fife & Son	Cutter	4	40	60.8		12.4		Mr. T.L. Arnott
BROWNIE	1877	William Fife II	William Fife & Son								
CLYTIE	1877	William Fife III	William Fife & Son	Cutter	5		28.2		6.6	6	R. Foley jun.
LEVERET	1877	William Fife III	William Fife & Son	Cutter	5						W. Fife
MIDA	1877	William Fife II	William Fife & Son	Schooner		112	85		17.7	10.4	Mr Buchanan, Glasgow
ROCKET	1877	William Fife II	William Fife & Son	Cutter	6		30.5		7	5	W. York
ST CLAIR	1877	William Fife II	William Fife & Son	Cutter	20						J. Kennedy
AGNES	1878	William Fife II	William Fife & Son	Yawl	13			76.4	10.1	6.1	Sir H. Berney Bart.
CONDOR	1878	William Fife II	William Fife & Son	Yawl		159	93.9		20.1	11.8	John Clark Paisley
CORAL	1878	William Fife II	William Fife & Son		10						C.H. Beloe
DINORAH	1878	William Fife II	William Fife & Son		89 / 38						G. Morrison
FAIRY	1878	William Fife II	William Fife & Son	Cutter	4						Mr McGill Glasgow
NANCY LEE	1878	William Fife II	William Fife & Son	Cutter	7		30.7		7.7	6	George Coates Paisley
VOLGA	1878	William Fife II	William Fife & Son	Cutter	10			37.4	8	6.4	Marquis of Ailsa
CYPRUS	1879	William Fife III	William Fife & Son	Cutter	5			30	6.3	5.4	W. Fife Fairlie & Mr Godwin of "Fiery Cross"
FREYIA	1879	G. N. Duck	William Fife & Son	Yawl	7	33			7.3	6.5	G.N. Duck, Fairlie
ST. BRYDE	1879	William Fife II	William Fife & Son	Schooner	109		84.7		17.5	10.5	Sir John Douglas, Greenock
THORA (ALCINIA)	1879	William Fife II	William Fife & Son	Cutter	20		46.8		10.1	6.9	Wm. Burnley Kirn
WRAITH	1879	William Fife II	William Fife & Son	Cutter	39		60.4		12.3	8.6	S.W. Fitzgerald Weymouth
WYVERN	1879	William Fife II	William Fife & Son	Yawl	20		47		10.1	7	Rev. J. Seton-Kerr Greenock
CYRENE	1880	William Fife II	William Fife & Son	Cutter	5		30		6.3	5	James Grant, Milport
MUNA	1880	William F fe II	William Fife & Son	Cutter	13						
NEPTUNE	1880	William Fife III	William Fife & Son	Cutter	10		40		7.3	6.5	John & Ninian Stewart Ascog
RIVAL	1880	William Fife III	William Fife & Son	Cutter	15			43.2	9		Andrew Bain
SHRIMP	1880	William Fife III	William Fife & Son	Cutter	6						Capt. C.A. Lodder RN Largs
THORA II	1880	William Fife III	William Fife & Son	Cutter	50		66.4		13.3	8.4	Wm. F. Burnley, Kirn
WAIF	1880	W. B. Forwood	W. B. Forwood	Sloop	2						Sir W.B. Forwood, Liverpool
ANNASONA	1881	William Fife II	William Fife & Son	Cutter	43		64		12	9.8	J.D. Hedderwick, Glasgow
EURELIA	1881	William Fife II	William Fife & Son	Schooner	62						George Elder Knock Castle
MOINA	1881	William Fife II	William Fife & Son	Cutter	110		81		17.9	10.7	Robert Stewart Ingleston
SLEUTH HOUND	1881	William Fife III	William Fife & Son	Cutter	43		64		12	9.8	Marquis of Ailsa
VESPA	1881	William Fife II	William Fife & Son	Cutter	22		50.5		9.8	8.7	J.C. Redie Weymes Bay
ERYCINA	1882	William Fife II	William Fife & Son	Cutter	96		87		15.93	12.39	Alexander Allan Glasgow
FLORENCE	1882	William Fife I & III	William Fife & Son	Cutter	8						J.G. Carrick Moore
LENORE	1882	William Fife II	William Fife & Son	Cutter	20		53		9.4	6.2	James Grant Jun. Glasgow & Millport
IOLANTHE	1883	William Fife III	William Fife & Son	Cutter	6		35.2		6	6.2	Howard Smith Port Jackson Australia
ULIDIA	1883	William Fife III	William Fife & Son	Cutter	10		45		7.3	7.3	William Corry London
YSO	1883	William Fife II	William Fife & Son	Trader	4		25.3		6.2		D. Campbell
DORMOUSE	1884	William Fife II	William Fife & Son	Yawl	24		48		11	9	P.A. Lloyd
KELPIE	1884	William Fife III	Elias Balmain Australia	Gaff cutter	5.65		37.5		6.5	5	John Fairfax
BEDOUIN	1884	William Fife III	Culzean Castle	Cutter	6		27		7.3	5.4	Henry C. Craig
CARISSIMA	1884	William Fife II	William Fife & Son	Cutter	32		56.1		11.6	8.8	George McRoberts
CLARA	1884	William Fife III	Culzean Castle	Cutter composite	20		57.5		9	8.5	J. Howard Adams
DELVIN	1884	William Fife III	William Fife & Son	Cutter	5		34		5.9	6.6	R.D. Jameson, Dublin

BOAT NAME	Yard NUMBER	YEAR	DESIGNER	BUILDER	TYPE	FIRST OWNER	Tonnage TM / Reg	LWL - ft	LBP - ft	LOA - ft	Beam - ft	Draft - ft
LADY GODIVA		1884	William Fife II	William Fife & Son	Cutter	F.W. Garnham	10		36		8.2	
MARGUERITE		1884	William Fife II	William Fife & Son	Cutter	Mr.J.B. McIndoe	10		45		7.3	7.3
SHEENA		1884	William Fife III	William Fife & Son	Cutter		3					
UNA		1884	William Fife III	William Fife & Son	Lug		2	18.7			6	
VAGRANT		1884	William Fife III	Culzean sc	Cutter Dublin Bay 18ft	Thomas Trocke Kingston	2	18			5.1	
AILSA		1885	William Fife II	William Fife & Son	Cutter	R.N.Y.C.	67		72.7		14.7	11.7
BLACK PEARL		1885	William Fife III	Culzean SBC 2cyr 55hp	Schooner	Marquis of Ailsa	345		144.5		23.15	13.15
CYMBA		1885	William Fife II	William Fife & Son	Cutter	William Fife son.	3					
DELTA		1885	William Fife II	W. McGlashan Paisley	Lug		2					
NEPTUNE		1885	William Fife II	William Fife & Son	Cutter	J.S. Stewart & N.B. Stewart jun.						
ARIEL		1886	William Fife II	William Fife & Son	Cutter	W. Peter Donaldson, Glasgow	3		33.6		4.6	6.25
BLACK & TAN		1886	William Fife III		Cutter	Marquis of Ailsa	7		28		8	
CASSANDRA		1886	William Fife III	Culzean SBC	Yawl	J. George Clark Paisley	109		100		15.16	10.7
CRUISER		1886	G. L. Watson	William Fife & Son	Cutter	James Coats		13.42			8.6	7.75
EILEEN		1886	William Fife II	William Fife & Son	Cutter	H. Trevor Henderson Belfast	3		22		6	
LILY		1886	William Fife III	Culzean SBC	Lug	Marquis of Ailsa	21		55		9.2	7.2
PRELEST		1886	William Fife II	William Fife & Son	Cutter	Alex. Metier Belfast	24		43.3	49.4	10.8	7.2
PRIMULA		1886	William Fife II	William Fife & Son	Cutter	Major C.B. Wynne Sligo	6		29.1		7.3	5.9
ZULU		1886	William Fife II	William Fife & Son	Cutter	K.M. Clark Weymss Bay	21		28		9	9.5
NELLIE		1887	William Fife III	William Fife & Son	Clyde 17/19							
DINORAH	186	1887	William Fife III	William Fife & Son	Schooner	J.B. Atkinson R.H.Y.C Leamington	35		68.6	76.8	15.1	10.7
MAGGIE MURRAY	187	1887	William Fife III	William Fife & Son	Coaster	J. Murray				66		
WINDWARD	188	1887/9	William Fife III	William Fife & Son	Cutter 20 Rater	Robert Cross Edinburgh	19		46.17	53	9.15	8.3
AYRSHIRE LASS	189	1887	William Fife II	William Fife & Son	Cutter 2.5 Rater	Thomas Reid Paisley	4	23	24	24	7	4.5
NOVA	191	1987	William Fife III	William Fife & Son	Cutter	F.C. Hill	12		31	33.1	9.76	6.3
CAPRICE	192	1888	William Fife II or III	William Fife & Son	Lug Clyde 17/19	R.M. Donaldson	2.5	17				
NELLIE TOO	193	1888	William Fife II or III	William Fife & Son	Lug Clyde 17/19	K.M. Clark	2.5	17				
194	194	1888	William Fife III	William Fife & Son	Steam launch	Thomas Hamilton	3.5					
DOROTHY	195	1888	William Fife III	William Fife & Son	Lug Clyde 17/19	John Tennant	2.5	17		19	6	4.6
196	196	1888	William Fife II or III	William Fife & Son	Steam launch	James Stevenson	3.5					
197	197	1888	William Fife II or III	William Fife & Son	Centre board cutter	J. George Clark	1	15				
PUFFIN	198	1888	G. L. Watson	William Fife & Son	Cutter	S.A. Hermon Crawley	32			46.35	13.5	7.7
MINERVA	199	1888	William Fife III	William Fife & Son	Cutter 40 LWL American Class	Charles H. Tweed New York		39.9		54	10.5	9
200	200	1889	William Fife III	William Fife & Son	Steam launch	James Stevenson	6		27		7	3' - 6"
OREAD	201	1889	William Fife III	William Fife & Son	Cutter 6 Rater	Andrew Jameson Dublin	6	28.22		32	7.3	5.5
ASTHORE	202	1889	William Fife III	William Fife & Son	1.5 Rater	T. Stephen Jun.						
J or LAPWING	203	1889	William Fife III	William Fife & Son	Bermudan Clyde 17/19	E.S. Parker	3	17		18.9	6.3	3.6
YVONNE	204	1889/90	William Fife III	William Fife & Son	Cutter 10 Rater	W. Peter Donaldson	20 / 8.21	33.95		42	8.3	7.7
DRAGON	205	1889	William Fife III	William Fife & Son	Cutter 20 Rater	F.C. Hill	24					
206	206	1889	William Fife III	William Fife & Son		W. Trevelyn		21				
MAGIC	207	1889	William Fife III	William Fife & Son	Cutter 2.5 Rater	W. Higgin	4	20.97	27	6	4.6	
IOTA	208	1889	William Fife III	William Fife & Son	Cutter 2.5 Rater	A.S. Marier	4	21		27	6	4.6
CLUTHA	209	1889	William Fife III	William Fife & Son	CB sloop 2.5 Rater	W.G. Mears	4	18.5		23	6.5	2.6
SHIBBEAL	210	1889	William Fife III	William Fife & Son	Cutter 2.5 Rater	H.J. Neil Jun. Co Down	4	20.93		27	6	4.6
IXXOT	211	1889	William Fife III	D. Stone Erith	Cutter 1.73 Rating	S. Satterthwait	3	21		26	5.1	4.6

BOAT NAME	Yard NUMBER	YEAR	DESIGNER	BUILDER	TYPE	FIRST OWNER	Tonnage TM / Reg	LWL - ft	LBP - ft	LOA - ft	Beam - ft	Draft - ft
KAHARA	212	1889	William Fife III	William Fife & Son	Lug & jib 1.5 Rater	A.H. Dexter	4	18.5	14	23.9	6.5	3.3
Rose		1889	T. B. Middle	William Fife & Son	Dublin Bay Waterwag	Louis Meldon						
IOLAIRE	213	1889	William Fife III	P. R. Mclean Rosneath	Lug 1.5 Rater	J.D.G. Hendry Glasgow	2	18.5		22	5.8	4.6
MOSQUITO	214	1889	William Fife III	William Fife & Son	Lug 2.5 Rater	Rupert & Sidney Mason	7		29.6		7.6	5.3
SEA GULL	215	1889/90	William Fife III	William Fife & Son	Cutter 1.5 Rater	Sydney R. Hermon	3	18		20	7.3	4
NAN	216	1890	William Fife III	William Fife & Son	Cutter 6 Rater	T.C. Burrows Co. Cavan	6	29.93		34	7.3	5.3
JABBERWOCK	217	1890	William Fife III	William Fife & Son	Lug	R.M. Donaldson, Glasgow	2	16.2		18.2	6.6	4
UVIRA	218	1890	William Fife III	William Fife & Son	Cutter	James Fraser	18	42.5		59	11.2	9.6
NELLIE	219	1890	William Fife III	Black & Co Southampton	Cutter	Dan Sutherland	4	21		26	7	4
220	220	1890	William Fife III	Black & Co Southampton	Cutter 40ft Class	J.G. Beecher, USA	18					
FAIRLIE	221	1890	William Fife III	Built USA	Cutter	A. Currie, Sandbank	2	17.5		19	6.6	4
222	222	1890	William Fife III	Alex. Robertson Sandbank		O. Rendal	3					
WHITE SLAVE	223	1890	William Fife III & F. L. Popham	G. Gausden Eastbourne	Lug schooner 40 Rating	F.W. Layborne Popham Hythe	53	60		65	14	9.2
ENCORE	224	1890	William Fife III	William Fife & Son	Cutter 10 Rater	K.M. Clark	13	36.35		42	8	6.6
WOODCOCK	225	1890	William Fife III	William Fife & Son	Cutter 10 Rater	Andrew Coats	13	36.8		42	8.6	6.6
JESSICA	226	1890	William Fife III	William Fife & Son	Cutter 20 Rater	W. O'B. MacDonough	27 / 17.76		56.6		10.45	8.5
227	227	1890	William Fife III	Finland	Cutter 6 Rater	E. Bindman, St. Petersburgh	6					
ISIS	228	1890	William Fife III	William Fife & Son	Cutter 40ft	L. Hoyack jun, Amsterdam, C. d'Anvers, Netherland	30 / 16.08	50.4		12.15	7.85	9
OSIRIS	229	1890	William Fife III	William Fife & Son	Cutter 40ft	P. Von Rath, Amsterdam Y.C. d'Anvers, Netherland	30 / 16.08	50.4		12.15	7.85	5
230	230	1890	William Fife III	William Fife & Son	CB Lug	K.R. McKenzie Helley	2	17				
BANDERSNATCH	231	1890	William Fife III	William Fife & Son	Lug 2.5 Rater	W.B. Richardson	5	24.85		28.3	6.3	5
QUINTA	232	1890	William Fife III	J. Ninian Largs	Cutter 5 Rater	A.T. King	7	28.85		32	7.3	5.3
ZWERVER	233	1890	William Fife III	William Fife & Son	Cutter 21 Rater	E. Kol. Amsterdam	28	40.74		47.3	12.3	7.6
MINERVA	234	1890	William Fife III	William Fife & Son	Cutter	W. Goucharoff	8	34			7.6	5.3
YAMA	235	1890	William Fife III	Wintringham Brooklyn NY	Cutter 40 CL	Allen Ames Oswego. N.Y.	10	36		52	9.2	9
PRINCESSIDA	236	1890	William Fife III	D. Mcglashan Paisley	Lug 2.5 Rater	D. McGlashan	5	25		28	6.3	5
RIPPLE	237	1890	William Fife III	William Fife & Son	Cutter 5 Rater	R. Hutcheson Fairlie	6	26		28	7.66	5
238	238	1890	William Fife III	William Fife & Son	CB Lug	Norman Clark		15				
BUL BUL	239	1891	William Fife III	T. Cubbit Sydney Australia	Cutter 2.5 Rater	J.G. Fairfax	2	31			6.3	5.1
ZOLOOSCHKA	240	1891	William Fife III	G. W. Esch St. Petersburgh	Cutter 10 Rater	J.W. Fansmith St Petersburgh	YRA 10					
THALIA	241	1891	William Fife III	William Fife & Son	Cutter composite 40 Rater	J. Anthony Inglis	59	59.37	70.2	70.75	13.9	9.75
DRAGON II	242	1891	William Fife III	William Fife & Son	Cutter 20 Rater	F.C. Hill	27	46.74		54.4	10.76	7.55
MYRTA	243	1891	William Fife III	William Fife & Son	Lug 2.5 Rater	J.C. Connell	5	24.5		28.9	6	5.5
THELMA	244	1891	William Fife III	William Fife & Son	Lug 2.5 Rater	W.C.S. Connell	5	25.45		32.6	6.2	5.4
VASHTI	245	1891	William Fife III	William Fife & Son	Cutter 2.5/3.5 Rater	P.M. Inglis	6	26.31		31.75	6.5	5.5
OLIVE	246	1891	William Fife III	William Fife & Son	Sloop 2.5 Rater	D. Campbell of Inverneill	5	25.9		28.9	6.5	5
VOLVA	247	1891	William Fife III	William Fife & Son	Cutter	G. Watson	YRA 6	30.2		34	7.9	5.3
ERICA	248	1891	William Fife III	William Fife & Son	Lug 2.5 Rater Clyde 23lwl	W.C. Teacher	7	23		30.7	7.5	5
KITE 2	249	1891	William Fife III	William Fife & Son	Cutter 10 Rater	J.H. Lister	14	36		44	8.6	7
CRANTARA	250	1891/92	William Fife III	George Gamble Liverpool	Cutter	George Gamble Liverpool	11	32.95		39.5	8	6.4
JEANNIE	251	1891	William Fife III	Bideford	0.5 Rater	Blair O. Cochrane	2					
BARBARA	252	1891	William Fife III	G. Lawley & Son Boston Massachusetts	Cutter Composite 46'	B.H.W. Foster	46		65	12.5	11.7	
HELEN	253	1891	William Fife III	Alex. Robertson Sandbank	Lug Bangor 1 Rater	A.P. Jenkins	3					

BOAT NAME	Yard NUMBER	YEAR	DESIGNER	BUILDER	TYPE	FIRST OWNER	Tonnage TM / Reg	LWL - ft	LBP - ft	LOA - ft	Beam - ft	Draft - ft
MOSQUITO	254	1891	William Fife III	Alex. Robertson Sandbank	Lug Bangor 1 Rater	R. Lepper	3	18		20	6.3	3.6
ULAH	255	1891	William Fife III	Alex. Robertson Sandbank	Lug Bangor 1 Rater	Vincent Craig	3					
MISS MOLLIE	256	1891	William Fife III	Alex. Robertson Sandbank	lug Bangor 1 Rater	R.G. Sharman-Crawford	3	18		20.2	6.2	3.6
LIZETTE	257	1891	William Fife III	William Fife & Son	Lug 2.5 Rater	Norman Clark	5	25.45		28.9	6.5	5
BUL-BUL	258	1891	William Fife III	T. Cubbit Sydney	Cutter 2.5 Rater	J.G. Fairfax. Sydney	5	31			6.3	5.1
IERNIA	259	1891	William Fife III	Camper &Nicholson	Lug 5 Rater	H.R. Langrishe	11	31.74	39.7	48	8	6.15
260	260	1891	William Fife III	Greenock	20 Rater	John Paterson						
NELLIE	261	1891	William Fife III	Manchester	CB Lug	M.H. Cameron	2.5	18				
GEW-GAW	262	1891	William Fife III	J. Doyle Kingston	Lug Dublin Bay Mermaid	T.C. Burrows, Co Cavan	2	18			6	
BONNIE DUNDEE	263	1891	William Fife III	William Fife & Son	29ft	W.C. Sproull						
264	264	1891	William Fife III	Glasgow	18lwl	J.C. Kemp. Glasgow		18				
265	265	1891	William Fife III	William Fife & Son	33lwl	Shannon		33				
YOULA		1891	William Fife III	Nova Scotia Building Co.	Cutter	J.P. Bell	7	26		32.5	7.3	6.9
ARLA		1891	William Fife III	Crigghton & Co. Abo Finland	Cutter		5		28.1		7	6.9
KIWI	266	1891	William Fife III	William Fife & Son	Cutter 1.5 Rater	H.H. Bell	4	18.9	21		7.2	
ISIS	267	1891/2	William Fife III	W. Reekes Sydney	Schooner steam yacht	J.R. Fairfax. Sydney	80			85.4	14.08	9.4
STORMY PETREL	268	1892	William Fife III	William Fife & Son	Bermudian 1 Rater	Rupert Colomb Kenmore	3	17		18.9	6.3	3.6
DOREEN	269	1892	William Fife III	William Fife & Son	Lug Composite 10 Rater	John Gretton jun.	20		38.59			
Zelma	270	1892	William Fife III	H. Staunton Toronto	Cutter	N.B. Dick	16	37				
KETCH	271		William Fife II	William Fife & Son	Coaster	W. Fife	140				10.5	
KATYDID	272	1892	William Fife III	William Fife & Son	Lug Clyde 17/19	P.P. Nicholl	3	17	19	19	6.5	4.2
ALEXA	273	1892	William Fife III	William Fife & Son	7 Rater	A.P. Wylie						
NIRVANA		1892	William Fife III	William Fife & Son	Cutter		10	30				
NAVETTE		1892	William Fife III	D. McGlashan Paisley	Lug 2.5 Rater	D. McGlashan	5	25		28	6.3	5
VEDETTE	274	1892	William Fife III	William Fife & Son	Lug 30 Clyde	F.M. Gray	10		30.3		9.5	5.2
LADY GRIZELL	275	1892	William Fife III	William Fife & Son	1 Rater	J. Blair Cochrane						
NOX	276	1892	William Fife III	Miller Bros NY	Cutter Clyde 25	W. Miller, Miller Bros Rochester NY		25		36	8	5.2
RED LANCER	277	1892	William Fife III	William Fife & Son	Lug 5 Rater	R.G. Sharman-Crawford	11	31.44				
PTARMIGAN	278	1892	William Fife III	William Fife & Son	Cutter	Andrew Coats	20	36.58		44.4	10.6	6
NANSHEEN	279	1892	William Fife III	J. Doyle Kingston	CB Lug Dublin Bay 1 Rater	T.C. Burrows Co. Cavan	3	20.95	20		6.6	2.3
VEDETTE	280	1892	William Fife III	William Fife & Son	Lug 2.5 Rater	J.C. Connell	11	26.5		36	8.5	3
YSEULT	281	1892	William Fife III	William Fife & Son	Cutter 20 Rater	P. Donaldson	18		35.5			
WHILIGIG	282	1892	William Fife III	William Fife & Son	Lug 21/2 Rater	R.M. Donaldson						
EILEEN	283	1892	William Fife III	J. Ninian Largs	Cutter 5 Rater	Sydney Mason	11		31.4	9	4.6	
MIMI-TOINON	284	1892/3	William Fife III	William Fife Hamburgh	Sloop 30 metres	Count Le Chabannes	4	20		27.5	6.1	
SIGRUN	285	1892	William Fife III	H. Heidtmann Hamburgh	Cutter	Kapt. A. Rittmeyer Kiel	4		24.4	6.5	4.1	
YOULA	286	1892	William Fife III	Nova Scotia S B Co	Cutter 3.6 Rater	W. Butler Duncan	7	26		32.5	7.3	5.4
NORKA	287	1893	William Fife III	William Fife & Son	Lug Clyde 23/30	R.M. Donaldson	9	23		30		
SNARLEYOW II	288	1893	William Fife III	William Fife & Son	Lug Clyde 17/19	A. Liddle McLaren. Skelmorlie	5	17				
LAIS	289	1893	William Fife III	B. Hansen& Sons Cowes	Cutter, composite 40 Rater	John Gretton jun.	80	59.92		76	17	8
290	290	1893	William Fife III	William Fife & Son		K.M. Clark				26.6		
THE SCOT	291	1893	William Fife III	William Fife & Son	Lug 1 Rater	George Gamble	3	20.8		21.5		
GODWIT	292	1893	William Fife III	William Fife & Son	Cutter	E. Gaskell London	43 / 25.15		63.3	13	8.4	
INFANTA	293	1893	William Fife III	Bristol R.I. USA	Cutter	J.B. Mills NY		30		40.5	9.4	5.5
ALMIDA	294	1893	William Fife III	William Fife & Son	Cutter 10 Rater	Alex. Scott Glasgow	20 / 11.70	30	47.8		11	7.3

BOAT NAME	Yard NUMBER	YEAR	DESIGNER	BUILDER	TYPE	FIRST OWNER	Tonnage TM/Reg	LWL-ft	LBP-ft	LOA-ft	Beam-ft	Draft-ft
DRAGON III	295	1893	William Fife III	William Fife & Son	Cutter 20 Rater	F.C. Hill	40 / 19.84	46.04		57.7	13.2	6.8
LALA	296	1893	William Fife III	William Fife & Son	Lug Clyde 23/30 2.5 R	Norman Clark	2.5					
CALLUNA	297	1893	William Fife III	A.& J Inglis Pointhouse	Cutter composite 125 Rater	P. Donaldson	260	81.95		106.6	24.3	11.2
ZINITA	298	1893	William Fife III	William Fife & Son	Cutter 20 Rater	W.C.S. Connell	40 /18.35	46.23		58.5	12.6	6.4
	299	1893	William Fife III	William Fife & Son		G.L. Blake		23				
SAUCY KIPPER	300	1893	William Fife III	J. Ninian Largs	Lug Clyde 17/19	A.C. Connell	3	17		19		
THABER	301	1893	William Fife III	William Fife & Son	Lug Clyde 23/30	P.M. Coats	9	23		30		
	302	1893	William Fife III	William Fife & Son.	Dublin Bay Waterwag				13			
	303	1893	William Fife III	William Fife & Son	CB	G.S. Parsons						
	304	1893	William Fife III	William Fife & Son				17				
MAY	305	1894	William Fife III	William Fife & Son	Bermudian Lug 1 Rater	W. Fife II	4	20		25.2	6.3	
	306	1894	William Fife III	William Fife & Son	10 Rater	F. Freichter Wasser						
LUNA	307	1894	William Fife III	William Fife & Son	Cutter 20 Rater	F.B. Jameson	27 / 17.74	45.66		55.3	12.75	5.8
EILEEN	308	1894	William Fife III	William Fife & Son	Lug 5 Rater	Sydney Mason Beaumaris	15					
FLEUR DE LYS	309	1894	William Fife III	C. Hanson & Sons Cowes	Lug 5 Rater	S.H. Montgomery France	15		35.5	8.7	3	
LILITH	310	1894	William Fife III	William Fife & Son	Cutter 10 Rater	Robert Collins	20					
FENELLA	311	1894	William Fife III	William Fife & Son	Lug 5 Rater	E.S. Parker	15 / 5.71	31.65		36	8.8	3.6
	312	1894	William Fife III	William Fife & Son	lug	F. Frichter Waser Zurich	4					
	313	1894	William Fife III	William Fife & Son	1.75 Rater	Nylandska Yaktklubben	3	17				
HATASOO	314	1894	William Fife III	C. Hanson & Sons Cowes	Cutter, composite 20 Rater	Andrew Bain Glasgow	3	17		19		
THELMA	315	1894	William Fife III	C. Hanson & Sons Cowes	Cutter, composite 20 Rater	A.B. Walker	27	41	45.78	56.2		
MYSTERY	316	1894	William Fife III	William Fife & Son	Lug 2.5 Rater Fin & Bulb	H.L. Mulholland	8		29.9	7.4	3.25	
SCOWDER	317	1894	William Fife III	William Fife & Son	Lug fishing yacht	Andrew Coats	6					
	318	1894	William Fife III	William Fife & Son	1 Rater	S.N. Nolan						
MINIME	319	1894	William Fife III	T. Orr jun. Greenock	Bermudian 2.5 Rater	Duncan F. D. Neill, Greenock	7	25.5		33	8.7	4.9
FAIRLIE	320	1894	William Fife III	R. Inches Hobart Tasmania	Cutter	F.N. Clark	2.5	21				
GENESTA	321	1894	William Fife III	Perth W. Australia	Cutter	R.B. Burnside, Perth	12	30				
NAPPER	322	1894	William Fife III	William Fife & Son	Gunter 0.75 Rating	J.C. Connell	3		16.5			
FRIMOUSSE	323	1894	William Fife III	Mors Freres Paris	Sloop 3 French metre class	De Boulogne	9	25.7		38.7	7.4	5.2
NINON		1894	William Fife III	E. Weglius Helsingfors	Lug 7.5 Rater	Dr T. Tallogoist	7	23.5		35	7	2.6
HELENA	324	1895	William Fife III	Robert Logan NZ	Lug 2.5 Rater	P.M. Coats, Paisley	8		40.7	8.5	4.5	
MIRU	325	1895	William Fife III	Alex. Robertson Sandbank	0.5 Rater	A.H. Turnbull Wellington	3					
VILL-U-AN	326	1895	William Fife III	William Fife & Son	Lug 1.5 Rater	Harry E. Smith Zurich	8	19.3	26.5	32	7.8	3.3
	327	1895	William Fife III	A.& J. Inglis Pointhouse	1 French Measurement	Jules Valton	3.5					
AILSA	328	1895	William Fife III	William Fife & Son	Cutter, composite 125 Rater	A.Barclay Walker	280	89.25		107	25.55	8.4
ALMIDA	329	1895	William Fife III	William Fife & Son	Lug 5 Rater	Alex. Scott Glasgow	14		30.98		9	
SPIDER	330	1895	William Fife III	William Fife & Son	Lug 1.5 Rater	K.M. Clark Paisley	3		22			
FLY	331	1895	William Fife III	William Fife & Son	Lug 1.5 Rater	N. Clark Paisley	3		22			
FAIRLIE	332	1895	William Fife III	William Fife & Son	Lug 2.5 Rater	Edward Jessop	2.5					
ISOLDE	333	1895	William Fife III	William Fife & Son	Cutter, composite 40 Rater	P.Donaldson Glasgow	81 / 36.92	59.56		71.25	16.8	
NANTA	334	1895	William Fife III	William Fife & Son	Lug sloop 2.5 Rater	T.C. Burrows	8		25.99			
CONTEST	335	1895	William Fife III	A. Taylor Sandown I.O.W.	Lug 5 Rater	J. Blair Cochrane & Sutton	14	31.7		46.2	8.8	4.9
KLYSMA	336	1895	William Fife III	William Fife & Son	Lug Clyde 23/30	R.M. Donaldson	9	23		30		
ELIZABETH	337	1895	William Fife III	H. C. Stulcken Hamburg	Cutter 20 Rater	Bolling & Lowe for Rbt. Loesner	40	47	46.9	67.2	12.7	7.7
HESTER	338	1895	William Fife III	A. Hansen & Sons Cowes	Cutter, composite 72 Rating	John Gretton jun.	110	68		82.2	17.95	8.7
	339	1895	William Fife III	William Fife & Son	5 Rater	Cumming						

BOAT NAME	Yard NUMBER	YEAR	DESIGNER	BUILDER	TYPE	FIRST OWNER	Tonnage TM / Reg	LWL - ft	LBP - ft	LOA - ft	Beam - ft	Draft - ft
SATANELLA	340	1895	William Fife III	J. Hilditch Carrickfergus	Lug 1.5 Rater	Bryce Smythe	5.5	19		32.5	7.1	3
LOUISE	341	1895	William Fife III	William Fife & Son	Bermudian - YRA rating 2	Hon. Thomas Cochrane MP. Androssan						
EVOE	342	1895	William Fife III	William Fife & Son	CB Lug 1 Rater	P.M. Inglis	3					
EUCHARIS	343	1895	William Fife III	William Fife & Son	Cutter 20 Rater	Earl of Lonsdale Penarth	35 / 15.27		52.15	13.1	4.1	
DICK		1895	William Fife III	Selcyer Courbevoie France	Lug bulb keel		2	18			5.5	
EVORA		1895	William Fife III	William Fife & Son	Lug		1	15.5			4.5	1.5
GENESTA		1895	William Fife III	A. R. Brown Freemantle Australia	Cutter	R. B. Burnside & F. Stevens Perth	17	30		36	10.2	
REDGAUNTLET		1895	William Fife III	Carrigaloe Works Cork Ireland	Lug 5 Rater		16	31		47.5	9.05	5
HELEN	344	1895/6	William Fife III	William Fife & Son	Schooner	Fred. Lobnitz Renfrew	25 / 16.11		54.6	12.15	6.7	
345	345	1896	William Fife III	William Fife & Son	0.5 Rater	Peter Donaldson						
SQUAW	346	1895	William Fife III	William Fife & Son	Lug	T.C. Burrows Co. Cavan	2					
MARJATTA	347	1896	William Fife III	Abo Batvarf Finland	Cutter 10 Rater	Gustav Lindlom	16					
FRICKA	348	1896	William Fife III	William Fife & Son	Lug Clyde 17/19	Robert M. Mann	3	17				
SAYONARA	349	1896	William Fife III	A. McFarlane Port Adelaide	Yawl	G.F. Garrard	18	38				
BUNYIP	350	1896	William Fife III	Carrigaloe Works Cork Ireland	Sloop Cork Harbour OD	Atwell H. Allen	6	24.4		30	7.3	4.3
ELSIE	351	1896	William Fife III	Carrigaloe Works Cork Ireland	Sloop Cork Harbour OD	P. Halloran	6	24.4		30	7.3	4.3
LITTLE DEVIL	352	1896	William Fife III	Carrigaloe Works Cork Ireland	Sloop Cork Harbour OD	G.H. Gubbins Glanire Co. Cork	6	24.4		30	7.3	4.3
MAUREEN	353	1896	William Fife III	Carrigaloe Works Cork Ireland	Cork Harbour OD	M.J. O'Sullivan	6			30	7.3	
MINX	354	1896	William Fife III	Carrigaloe Works Cork Ireland	Cork Harbour OD	Arthur Julian Cork	6	24.4		30	7.3	4.3
QUERIDA	355	1896	William Fife III	Carrigaloe Works Cork Ireland	Cork Harbour OD	Adolphus Fowler Cork	6	24.4		30	7.3	4.3
ISA	356	1896	William Fife III	William Fife & Son	Cutter CB	G. Bulloch Rhum	2	20				
MORNA	357	1896	William Fife III	William Fife & Son	Cutter	G. Bulloch Rhum	2	20				
TRILBY	358	1896	William Fife III	Tellier Paris	Lug 1 French Rater	Harry A. van Bergen	2	18.5				
THELLA	359	1896	William Fife III	William Fife & Son	Lug Clyde 23/30	K.M. & N. Clark	9	23		30		
360	360	1896	William Fife III	William Fife & Son		McPhail	2	18				
ALBICORE	361	1896	William Fife III	William Fife & Son	Yawl	W.D. Howland	18	36				
362	362	1896	William Fife III	William Fife & Son	Rater - Benson Rule	Johan Wessman	2					
363	363	1896	William Fife III	William Fife & Son	Lug 1 Rater	A.B. Walker Sligo	3					
FLIP	364	1896	William Fife III	William Fife & Son	Cutter	Max Aschmann Koningsburgh	9	31				
CERIGO	365	1896	William Fife III	William Fife & Son	Cutter 42 Rater	W. Fife III	20	38		49	10.5	7.5
366	366	1896	William Fife III	William Fife & Son		George Bulloch						
JURA	367	1896	William Fife III	William Fife & Son	Lug 2.5 Rater	J. Stewart Clark	6	30				
THE SAINT	368	1896	William Fife III	William Fife & Son	Cutter 20 Rater	Frank B. Jameson Dublin	37 / 18.47			30		
SNARLEYOW	369	1896	William Fife III	William Fife & Son	Lug Clyde 17/19	A.F. McLaren Skelmorlie	3	17				
VIXEN	370	1896	William Fife III	P. McKeown Belfast	Lug 18.5 LR	K. Johson & E.N. Hodgeson	2	15.4		22	6.2	3.1
371	371	1896	William Fife III	William Fife & Son		Brenner Helsingfors	5	20				
CANADA	372	1896	William Fife III	Jas. Andrews Oakville Ontario	Cutter 42 Canadian Length	Emelius Jarvis	24	37				
TURQUOISE	373	1896	William Fife III	E. S. Luard Bombay	Lug 2.5 Rater fin keel	E.S. Luard Bombay	6	26.7		37.3	7.5	
THE FERN	374	1896	William Fife III	William Fife & Son	Lug 5 Rater	A. Barclay Walker	14	30.6			8.6	
AILSA	375	1896	William Fife III	William Fife & Son		F.N. Clark	6	21				
MARGARET	376	1896	William Fife III	William Fife & Son		C.S. Parker						
NAN	377	1896	William Fife III	William Fife & Son	Cutter LR 49 14	T. Corby Co. Cavan	20	44.89	53.6	11.63	7.8	
MERCIA	378	1896	William Fife III	William Fife & Son	Sloop	Alex. Scott Dunbar	5	19				
DORIS	379	1896	William Fife III	P. McKeown Belfast	Lug	Dr R.L. Moore	3	19.9		22		
NIALL	380	1896	William Fife III	P. McKeown Belfast	Lug	George Rogers	3	15.4		22	6.2	3.1

BOAT NAME	Yard NUMBER	YEAR	DESIGNER	BUILDER	TYPE	FIRST OWNER	Tonnage TM / Reg	LWL - ft	LBP - ft	LOA - ft	Beam - ft	Draft - ft
THE SULKY		1896	William Fife III	William Fife & Son	Lug 18 LR	Mary Fife	1					
GEISHA	381	1897	William Fife III	William Fife & Son	Schooner LR 48.97	A.R. Brown Glasgow	30	45.6	46.8	58.6	12.6	7.15
382	382	1897	William Fife III	William Fife & Son		Sydney Mason (order suspended)						
383	383	1897	William Fife III	William Fife & Son		T. Shirley Gooch (order suspended)						
SENGA	384	1897	William Fife III	William Fife & Son	Cutter 52 LR	Frank A. Dubbs Glasgow	37	47.9			12.2	
FELTIE	385	1897	William Fife III	J. Hilditch Carrickfergus	Cutter Belfast Lough OD 25ft.Class	George S. Clark	9	25		31.8	8.65	5.8
FLAMINGO	386	1897	William Fife III	J. Hilditch	Cutter Belfast Lough OD 25ft.Class	John B. Pirrie	9	25		31.8	8.65	5.8
HALCYONE	387	1897	William Fife III	J. Hilditch	Cutter Belfast Lough OD 25ft.Class	J. Herbert Brown	9	25	31.8		8.65	5.8
HOOPOE	388	1897	William Fife III	J. Hilditch	Cutter Belfast Lough OD 25ft.Class	R.G. Sharman-Crawford	9	25		31.8	8.65	5.8
MERLE	389	1897	William Fife III	J. Hilditch	Cutter Belfast Lough OD 25ft.Class	Bryce Smith	9	25		31.8	8.65	5.8
ARROW II	390	1897	William Fife III	A. Hutcheson & CO Belfast	Lug Belfast Lough OD 15 ft. Class	H. Fulton	3	15		20.2	6.2	3
BOLIVAR	391	1897	William Fife III	Carsewell Belfast	Cutter	Sam Rose & W. Calvert	4	23			6.6	
LA POUPEE	392	1897	William Fife III	A. Hutcheson & Co Belfast	Lug Belfast Lough OD 15 ft. Class		2	15			6.2	
MORNING STAR	393	1897	William Fife III	William Fife & Son	Cutter 52 LR	Andrew Coats Paisley	37	47.74		58	11.9	7
FORELLA	394	1897	William Fife III	William Fife & Son	Cutter 36 LR	Evelyn S. Parker	14 / 7.53		33.29		8.4	
RONA	395	1897	William Fife III	A. J. Freyers Largs	Lug Clyde 23/30	J. Stewart Clark	9	23		30		
VERENIA	396	1897	William Fife III	William Fife & Son	Sloop Clyde 19/24	A.W. Steven Helensburgh	5	19.2				
MAGDA	397	1897	William Fife III	S. Gudmansen Norway	Cutter 10R Benson Rule	A.W.G. Larsen Christiana Norway	16		35.1		8.6	
NELLIE	398	1897	William Fife III	S. Bond Birkenhead	CB Lug IR	Edmund Johnston Liverpool	4	20		28	6.8	4
TERN	399	1897	William Fife III	Hilditch	Cutter Belfast Lough OD 25ft. Class	W.A.A.G. & T.J. King	9	25		31.8	8.65	5.8
THELMA	400	1897	William Fife III	Hilditch	Cutter Belfast Lough OD 25ft. Class	John A. Black	9	25		31.9	8.6	5.9
SHULAH	401	1897	William Fife III	A. Hutchinson & Co. Belfast	Lug Belfast Lough OD 15ft. Class	A. Norman Stanley	3	15		20.2	6.2	3
UANDI	402	1897	William Fife III	Hutchison Belfast	Lug Belfast Lough OD 15ft. Class	T.V.P. McLammon Hollywood	3	17		20.2	6.2	3
KESTREL	403	1897	William Fife III	B. F. Wood City Is.NY	Cutter	J.B. Mills	33	43.4		51	12	9
404	404	1897	William Fife III	William Fife & Son	Half Rater	W.H. Orvis	2	17.38				
JULIA	405	1897	William Fife III	William Fife & Son	Lug 1R 24 LR	J.J. Greenshields Lesmahago	3		21.41		6.35	
JAP		1897	William Fife III	Teignmouth S & Y Co	Cork Harbour OD	Adolphus Fowler	6	22.4		30	7.3	4.8
CIRCE	406	1897	William Fife III	W & SL Lawrence Perth W. Australia	CB Sloop 24 LR	H.R. & F.E. England	7.5		20		8	
IMP		1897	William Fife III	T. Roche Passage West	Cork Harbour OD	B.A. Morrison & J. L. Seymore	6	22		28	7.2	4.2
REVERIE	407	1897	William Fife III	A. McFarlane Adelaide	CB sloop	W. Fisher Pt Adelaide	10	27		33.6	9	4.2
408	408	1897	William Fife III	W. Finn Carrigloe	Lug	W. Finn Carrigloe	1		17		6.9	
WHIMBRIL		1897	William Fife III	J. Hilditch Carrickfergus	Belfast Lough OD LR 30.35	H. Trevor Henderson	9	25		31.8	8.65	5.8
WIDGEON		1897	William Fife III	J. Hilditch Carrickfergus	Belfast Lough OD LR 30.35		9	25		31.8	8.65	5.8
COLLEEN II		1897	William Fife III	T. Roche Passage West	Cork Harbour OD	A.F. Sharman-Crawford	6	24		30	7.3	4.3
VOL-AU-VENT II		1897	William Fife III	A. Hutchinson & Co. Belfast	Lug	J. Crawford jun.	2	15	15		6.5	3.5
NAPPER	409	1897	William Fife III	William Fife & Son	Sloop	A.M. Connell	4.5	18.6	18	23	7.6	4
DONCELLA	410	1897	William Fife III	William Fife & Son	Sloop Clyde 23/30	A.H.M. Jameson	7	23		30	8	5.8
YUM	411	1898	William Fife III	Carrigloe G7 W Co	Cutter 36LR	W.J.C. Cummins	15	33.6		42	9.4	6.9
412	412	1898	William Fife III	William Fife & Son	17 ft WL	Miss Lillingston	1	17				
LEHETETLLEN	413	1898	William Fife III	William Fife & Son	Cutter	Count Francis, Nadasty Budapest	11	27		33.5	8.75	5.75
414	414	1898	William Fife III	J. Hilditch Carrickfergus	4.5R Benson Rule	James Cable	11					
415	415	1898	William Fife III	William Fife & Son	5R	Edwin Bindeman	12					
SENTA	416	1898	William Fife III	William Fife & Son	Cutter 65LR or 40R, composite	Adolf Bussing Hamburgh	72		72		15.5	8.4
ESPADA	417	1898	William Fife III	William Fife & Son	Lug Clyde 23/30	Andrew Bain	9	23		30		
VIERA	418	1898	William Fife III	William Fife & Son	Cutter 52 LR, composite	W.C.S. & J.C. Connell	37		55		12.5	

Yard number omitted

BOAT NAME	Yard NUMBER	YEAR	DESIGNER	BUILDER	TYPE	FIRST OWNER	Tonnage TM / Reg	LWL - ft	LBP - ft	LOA - ft	Beam - ft	Draft - ft
PUNCTILIO	420	1898	William Fife III	C. Sibbick & Co Cowes	Cutter Dublin Bay 25	G.A. Newson & J.B. Stephens Kingston	9	26.2		32	8.7	6.3
Countermanded	421		William Fife III	William Fife & Son								
EILEEN	422	1898	William Fife III	William Fife & Son	Lug	Sydney Mason	16	32	36	47	9	4.5
FAIRLIE	423	1898	William Fife III	Shepherd & Borwick Windermere	Sloop	Herbert P.C. Crossley	6		27		7.75	
FUJI	424	1898	William Fife III	William Fife III	Lug Clyde 23/30	Andrew Coats	9	23		30		
CORA	425	1898	William Fife III	P. R. McLean Rosneath	Cutter Clyde 23/30	D. Ralston Holms Kerr. Largs	9	23		30		
MAVIS	426	1898	William Fife III	P. R. McLean Rosneath	Lug Clyde 23/30	Henry Allen Glasgow	9	23		30		
MIGNON	427	1898	William Fife III	William Fife & Son	Cutter	Nelson Mitchell Glasgow	3					
NETA	428	1898	William Fife III	William Fife & Son	Cutter 34 LR	A. Liddle McLaren Skelmorlie	12 / 7.48	29.6		42.5	6.8	5.8
GWENDOLIN	429	1898	William Fife III	Paul Jones & Sons Gourock	Lug Clyde 23/30	E.D. Hargreaves Ardrishaig	9	23		30		
RED SPIDER	430	1898	William Fife III	S. Bond Birkenhead	CB Lug Mersey 1 Rater	Rupert Mason	4					
WHITE WINGS	431	1898	William Fife III	W. M. Ford Sydney	CB Cutter 5R	Samuel Harden Sydney	18	30		37.5	11.5	
432	432	1898	William Fife III	William Fife & Son	21 ft. bulb and fin	Karl Soderman	6.5	21				
CLUTHA	433	1898	William Fife III	William Fife & Son	21 ft. bulb and fin	F.N. Clarke		21				
MIRZA	434	1898	William Fife III	William Fife & Son	Cutter	J. Robertson Blackie Cove	24	37.6		46.3	11.3	6.7
UMSLOPOGAS			William Fife III	William Fife & Son	Cutter	L. McLaren	12		37		9	6
SHAMROCK I	435	1898	William Fife III	J.I. Thorneycroft Chiswick	Cutter steel frame bronze & aluminium plating	Sir T.J. Lipton	260	89		105.5	24.55	10.55
Nance	436	1898	William Fife III	William Fife & Son	Cutter Dublin Bay 25	T.C. Burrows, Dublin	9	25				
TRINGA	437	1898	William Fife III	William Fife & Son	Sloop Clyde 19/24	W.C. & J.H. Teacher	5	19	25	24		
IRMA	438	1899	William Fife III	Abo Batvarf Finland	Cutter	Axel Palander Helsingfors	22	33.9		44.7	11	5.4
KISMET	439	1899	William Fife III	William Fife & Son	Cutter	Latham Blacker Carlingford	16					
CHALLENGE	440	1899	William Fife III	J. Clancy Kingstown	Cutter Dublin Bay 25	Fred Thomson		25.8		32	8.7	
WHISPER	441	1898	William Fife III	Doyle Kingston	Cutter Dublin Bay 25	L. Meldon, W. Richardson & J. Mooney	6	25			8.6	6.1
NEPENTHE	442	1898	William Fife III	J. Doyle Kingston	Cutter Dublin Bay 25	H.A. Robinson	6	25			8.6	6.1
MAVIS	443	1898	William Fife III	P. Holloway & Sons Dublin	Cutter Dublin Bay 25	J.W. Chancellor & F. North	6	25			8.6	6.1
ZISKA	444	1898	William Fife III	Paul Jones Gourock	Cutter Dublin Bay 25	J. Lamont Brown Dublin	6	25			8.6	6.1
ACUSHLA	445	1898	William Fife III	J. Clancy Kingston	Cutter Dublin Bay 25	R.J. McDermott Dalkey	6	25			8.6	6.1
DARTHULA	446	1898	William Fife III	J.E. Doyle Kongstown	Cutter Dublin Bay 25	F. St.J. Worrall	6	25			8.6	6.1
FINVOLA	447	1898	William Fife III	J. Hildtich Carrickfergus	Lug Belfast OD 15ft	Richard McGiffin	3	15		20.2	6.2	3
FUGITIVE	448	1898	William Fife III	J. Hildtich Carrickfergus	Lug Belfast OD 15ft	J. Craigjun. Bangor	3	15		20.2	6.2	3
YVETTE	449	1899	William Fife III	William Fife & Son	Lug LR21	P. & Miss Donaldson Kilcreggan	3	16.54				
PIERETTE	450	1899	William Fife III	William Fife & Son	Lug LR21	Peter Donaldson	3	16.57				
ASTRID	451	1899	William Fife III	C. Jensen Christiana Norway	Cutter	P.A. & A.W.G. Larsen	35	41.2		51.5	13	7.5
BLUE ROCK	452	1899	William Fife III	S. Bond Birkenhead	CB Lug Mersey 1 Rater	E. & Arthur C. Davis Beaumaris	4	24			6.6	3.5
PETULA	453	1899	William Fife III	William Fife & Son	Cutter	A.H.M. Jamieson Edinburgh	- / 12.09	34	41.7	42	10.3	7
454	454	1899	William Fife III	William Fife & Son	Lifeboat cutter	Sir T. Lipton						
ACSENOV	455	1899	William Fife III	William Fife & Son	Ketch	Robert Brown Largs	19.5 / 13.95	33.2	39.2	42.1	11.5	6.5
FAIRLIE II	456	1899	William Fife III	R. Inches Hobart Tasmania	Cutter	F.N. Clarke Hobart	6	25		26	8.2	6
AOTEA	457	1901	William Fife III	A. Blunt Victoria	Lug	Osmond H. Alsop Melbourne	8	22		29	8.9	6
HILDA	458	1899	William Fife III	Abo Batvarf Finland	Cutter		14	30.1		42.4	9	4.6
ZELDA		1900	William Fife III	William Fife & Son	Steam yacht	Alex. Scott Dunbar	18	39.8			10.8	5.14
KHAMA	459	1900	William Fife III	William Fife & Son	Cutter 65LR composite nickle steel frames	Kenneth M. Clark, Paisley	74 / 38.74		71.1		15.8	9.9
ULVA	460	1900	William Fife III	William Fife & Son	Lug Clyde 23/30	J. Stewart Clark, Paisley	9	23		30		
POWERFUL	461	1900	William Fife III	William Fife & Son	Lug	A.C. Connell	2.5	15		21	5.6	2.7

BOAT NAME	Yard NUMBER	YEAR	DESIGNER	BUILDER	TYPE	FIRST OWNER	Tonnage TM / Reg	LWL- ft	LBP- ft	LOA- ft	Beam- ft	Draft- ft
MAJESTIC	162	1900	William Fife III	William Fife & Son	Lug	W.C.S. Connell	2.5	15		21		
TERRIBLE	463	1900	William Fife III	William Fife & Son	Lug	A.M. Connell	2.5	15		23		
Cancelled	464	1900		William Fife & Son		T.G. Burrows						
EIDELVEISS	465	1901	William Fife III	William Fife & Son	Cutter	Jules Valton Paris	35	42		54	12.6	7.62
SAPPHIRE	466	1901	William Fife III	E. S. Luard Bombay	Lug 30LR	E. S. Luard Bombay	6	27			7.6	
TOPSY	467	1901	William Fife III	William Fife & Son	cb-Lug	Sydney Mason Beaumaris	2	17				
SUNSHINE	468	1901	William Fife III	William Fife & Son	Schooner	F. Glen McAndrew Knock, Largs	115 /54.86		83		18.2	11
FLEETWING	469	1901	William Fife III.	William Fife & Son	30R	Anthoney Horden	8					
ULIDIA	470	1901	William Fife III	William Fife & Son	Sloop Clyde 19/24	Sir W. Corry London	5	19		24		
PUKAKI	471	1901	William Fife III	G. Lavis Portsmouth	Cutter	Louis Bamberger Excmouth	19	36.3		44	10.5	7.5
CHINOOK	472	1901	William Fife III	Hamilton Ontario	Cutter 40R	S.E. Malloch Hamilton, Ontario	18	34.6		40	10	6.2
COILA	473	1901	William Fife III	William Fife & Son	Cutter	Edward Hunter Kilmarnock	/6.69	31.6		42.27	9.6	6.4
ZINITA	474	1901	William Fife III	William Fife & Son	Cutter 30LR	W.C.S. & J.G. & A. Connell	7					
MAGDALEN	475	1901	William Fife III	William Fife & Son	Cutter 52LR composite nickle steel frames	Baron de Forest	47 / 23.12	63.3			13.15	6.65
476	476	1901	William Fife III	William Fife & Son	Yawl	F.N. Clarke	13.5	30				
YVALDA	477	1901	A. Mylne	William Fife & Son	Cutter Clyde 20 Y.R.A Rating	Peter Donaldson	21 / 12.25		42		11	7.6
Not built	478											
479	479	1901	William Fife III	William Fife & Son	Yawl 52LR	C.D. Wallace		49.8				
PICCOLO	480	1901	William Fife III	William Fife & Son	Cutter 36LR	Capt. J. Orr-Ewing	16	34.15			9	6.6
ASTHORE	481	1902	William Fife III	William Fife & Son	Schooner	Walter Runciman Newcastle	115 / 55		84		18.3	10.65
EILEEN IV	482	1902	William Fife III	William Fife & Son	Cutter 36LR	Sydney Mason,Beaumaris	15					
TRINGA II	483	1902	William Fife III	William Fife & Son	Sloop Clyde 19/24	W.C. & J.H. Teacher	5	19		24		
FAIRLIE III	484	1902	William Fife III	R. Inches Hobart	Cutter	F.N. Clarke Hobart	17	30		36.4	11.5	5.3
CICELY	485	1902	William Fife III	J. G. Fay Southampton	Schooner	Cecil Qentin Lipbook Hants	263	90		112	23.5	12.58
ENSAY	486	1902	William Fife III	William Fife & Son	Cutter 36LR	J. Stewart Clark S. Queensferry	16					
487	487	1902	William Fife III	William Fife & Son	52LR	Baron von Prenschen	47					
NYAMA	488	1902	William Fife III	William Fife & Son	Cutter 36LR	Capt. J. Orr-Ewing	16					
CARMEN	489	1902	William Fife III	C. Jensen Asker Norway	Cutter	F.C. & J.C. Roschauw Christiana	8					
LUCIDA	490	1902	William Fife III	William Fife & Son	Cutter 52 LR composite	W.P. Burton Ipswitch	47 / 22.29	47.82		62.5	13	7.15
MOONBEAM	491	1903	William Fife III	William Fife & Son	Yawl	Charles P. Johnson	65 / 37.27	59.26		68	15.55	10.8
VALDORA	492	1903	William Fife III	William Fife & Son	Yawl	Dr J.G. Douglas Kerr Bath	106 /55.64	68.25		79.2	18.1	12.17
SCOTIA	493	1903	William Fife III	H. T. Green Sydney	Cutter 30LR	T.W. Bremner, Sydney	9.5	28.94		37	7.9	4.1
CRIMSON RAMBLER	494	1903	William Fife III	William Fife & Son	Aux. steam schooner	W.G. Jameson	40 / 15.78	50		60.4		
SHAMROCK III	495	1903	William Fife III	Denny Bros Dumbarton	Cutter steel	Sir T. Lipton	278	89.81		109.35	24.85	10.7
496	496	1903	William Fife III	William Fife & Son	Motor launch	E.S. Parker						
497	497	1903	William Fife III	William Fife & Son		Alfred Gollin	40					
NINIA	498	1903	William Fife III	C. Jensen Asker Norway	Cutter	Christian Wisbech Christiana	9	27.7			9.5	6.1
499	499	1903	William Fife III	William Fife & Son	CB cutter	K.M. Clark						
ANDRUM	500	1903	William Fife III	William Fife & Son	Cutter 30LR	Capt. J. Orr-Ewing	9.5	28.37		30.7	7	7.85
ZINITA	501	1904	William Fife III	J. Clancy Kingstown	Cutter 65LR, composite	W.C.S. Connell	/42.12	61.75		79.5	16.6	
CHECKMATE		1904	William Fife III	J. Clancy Kingstown	Cutter							9.14
FALCON	502	1903	William Fife III	William Fife & Son	Cutter 36LR	W.S. &J.C. Connell	16	33.74				
TANJA		1904	William Fife III	C. Jensen Christiana Norway	Cutter	J.C. Rowshaw	9	27.7			9.5	6.2
503	503	1903	William Fife III	William Fife & Son	CB cutter	W.G. Jameson London	5	25.2		32	6	
ALANA		1904	William Fife III	J.E. Doyle Kingston	Cutter Dublin Bay 25		9	26		31.8	8.5	6.2
LADA	504	1904	William Fife III	St. Petersburgh River YC	Cutter	Alex. Korowin St Petersburgh	30	35.4	47.6	12.6		

BOAT NAME	Yard NUMBER	YEAR	DESIGNER	BUILDER	TYPE	FIRST OWNER	Tonnage TM / Reg	LWL - ft	LBP - ft	LOA - ft	Beam - ft	Draft - ft
EVA	505	1906	William Fife III	William Fife & Son	Cutter	F. Glen McAndrew Largs	8	28.6		67.7	15.04	10.2
ROSAMOND	506	1904	William Fife III	William Fife & Son	Yawl	A. K. Stothert London	63 / 34.49	56.5				
WHITE HEATHER	507	1904	William Fife III	J. G. Fay & Co Southampton	Yawl 82.6 LR, composite	Myles B. Kennedy	151	74.2	77	91.2	19.95	11.2
MAGDA IV	508	1904	William Fife III	C. Jensen Christiana Nor	Cutter	P.A. & A.W.G. Larsen Christiana	18	34.88	36	46	9.3	
MIKADO	509	1904	William Fife III	William Fife & Son	Cutter 30LR	Sir W. Corry	10	26.4		35.7	8.3	
SUSANNE	510	1904	William Fife III	A & J Inglis Pointhouse	Schooner 79.07 LR, composite	O. Huldschinsky Berlin	/ 69.54	74.3	75.03	93.7	19.8	10.25
LILIAN	511	1904	William Fife III	William Fife & Son	Cutter Clyde 30R	James S. Craig	10 / 6.03	26.4		35.7	8.3	
MAYMON	512	1904	William Fife III	William Fife & Son	Cutter 52 LR composite	Samuel Butler Bristol	46 / 22.03	48.75	48.1	63.2	13.2	6.5
SAGA	513	1904	William Fife III	Moskin & Brobygg Finland	Cutter	Karl Soderman Helsingfors	13	28.45	30.5	36	9.8	4.9
SU SU	514	1904	William Fife III	William Fife & Son	Sloop 24 LR	Mrs H.G. Allan Southsea	4	22.85	23.5	30.5	6.26	3.7
515	515	1904	William Fife III	William Fife & Son	Motor launch	William Fife III		30				
ROSE	516	1906	William Fife III	William Fife & Son	Yawl	James J. Frame Glasgow	80	60	61	73.25	16.2	10.7
KARMA	517	1905	William Fife III	William Fife & Son	Cutter 32 LR	W.C. & J.H. Teacher	11 / 6.92	27.21	27.34	33.7	9.2	6.1
LAFONE	518	1906	William Fife III	J. Kelly Portrush	Cutter	G.H. Moore Brown Dublin	38	45.55		54	13.3	
TARPON	519	1905	William Fife III	William Fife & Son	Cutter Clyde 30 LR	T.K. Laidlaw Largs	10	26.3		43.5		5
AWANUI	520	1905	William Fife III	W.M. Ford jun. Sydney	Cutter 36 R		16	33.7				
MAGDA V	521	1905	William Fife III	C. Jensen Christiana	Cutter 11 metre Norway	P.A. & A.W.G. Larsen Christiana	17	36.7			10.8	
VANESSA	522	1905	William Fife III	William Fife & Son	CB sloop	Earl of Dudley Dublin	8	20.5				
GREAT AUK	523	1905	William Fife III	William Fife & Son	Cutter Clyde 30LR	Andrew Coates Paisley	10 / 6.23	26.7	30	36.3	8.2	4.9
TEMERAIRE	524	1905	William Fife III	J. Andres Ontario framed	Cutter	Fred Nicholls	17	29.75		30		
ULDRA	525	1905	William Fife III	William Fife & Son	Cruising cutter 57 LR	J. Robertson Blackie Cove	56 / 27.13	50	50.5	64.5	14.5	8.8
NENUFAR	526	1905	William Fife III	William Fife & Son	Cutter	Gabiel Roiz Parra Santander	15	29.75				
NORTH STAR	527	1905	William Fife III	William Fife & Son	Sloop	Robert Brown Largs	4			20.5	7	
MANORA	528	1905	William Fife III	William Fife & Son	C.T.R. Sevell	J.C. Connell	115	83.25			18.25	
529	529	1905	William Fife III	William Fife & Son	Motor launch		8	25				
SEAGULL		1905	William Fife III	William Fife & Son	CB. sloop	Hon. Cyril Ward						
MARGUERITE	530	1905	William Fife III	William Fife & Son	Cutter	J. Wotherspoon Seamill	4	17		21		
ALFHILD	531	1906	William Fife III	A. Hansen Arendal Norway	Cutter		9	27.7			9.5	
CLIO	532	1906	William Fife III	William Fife & Son	Cutter	William Fife III	18	32.5		41	10.7	5.8
532	533	1906	William Fife III	William Fife & Son		Fred Nicholls		30				
SORAIS	534	1906	William Fife III	William Fife & Son	Lug 24 LR	Mrs H.G. Allan	5	22.75				
OCEAN	535	1906	William Fife III	Anker & Jensen Norway	Cutter	Olaf Bronn Christiania	9	27.9			9.5	
534	536	1906	William Fife III	Cancelled, design partly paid		Hon Gervais Beckett						
MAGDA VI	537	1906	William Fife III	Anker & Jensen Asker Norway	Cutter	P.A. & A.W.G. Larsen, Christiana	24	34.4		46.7	11.2	8.5
THE KETCH	538	1906	William Fife III	William Fife & Son	Aux TS ketch motor fishing yacht	Kenneth M. Clark Suffolk	108	75.1		19	10	
ANITRA	539	1906	William Fife III	William Fife & Son	Lug 24 LR	W. Hargreaves Brown London	5	22.75				
MIRAGE (MNPAEKB)	540	1906	William Fife III	William Fife & Son	Cutter	P. Yuritsin (Nicolaeff)	71	70.5		62.1	15.6	8.5
ZWERVER	541	1906	William Fife III	William Fife & Son	Cutter	E. Kol Amsterdam	55 / 28.25	50			14.9	8.9
TEMERAIRE II	542	1907	William Fife III	Framed+ Andrews Ontario	Sloop	Fred Nicholls Toronto	12	30		37.7	8.9	4.7
541	543	1907	William Fife III	Not built	Motor launch	Argyll Motor Co		64				
WANDA	544	1907	William Fife III	Anker & Jensen Christia	Cutter 10 metre	Frantz Rosenburgh, Christiana	15	33.1		42.6	9.3	5.7
WHITE HEATHER II	545	1907	William Fife III	William Fife & Son	Cutter 23 metre Composite	Myles B. Kennedy	179 / 89.89	96.6			21.7	10.95
544	546	1907	William Fife III	William Fife & Son	Motor launch	Miss Winifred Parker				25		
SHIMINA	545	1907	William Fife III	Alex. Robertson Sandbank	Cutter 15 metre Composite	William Yates	49	62.75			13.9	7
ALEXANDRA	546	1907	William Fife III	Vancouver Shipyard	Sloop	Fred Lucas Vancouver	11	29.3		38.1	8.2	4.9

Name	No.	Year	Designer	Builder	Type	First owner	Tonnage TM / Reg	LWL-ft	LBP-ft	LOA-ft	Beam-ft	Draft-ft
LILIAN	547	1907	William Fife III	William Fife & Son	Cutter Clyde 30R	James S. Craig Glasgow	9.5	36			8	4.3
OSBORNE	548	1907	William Fife III	William Fife & Son	Cutter 6 metre	HM King of Spain	4	22.03		26.2	5.9	3.3
ALMORAIMA	549	1907	William Fife III	William Fife & Son	Cutter 6 metre	Duque de Medinacelli Barcelona	4	21.98		26.2	5.9	3.3
SORAIS	550	1907	William Fife III	William Fife & Son	Cutter 8 metre	Mrs R.G. Allen	8	34.2			7.7	4.3
YA VEREMOS	551	1907	William Fife III	William Fife & Son	Cutter 8 metre	Enrique Careaga	8	34.2			7.7	4.3
EILEEN VI	552	1908	William Fife III	William Fife & Son	Cutter	Sydney Mason	25 / 12.85	35.5		45.2	9	4.5
MARISKA	553	1908	William Fife III	William Fife & Son	Cutter 15 metre	A.K. Stothert	50 / 27.87	63.8			13.7	7.2
554	554	1908	William Fife III	William Fife & Son	Motor gig							
SHAMROCK	555	1908	William Fife III	William Fife & Son	Cutter 23 metre composite	Sir T. Lipton	176 / 94.82	96.6			21	11.1
ALACHIE	556	1908	William Fife III	William Fife & Son	Cutter 15 metre	George Coats Ayr	26 / 14.94	51.6			11.1	6.1
VIOLA	557	1908	William Fife III	William Fife & Son	Cutter	T.M. Hunter Cove	12 / 8.32	34.2			9.5	5.9
CORRIE	558	1908	William Fife III	A. Robertson Sandbank	Cutter Clyde 30 LR	W.A. Collins Glasgow	10	37		34.9	8	4.3
COBWEB	559	1908	William Fife III	William Fife & Son	Cutter 8 metre	Blair O. Cochrane Ryde	9	25.98		34.9		4.7
560	560	1908	William Fife III	William Fife & Son	Motor gig for Moonbeam III	Charles P. Johnson			17			
SPERO	561	1909	William Fife III	William Fife & Son	Cutter 8 metre	Rev. Charles Progers	9	33.9			7.8	4.7
ENDRICK	562	1909	William Fife III	William Fife & Son	Cutter 8 metre	Sir A. Orr-Ewing	9	33.9			7.8	4.7
ENDRICK	562	1909	William Fife III	William Fife & Son	Cutter 8 metre	Sir A. Orr-Ewing	9	33.9			7.8	4.7
CINTRA	563	1909	William Fife III	William Fife & Son	Cutter 12 metre	Andrew Coats	27 / 15.06	51.5			11.1	6.3
VANITY	564	1909	William Fife III	William Fife & Son	Cutter 15 metre	J.R. Payne, A.E. Watson, I. Hamilton Bell	50 / 27.55	63.6			13.7	8.1
JULNAR	565	1909	William Fife III	Summers & Payne Southampton	Ketch composite	Sir M. Fitzgerald London & Valencia	135	79.3		89.1	19.03	10.1
MAGDA VIII	566	1909	William Fife III	Anker & Jensen Norway	Cutter 12 metre	P.A. & A.W.G. Larsen Christiania	27	39.4		51.3	11.1	6.3
CHAMELEON	567	1909	William Fife III	William Fife & Son	Aux. cutter	Philip Herbert Plymouth	28 / 15.20	48		48.2	12	8.4
HISPANIA	568	1909	William Fife III	Astilleros Karrparo	Cutter 15 metre	HM King of Spain Pasages	50	49.2		63.5	13.7	8.1
TUIGA	569	1909	William Fife III	Abo Batvarf Finland	Cutter 15 metre	Duque de Medinacelli Santander	50 / 28.5			63.5	13.7	8.1
LUCKY GIRL	570	1909/10	William Fife III	William Fife & Son	Cutter 8 metre	Karl Soderman	9	26.7		33.9	7.78	4.7
SAUNTERER IV	571	1909	William Fife III	William Fife & Son	Cutter	John Simpson	20	34.9		39.3	11.6	6.9
571	571	1909	William Fife III	William Fife & Son	CB cutter	Sir M. Fitzgerald	2					
SON II	572	1909	William Fife III	D.N.K. Barth Christiania	Cutter 9 metre	C.N.V.K. Barth, Christiania	13	39.5			8.6	5.2
VESANIA	573	1909	C. Dekke	William Fife & Son	Cutter 8 metre	Duque d'Alba Madrid	9	26.38		34.5	7.8	4.7
MINORU	574	1909	William Fife III	William Fife & Son	Aux cutter	John Simpson London	21 / 13.59	34.9		41.5	11.4	4.9
SHAHEEN	575	1910	William Fife III	William Fife & Son	Aux ketch	L.M. Torin London	82 / 43.07	67.9			17.6	10.4
PRO TEA	576	1910	William Fife III	Woodstock Naval cadets	Cutter 8 metre	Sir T. Lipton for cadets Capetown, S. Africa	9	34.7			7.8	4.7
ELLA	577	1910	William Fife III	W. E. Thomas Falmouth	Yawl	Col. David Wilkie	9	25		29.4	9.23	5.4
IREX	578	1910	William Fife III	William Fife & Son	Cutter 10 metre	H. Marzetti London	15 / 14.92	32.4		43	9.7	6
GANNET	579	1910	C. Dekke	William Fife & Son	SC ketch paraffin engine	Sidney A. Hermon Crawley	37 / 18.53	47.4			14.5	7.5
SOPHIE ELIZABETH	580	1910	William Fife III	William Fife & Son	Cutter 15 metre	Leopold Biermann, Bremen	50 / 30.11	64.25			13.4	9
WOGE IV	581	1910	William Fife III	Abeking & Rassmusson	Cutter 8 metre	Otto C. Ernst Hamburg	9	36.4			7.7	4.7
CLIO	582	1910	William Fife III	J. Goudie	Cutter 6 metre	J. Goudie	4	20.33		27	5.93	3.8
SANTANDER	583	1910	William Fife III	Tailles de San Martin	Cutter 7 metre	V.L. Doriga Santander	5.5	23.2	30.8		6.6	4.2
IRENE	584	1910	William Fife III	William Fife & Son	Cutter 8 metre	H.T. Henderson Belfast	9	35.4			7.7	4.7
THE TRUANT	585	1910	William Fife III	William Fife & Son	Cutter 8 metre	Sir Ralph Gore Warsash	9	35.4			7.7	4.7
CINGALEE	586	1910	William Fife III	William Fife & Son	Cutter 6 metre	Algernon Maudesley	4	20.3		27.1	5.9	3.7
587	587	1910	William Fife III	William Fife & Son	Port Motor launch for SY ERIN	Sir T. Lipton						
588	588	1910	William Fife III	William Fife & Son	Starboard Motor launch for SY 'ERIN'	Sir T. Lipton						
589	589	1910	William Fife III	Cardona & Palon Barcelona	7 metre	Pedro Ma de Reynoso	5.5		30.3		6.7	

BOAT NAME	Yard NUMBER	YEAR	DESIGNER	BUILDER	TYPE	FIRST OWNER	Tonnage TM / Reg	LWL - ft	LBP - ft	LOA - ft	Beam - ft	Draft - ft
CLIO	590	1911	William Fife III	William Fife & Son	Twin screw yacht	W. Fife III	42	61.1	58.5	65.3	12.3	4.4
IERNE	591	1911	William Fife III	William Fife & Son	Cutter 12 metre	A.F. Sharman-Crawford Cork	28 / 15.98		52.6		11.25	6.25
CORONA	592	1911	William Fife III	William Fife & Son	Cutter 19 metre composite	William Yates	99 / 60.25		81.5		17	9.8
WATERWITCH	593	1911	William Fife III	Ailsa Shipbuilding Troon	Schooner, steel, A class	Cecil Whitaker	352		120		26.6	
ERNA SIGNE	594	1911	William Fife III	Stockholm Barbygge	Cutter 12 metre Prt steel frame	C.L. Hellstrom jun.	28	39.2		52.6	11.25	6.4
MARIQUITA	595	1911	William Fife III	William Fife & Son	19 Metre composite	A.K. Stothert	99 / 59.90		81.5		17	9.8
ENDRICK	596	1911	William Fife III	William Fife & Son	Cutter 8metre	Sir Arch. Orr-Ewing	8		35.1		7.5	
NORMAN	597	1911	William Fife III	William Fife & Son	Cutter 8metre	Capt. J. Orr-Ewing	8		35.1		7.5	
598	598	1911	William Fife III	William Fife & Son	7 Metre	Don Enrique Pardinas		23.04				
TONINO	599	1911	William Fife III	Astilleros del Nervion	Cutter 10 metre	HM King of Spain	16	32.7		43.6		
RED SPIDER	600	1911	William Fife III	William Fife & Son	CB cutter Mersey 1 Rater	Rupert Mason	4		24.9		6.5	2.7
ELISE	601	1911	William Fife III	William Fife & Son	Aux Schooner	W.A. Young Paisley	39 / 13.28	46	56.4		12.5	7.7
602	602	1911	William Fife III	William Fife & Son	Sailing cutter	Myles B. Kennedy						
MAYA	603	1911	William Fife III	William Fife & Son	Cutter 6 metre	V.T. Janson Bombay	4		27.3		5.77	3.8
MARITHEA	604	1911	William Fife III	William Fife & Son	Cutter 8 metre	Prince of Saxe Coburg Gotha		26.4		35	7.53	4.8
ENARA	605	1912	William Fife III	William Fife & Son	Aux yawl	Wm. C. Teacher	26 / 15.12	37		45.8	11.9	7
ENDRICK	606	1912	William Fife III	William Fife & Son	7 Metre gunter	Sir Arch. Orr-Ewing	6		30.7		6.6	4.5
607	607	1912	William Fife III	William Fife & Son	10 metre	Enrique Pardinas						
MARSINAH	608	1912	William Fife III	William Fife & Son	7 Metre gunter lug	Walter W. Greenhill Warsash	6		30.7		6.6	4.5
VENTANA	609	1912	William Fife III	William Fife & Son	Cutter 8 metre	A.J.H. Hamilton	8		34.6		7.5	4.9
THE LADY ANNE	610	1912	William Fife III	William Fife & Son	Cutter 15 metre	George Coats	51 / 31.13		64.1		13.8	7.9
LEILA	611	1912	William Fife III	William Fife & Son	Cutter 6 metre	Charles G. McAndrew Ayr	3		20.3		5.8	
NYMPHEA	612	1912	William Fife III	William Fife & Son	Cutter 8 metre	Richard Thomas	8		35.2		7.49	
ORN	613	1912	William Fife III	Helsingfors Barvarf Finland	Cutter 8 metre	Gustaf A. Estlander	8	26.4		34.6	7.5	4.9
MORNA	614	1912/13	William Fife III	Morrison & Sinclair NSW	Aux Cutter	Sir Alex. McCormack Sydney	38	4.6		55.2	13	8.7
ERICA	615	1912	William Fife III	William Fife & Son	Cutter 8 metre	Mr Advocate House Cape Town	8		35		7.49	4.9
SKEBENGA	616	1912	William Fife III	William Fife & Son	Cutter 8 metre	A. Suttie Secy. Point YC, Durban SA	8		35		7.49	4.8
GALLIA III	617	1912	William Fife III	P. Barre Lormont France	Cutter 8 metre	Joseph Loste Arachon	9					
618	618	1912	William Fife III	William Fife & Son	8 metre	A. Winterbeck						
BEDUIN	619	1912	William Fife III	William Fife & Son	15 metre	C.L. Hellstrom jun.		26.4				
IERNE	620	1913	William Fife III	William Fife & Son	Cutter 8 metre	A.F. Sharman-Crawford	8		35.3		7.5	4.8
STRATHENDRICK	621	1913	William Fife III	William Fife & Son	Cutter 7 metre	Sir Arch. Orr-Ewing	6		31.6		6.6	4.7
MAUDRY	622	1913	William Fife III	William Fife & Son	Cutter 15 metre Prt steel frame	W. Blatspiel Stamp London	51		65.2		13.7	7.9
LARSKAGG	623	1913	William Fife III	G.R. Liljegren Gothenburgh	Cutter 8 metre	Gothenburg Yacht Union	8	26.2		35.5	7.5	5.3
NITA	624	1913	William Fife III	William Fife & Son	6 metre gunter	J. Bryce Allan	4	27.7		41.4	5.8	4.1
CHAMELEON	625	1913/14	William Fife III	William Fife & Son	Aux cutter	Philip Herbert	20	33	34		11.3	7.7
RENDEVOUS	626	1913	William Fife III	William Fife & Son	17 metre steel frame	Gunnar Setterwall Stockholm		55	73.6		15.35	9.2
SCIGLINDA	627	1913	William Fife III	William Fife & Son	Twin screw yacht	Walter M. Bergius	52		64.2		13.9	7
628	628	1913	William Fife III	Cancelled order	6 metre	Charles Prince						
629	629	1913	William Fife III	William Fife & Son	12 metre	Nicoliev YC						
CYPRIS	630	1913	William Fife III	William Fife & Son	Cutter 5 metre	Louis Renault Meulan	3		24		5	3.2
631	631	1913	William Fife III	William Fife & Son	8 metre	Norman Murray Sydney						
NORMAND	632	1914	William Fife III	William Fife & Son	6 metre bermudian	Marquis de Cussy Le Havre	4		28.4		5.65	3.9
MARGA II	633	1914	William Fife III	G.R. Liljergen Gothenburgh	10 metre cutter	Gothenburg Yacht Union	26	32.4	44.9		9.1	6.6
PEGGY	634	1914	William Fife II	William Fife & Son	8 metre bermudian	Charles Prince Normoutier	9					

APPENDIX III — YARD LIST

BOAT NAME	Yard NUMBER	YEAR	DESIGNER	BUILDER	TYPE	FIRST OWNER	Tonnage TM/Reg	LWL-ft	LBP-ft	LOA-ft	Beam-ft	Draft-ft
ROULIS	635	1914	William Fife III	Chantier Nav du Leman	Lug	Chantiers Navale de Construction du Leman Copper	3	17.3		21.32	5.2	
MARMI	636	1914	William Fife III	William Fife & Son	6 metre bermudian	Norman Clark Neill	4		28.5		5.6	3.9
GALLIA IV	637	1914	William Fife III	P. Barre Lormont France	8 metre	Joseph Loste Bordeaux	8		35.1		7.3	5.1
IERNE	638	1914	William Fife III	William Fife & Son	8 metre cutter	A.F. Sharman-Crawford	9					
SKEAF	639	1914	William Fife III	Abeking & Rasmussen	Cutter 12 metre	Henry Horn	28					
SUMURUN	640	1914	William Fife III	William Fife & Son	Yawl	Lord Sackville	90	63.5		78.5	16.5	
SOGALINDA VI	641	1914	William Fife III	Astilleros del Nervion	Cutter 10 metre	Conde de Zubiria Bilbao	16	32.5		44.5	9.1	7
SILDA II	642	1914	William Fife III	Astilleros del Nervion	Cutter 8 metre	Angel F. Perez Santander	8	26.1		36	7.4	5.2
	643	1914	William Fife III	William Fife & Son	Launch for Sumurum	Lord Sackville						
MEKTOUB	644	1914	William Fife III	Astilleros del Nervion	Cutter 8 metre	HRH Don Carlos de Bourbon per E. Carraga	9	26.1		36	7.4	5.2
GIRALDA IV	645	1914	William Fife III	Astilleros del Nervion	7 metre bermudian	HM King of Spain Per E. Carraga	6	2.9		32.1	6.4	5.2
	646	1914	William Fife III	William Fife & Son	6.5 metre. Railway series	Robert Coutant						
	647	1914	William Fife III	William Fife & Son	De Horsey rig CB sailing cutter	Admiralty		34				
	648	1914	William Fife III	William Fife & Son	De Horsey rig sailing cutter	Admiralty		32				
	649	1914	William Fife III	William Fife & Son	De Horsey rig sailing cutter	Admiralty		32				
	650	1914	William Fife III	William Fife & Son	De Horsey rig sailing cutter	Admiralty		32				
	651	1914	William Fife III	William Fife & Son	Motor boat	Admiralty		35				
	652	1914	William Fife III	William Fife & Son	7 metre	Robert Coutant						
MOONBEAM IV	653	1915	William Fife III	William Fife & Son	Cutter composite	Charles P. Johnson	90		82		16.6	10
	654	1915	William Fife III	William Fife & Son	Motor launch	E.S. Parker		22				
	655	1915/16	William Fife III	William Fife & Son	Six motor boats	Admiralty		20				
	656	1915	William Fife III	William Fife & Son	Launch for Moonbeam	C.P. Johnson						
	657	1915/16	William Fife III	William Fife & Son	Five whalers	5 for Admiralty, 1 for Cammel Laird		27				
	658	1915/16	William Fife III	William Fife & Son	Three gigs double skin	Admiralty		30				
	569	1915	William Fife III	William Fife & Son	Whaler	Cammell Laird		25				
	660	1915	William Fife III	William Fife & Son	Skiff dinghy	Cammell Laird		16				
	661	1915/16	William Fife III	William Fife & Son	Two motor boats	Admiralty		20				
	662	1915	William Fife III	William Fife & Son	Two steam pinnaces	Admiralty		50				
	663	1915/16	William Fife III	William Fife & Son	Two motor boats	Admiralty		20				
	664	1916	William Fife III	William Fife & Son	Motor boat for stock	Sold to James Litster Kirn		26				
	665	1916	William Fife III	William Fife & Son	Motor boat	Bergius Launch & Engine Co. for War Office		26				
	666	1916	William Fife III	William Fife & Son	Motor boat	Bergius Launch & Engine Co. for War Office		26				
	667	1917	William Fife III	William Fife & Son	Motor boat	Bergius Launch & Engine Co. for War Office		36				
	668	1917	William Fife III	William Fife & Son	Motor boat	Bergius Launch & Engine Co. for War Office		36				
	669	1917	William Fife III	William Fife & Son	Motor boat	Bergius Launch & Engine Co. for War Office		36				
	670	1917	William Fife III	William Fife & Son	Water boat	Bergius Launch & Engine Co. for War Office		42				
	671	1917	William Fife III	William Fife & Son	Water boat	Bergius Launch & Engine Co. for War Office		42				

BOAT NAME	Yard NUMBER	YEAR	DESIGNER	BUILDER	TYPE	FIRST OWNER	Tonnage TM / Reg	LWL - ft	LBP - ft	LOA - ft	Beam - ft	Draft - ft
POPPY	672	1917	William Fife III	William Fife & Son	Motor boat	Bergius Launch & Engine Co. for War Office		36				
LILY	673	1917	William Fife III	William Fife & Son	Motor boat	Bergius Launch & Engine Co. for War Office		36				
674	674	1918	William Fife III	William Fife & Son	Motor boat	Admiralty RNAS		54				
675	675	1918	William Fife III	William Fife & Son	Motor boat	Admiralty RNAS		54				
676	676	1918	William Fife III	William Fife & Son	Water boat	Bergius Launch & Engine Co. for War Office		42				
677	677	1918	William Fife III	William Fife & Son	Water boat	Bergius Launch & Engine Co. for War Office		42				
678	678	1918	William Fife III	William Fife & Son	Steam pinnace	Admiralty		50				
679	679	1918	William Fife III	Cancelled	Steam pinnace	Admiralty		50				
ST ANDREW	680	1919	G. L. Watson	William Fife & Son	CB sloop Salcombe St OD	Capt. L. Lindsay-Smith	3	18		21	6	
ST GEORGE	681	1919	G. L. Watson	William Fife & Son	CB sloop Salcombe St OD	Capt. L. Lindsay-Smith	3	18		21	6	
ST PATRICK	682	1919	G. L. Watson	William Fife & Son	CB sloop Salcombe St OD	Capt. L. Lindsay-Smith	3	18		21	6	
ST DAVID	683	1919	G. L. Watson	William Fife & Son	CB sloop Salcombe St OD	Capt. L. Lindsay-Smith	3	18		21	6	
ASPHODEL	685	1919	William Fife III	William Fife & Son	Sloop 18 ft BRA	Algernon Maudesley	3	18				
ATHENE II	684	1919	William Fife III	William Fife & Son	Yawl 14 metre	Finn Wilhelmsen, Tonsberg Norway	32	45.6			13.7	8.2
CLIO	686	1919	William Fife III	William Fife & Son	Berm Sloop 30 ft	W. Fife III	14	30	38		9.6	5.1
IERNE	687	1920	William Fife III	William Fife & Son	Bermudian sloop Nat 30 ft	A.F. Sharman-Crawford	14		38		9.64	5.1
ANTWERPIA V	688	1920	William Fife III	William Fife & Son	Bermudian 8 metre	RYC de Belgique per Albert Grisar	8		34.5		7.75	
PRUDENCE	689	1920	William Fife III	William Fife & Son	Cutter 18ft BRA	Sir Ralph G. Gore	3	18				
DODO III	690	1920	William Fife III	William Fife & Son	Aux ketch	William M. Bergus	21		42.2		11.2	4.9
VANITY	691	1920	William Fife III	William Fife & Son	18ft BRA	Lt. Comm A.H.J. Hamilton	3	18				
CARYL	692	1920	William Fife III	William Fife & Son	Sloop 6 Metre	W.F. Robertson	5		28.7		6.45	3.85
FREEZIA	693	1920	William Fife III	William Fife & Son	Bermudian 6 metre	Algernon Maudsley	5		29.5		6.6	4
FLYA	694	1920	William Fife III	William Fife & Son	Bermudian 6 metre	E.S. Parker	5		29.5		6.6	4
POLLY	695	1920	William Fife III	William Fife & Son	Bermudian 6 metre	Basil J. Gould	5		29.5		6.6	4
MAID MARION	696	1920	William Fife III	William Fife & Son	Bermudian 6 metre	John Parkinson & Hamilton Emmons	5	29.5			6.6	4
FIRE FAY	697	1921	William Fife III	William Fife & Son	SC Motor Yacht	E.S. Parker	11 / 6.04	35.9	37.5		8.5	4.05
SUZETTE	698	1921	William Fife III	William Fife & Son	Bermudian sloop 6 metre	Col. F.T. Peel Alexandria Egypt	5					
GAIRNEY	699	1921	William Fife III	William Fife & Son	Bermudian sloop 6 metre	Lord Glentanner	5 / 3.48					
REG	700	1921	William Fife III	William Fife & Son	Bermudian sloop 6 metre	Norman Clark-Neill	5 / 3.39		29		6.9	4.25
AYESHA	701	1921	William Fife III	William Fife & Son	Bermudian sloop 6 metre	George F.Paisley	5					
ANNICK II	702	1921	William Fife III	Cantiere Baglietto	Bermudian sloop Int 18 class	Eddie Isnardi Genoa per Italian Shipping & Coal	2	18				
LADY EDITH	703	1922-23	William Fife III	William Fife & Son	Aux cutter 12 metre	Alfred Melson	33 / 16.87	31		50.3	12.4	8.3
ADA	704	1922-23	William Fife III	William Fife & Son	Aux schooner	Sir A. MacCormick Sydney	59 / 26.72	60		62	15.4	8.3
CELINA	705	1922	William Fife III	Kobenhavens Yr & Mtr Yt Copenhagen	6 metre bermudian sloop	C. Herforth Copenhagen	5	21.3				
ACACIA	706	1922	William Fife III	William Fife & Son	6 metre bermudian sloop	George F. Paisley	6 / 2.84	28.25			6.7	4.2
KENTRA	707	1922	William Fife III	William Fife & Son	Aux ketch	Kenneth M.Clark Acharacle	85 / 45.04	71			17.2	10.2
GEEJAN	708	1922	William Fife III	Abraham & Son Gothenberg	6 metre bermudian sloop	Gideon Falk	5	21.3		35.1	6.9	2.8
VANITY	709	1922	William Fife III	William Fife & Son	Cutter 12 metre	John R. Payne	33 / 19.47	52.5			12.1	6.5
Betty	710	1922	William Fife III	William Fife & Son	6 metre bermudian sloop	G.E. Halinstein & J.C. Newman, Norwich	5	28.2			6.7	4.2
WILLEM VI	711	1922	William Fife III	De Vries Lentsch Amsterdam	6 metre bermudian sloop	P. Blom & C.J. Laan	5	21.3			6.5	4.9
THISTLE	712	1922	William Fife III	William Fife & Son	6 metre bermudian sloop	Lady C. Baird N. Devon	3	19.6			6.76	4.2

Name	No	Year	Designer	Builder	Type	Owner	Tonnage TM / Reg	LWL-ft	LBP-ft	LOA-ft	Beam-ft	Draft-ft
713	713	1922	William Fife III	William Fife & Son	Launch for Kentra	K.M. Clark		16				
714	714	1922	William Fife III	William Fife & Son	Launch for Kentra	K.M. Clark		14				
FIFE	715	1922	William Fife III	Australia	21 restricted class	L.T. Bennett S. Australia						
716	716	1922	William Fife III	William Fife & Son	Launch Kelvin sleeve valve	E.S. Parker		25				
PUKI	717	1922	William Fife III	V. Despujols Arachon	International 18ft class	C.H. Black, Lisbon		18				
ADVENTURESS	718	1923	William Fife III	William Fife & Son	Aux schooner	Norman Clark Neill London	83 / 34.92	69.9		70.8	17	10
ZENITH	719	1923	William Fife III	William Fife & Son	6 metre bermudian sloop	J. Lauriston Lewis Somerset	5	28.8			6.8	4.2
JACQUELINE	720	1923	William Fife II.	Chantiers de la Heve, Havre	6 metre bermudian sloop	J.E.J. Taylor Paris	5	21.9		29.9		
THE FAN	721	1923	William Fife III	Design only	21ft restricted class	Col. Sir R. Waldie Griffith Bt.						
BONZO	722	1923	William Fife III	Thornycroft Kobnhaven	6 metre bermudian sloop	Wm. Vett, Copenhagen	4					
LINDA	723	1923	William Fife III	Kobenhavns Yt. & Mtr. Koben	6 metre bermudian sloop	H.L. Wessel Copenhagen	5	21		28.88	7	
CISS	724	1923	William Fife III	Abeking&Rasmussen Germa	6 metre bermudian sloop	RYC de Belgique Syndicate per A. Grisar	5		28.9		6.8	4.2
EMILY	725	1923	William Fife III	William Fife & Son	8 metre bermudian	Sir Ernest Roney Aldeburgh	12 / 6.73	34.8		36.7	8.6	4.9
GOLDEN ORFE	726	1923	William Fife III	William Fife & Son	Motor boat	Stock Leslie Wilson	11			36		
MAGIMA	727	1924	William Fife III	William Fife & Son		Count Pavlovic	6					
AWANUI IV	728	1924	William Fife III	Hays & Son Sydney	Bermudian sloop	A.C. Saxton Sydney	14	30.7		47	10	6.8
CARYL	729	1924	William Fife III	William Fife & Son	6 metre bermudian sloop	W.F. Robertson	6					
FINVOLA	730	1924	William Fife I.C.I	William Fife & Son	6 metre bermudian sloop	E.S. Parker Liverpool	5		28.9		6.67	4.29
ROSEMARY III	731	1924	William Fife III	William Fife & Son	Bermudian sloop	Arthur G. Ramage Edinburgh	10 / 6.07	25.57		32.05	8.8	
COLLEEN II	732	1924	William Fife III	William Fife & Son	8 metre bermudian	H.G. Meade Santander	12		37.2		8.5	4.7
TUTTI	734	1924	William Fife III	William Fife & Son	6 metre bermudian sloop	Emil Fahle, Reval Estonia	5		28.9		6.67	4.29
FELMA	733	1924	William Fife III	William Fife & Son	6 metre bermudian sloop	F.A. Richards Eversley Hants	5		28.9		6.67	4.29
FIFI	735	1924	William Fife III	H.B. Nevins NY	R Class bermudian	H.L. Maxwell, NY	6					
RITA IV	736	1924	William Fife III	Thorneycroft Copenhagen	10 metre bermudian sloop	HM King of Denmark	17	36.7	46	57	9.3	6.2
VELLELLA	737	1924	William Fife III	Cantiere Baglietto Vara	6 metre bermudian sloop	Capt. Leslie Richardson	5					
738	738	1924	William Fife III	Design only	Conway One Design							
739	739	1924	William Fife III	William Fife & Son	Launch	E.S. Parker			25			
ROSEMARY IV	740	1925	William Fife III	William Fife & Son	Aux bermudian sloop	Stock sold to Arthur Ramage Edinburgh	28	36.3	45.85	54	11.8	6.3
MODESTY	741	1925	William Fife III	William Fife & Son	11 metre part steel frame	Sir Mortimer Singer	33 / 19.96	52.9	53.75		12.15	6.7
MOYANA	742	1925	William Fife III	William Fife & Son	12 metre part steel frame	Wilfred Leuchars, Durban, Natal	33 / 19.96	52.9	53.75		12.15	6.7
REG	743	1925	William Fife III	William Fife & Son	6 metre bermudian sloop	Norman Clark Neill	5		29		6.8	4.3
SAGA	744	1925	William Fife III	William Fife & Son	6 metre bermudian sloop	A.S.L. Young Cove	5		29		6.8	4.1
HALLOWEEN	745	1925	William Fife III	William Fife & Son	Bermudian cutter	Lt. Col. J.F.N. Braxendale	51 / 28.92		59.5		14.55	11.7
CERIGO	746	1925	William Fife III	William Fife & Son	12 metre part steel frame bermudian cutter	Leon Becker Antwerp	33		53.75		12.15	6.7
FAIRLIE	747	1925	William Fife III	A.S. Holmanhvalstad Norway	6 metre bermudian sloop	Gunerius Pettersen	4					
RHONA	748	1926	William Fife III	William Fife & Son	12 metre part steel frame bermudian cutter	J. Lauriston Lewis	35 / 19.92		54.2		12.4	6.3
ZINITA	749	1926	William Fife III	William Fife & Son	12 metre part steel frame bermudian cutter	A.C. Connell	35 / 19.92		54.2		12.6	6.3
SUNSHINE	750	1926	William Fife III	William Fife & Son	6 metre bermudian sloop	George H. Goodricke Durban, Natal	4 / 3.24		27.8		6.85	4.2
DODO IV	751	1926	William Fife III	William Fife & Son	Aux bermudian ketch	William M. Bergius	63 / 33.83	60.2	59.6	63.5	15.8	6.6
CLUARAN	752	1926	William Fife III	William Fife & Son	8 metre	W. Betts Donaldson	8		37.37		8.7	
CARYL	753	1926	William Fife III	William Fife & Son	8 metre bermudian cutter	W.F. Robertson	8		37.7		8.7	
UBU	754	1926	William Fife III	William Fife & Son	6 metre bermudian cutter	Syndicate 'UBU' L. Becker RYC Belgique	4		29.7		6.9	
FINOLA	755	1926	William Fife III	William Fife & Son	8 metre bermudian cutter	Herbert Johnson JP	8		38.25		8.8	
756	756	1926	William Fife III	design only	8 metre	Rt Hon Earl of Dudley						
UNITY	757	1927	W. Fife	W. Fife	8 metre bermudian cutter	Lord Forster & Sir Fisher Dilke Bt.	12		37.95		8.72	4.75
CAMBRIA	758	1927	William Fife III	William Fife & Son	23 metre bermudian cutter, composite	Sir W. Berry	162 / 85.95	75		93.1	20.5	9.3

BOAT NAME	Yard NUMBER	YEAR	DESIGNER	BUILDER	TYPE	FIRST OWNER	Tonnage TM / Reg	LWL · ft	LBP · ft	LOA · ft	Beam · ft	Draft · ft
NAUSHABAH	759	1927	William Fife III	William Fife & Son	6 metre bermudian sloop	HH the Nawab of Bhopal	6		29.8		6.94	3.9
FINTRA	760	1927	William Fife III	William Fife & Son	6 metre bermudian sloop	E. S. Parker	6		29.8		6.94	3.9
CARIAD	761	1927	William Fife III	Morrison & Sinclair Sydney	Aux bermudian sloop	W.G. McBeath	16	31	39.7	47.3	10.5	6.1
LUCILE	762	1927	William Fife III	W.&R.B McGruer	6 metre bermudian sloop	J. Bryce Allan	4		22.44		6.94	5.17
NOORNA	763	1927	William Fife III	White Southampton	6 metre bermudian sloop	P & L Runciman	6		29.5		6.9	4
764	764	1927	William Fife III	Vancouver	R Class bermudian sloop	B.L. Johnson						
VANESSA	765	1927	William Fife III	J. Hayes Sydney	8 metre bermudian cutter	Percy Arnott	12	30.2	38.4	47.5	8.7	4.4
MARYK	766	1928	William Fife III	William Fife & Son	Aux bermudian sloop	Norman Clark Neill	34 / 16.90	40.1	51.5	60.4	12.96	7.75
VIM	767	1928	William Fife III	G. Bonnin, Lormont,France	8 metre bermudian sloop	Charles Prince Paris	12		38.2		8.8	4.4
REG	768	1928	William Fife III	Attilio Chiesa et Fils, Cannes	8 metre bermudian sloop	Capt. Arthus Paget Cannes	11					
EILEEN	769	1928	William Fife III	William Fife & Son	Aux. bermudian cutter	James V. & R.W. Fulton Greenock	33 / 16.90	40.1	50.4	60.4	12.96	7.7
CORAL	770	1928	William Fife III	William Fife & Son	6 metre bermudian sloop	Major A.A. Stuart Black Shandon	6		30.1		7	4.1
SULAIRE	771	1928	William Fife III	William Fife & Son	8 metre bermudian sloop	Robert B. & John A. Aspin Glasgow	12 / 7.76		38.3		8.7	4.5
EILEEN	772	1928	William Fife III	William Fife & Son	Aux. bermudian ketch	Lewis V. Fulton Greenock	94 / 41.41	60.5	73.6	84.6	17.74	11.25
FELMA	773	1928	William Fife III	William Fife & Son	6 metre bermudian sloop	F.A. Richards Hants	6		30		7	4.8
CARYL	774	1928	William Fife III	William Fife & Son	8 metre bermudian sloop	W.F. Robertson Glasgow	12		39		8.79	4.6
MOYANA	775	1928	William Fife III	William Fife & Son	12 metre bermudian sloop part steel frame	Wilfred Leuchars Durban Natal	36 / 22.83		56.35		12.5	6.75
OSBORNE	776	1928	William Fife III	Sagreda Hermanos, Bilbao, Spain	8 metre bermudian sloop	HM Queen of Spain	11	28.8	36	45.2	8.6	5
QUEST	777	1928	William Fife III	Oakville Yacht Building Co., Ontario	8 metre bermudian sloop	George H. Gooderham Toronto	8	29.3	38.8	48	8.8	6.3
FINOLA	778	1929	William Fife III	William Fife & Son	8 metre bermudian sloop	Herbert Johnson Hants	13		39.5		8.9	4.6
PRISCILLA II	779	1929	William Fife III	William Fife & Son	6 metre bermudian sloop	S. Russell Cooke Newport, IOW	6		29.3		6.9	4.1
REG	780	1929	William Fife III	William Fife & Son	6 metre bermudian sloop	Norman Clark Neill	6 / 3.85		29.5		7	4.1
SOUTHERN CROSS	781	1929	William Fife III	William Fife & Son	6 metre bermudian sloop	D. Guthrie Dunn Largs	6		29.5		7	4.1
DANA II	782	1929	William Fife III	William Fife & Son	8 metre bermudian sloop	Valdemar Graae	6		29.3		6.9	4.1
FALCON	783	1929	William Fife III	William Fife & Son	8 metre bermudian sloop	W.B. and N.P. Donaldson	13		39.2		8.87	4.6
AMITA	784	1929	William Fife III	William Fife & Son	8 metre bermudian sloop	John W. Hamilton Coulport	13 / 8.32		39.5		8.9	4.6
OONAH	785	1929	William Fife III	William Fife & Son	8 metre bermudian sloop	H. Catron Scrimgerour Woodbridge	13 / 7.68		39.3		8.9	4.6
SEVERN	786	1929	William Fife III	William Fife & Son	8 metre bermudian sloop	Roland B. Worth,Stourport	12		38.55		8.9	4.6
PRUDENCE	787	1929	William Fife III	William Fife & Son	6 metre bermudian sloop	Kenneth H. Preston London	6		29.3		6.9	4.1
SOGALINDA VII	788	1929	William Fife III	Sagreda Hermanos, Bilbao, Spain	8 metre bermudian sloop	HE Count de Zubiria Bilbao	12	30	38.5	47.5	8.7	6.3
ALTAIR	789	1930	William Fife III	William Fife & Son	Aux. gaff schooner	Capt. Guy H. MacCaw, London	161 / 77.54	77.9	92.5	107.8	20.5	13.2
TOOGOOLOOWOO II	790	1930	William Fife III	J.J. Savage. Melbourne, Australia	6 metre bermudian sloop	William S. Dagg, Melbourne	6	22.6	29.5	36.6	6.99	5.2
791	791	1930	William Fife III	William Fife & Son	Motor launch for Altair	Capt. Guy MacCaw London		18				
ZORAIDA	792	1930	William Fife III	William Fife & Son	12 metre bermudian sloop, part steel frame	Arthus C. Connell Dougalston	33 / 21.72		56.4		11.8	6
SASKIA	793	1930	William Fife III	William Fife & Son	6 metre bermudian sloop	A.S.L. Young Cove	12 / 7.46		39.07		8.5	4.8
INVADER II	794	1930	William Fife III	William Fife & Son	8 metre bermudian sloop	George Gooderham Royal Canadian YC	12		39.07		8.51	4.85
ANCORA II	795	1931	William Fife III	William Fife & Son	6 metre bermudian sloop	Cyrill M. Wright & Cecil R. Dormer London	5 / 3.67		29.65		6.6	4.3
EWYN		1931	William Fife III	A.M. Dickie Bangor N. Wales	Conway OD	John F. Burton	3					
JACQUAY		1931	William Fife III	Guidon Marseilles	Aux. schooner		21					
FIONA	796	1931	William Fife III	William Fife & Son	Aux. yawl, composite, 4cy.par, Bergius	Archie Watson	61 / 32.87	52.5	61	74.5	16	9.7
PICCOLO	797	1931	William Fife III	William Fife & Son	6 metre bermudian sloop	F.A. Richards & R. Steele Hants	5		29.75		6.62	
798	798	1932	William Fife III	William Fife & Son	Motor boat for stock				26			

BOAT NAME	Yard NUMBER	YEAR	DESIGNER	BUILDER	TYPE	FIRST OWNER	Tonnage TM / Reg	LWL - ft	LBP - ft	LOA - ft	Beam - ft	Draft - ft
FINTRA	799	1932	William Fife III	William Fife & Son	6 metre bermudian sloop	Evelyn S. Parker Liverpool & Little Cumbrae	5		28.65		6.68	4
ZELITA	800	1932	William Fife III	William Fife & Son	12 metre bermudian sloop	A.C. Connell	31 / 22.74		54		11.8	6.3
801 cancelled order	801	1932	William Fife III	William Fife & Son								
MINETTE	802	1932	William Fife III	William Fife & Son	18ft YRA class bermudian sloop	A.S.L. Young Cove	1.5		18		5.6	2.2
803	803	1932	William Fife III	William Fife & Son	16ft centre board dinghy	Sir Thomas W. Inskip				16		
MELITA	804	1933	William Fife III	William Fife & Son	6 metre bermudian sloop	R.M. Teacher Rhu	5		29.3		6.46	4.7
CARRON	805	1933	William Fife III	William Fife & Son	8 metre bermudian sloop	J. Lauriston Lewis, Templecombe	13		39.44		8.26	5.2
FREA	806	1933	William Fife III	William Fife & Son	Aux. ketch composite	Sir Alexander MacCormick St. Peters Jersey	45 / 20.59	47.37	54.66	64.28	14.52	8.3
SASKIA II	807	1933	William Fife III	William Fife & Son	6 metre bermudian sloop	A.S.L. Young Cove	4		23.75	6.55	4.7	
MIQUETTE	808	1933	William Fife III	William Fife & Son	12 metre bermudian sloop, composite	Major Ralph S. Grigg London	33 / 22.61		55.9		11.8	7.5
INTOMBI	809	1933	William Fife III	William Fife & Son	Conway OD	Wilfred Leuchars	3	16		24.4	6.2	3.2
GITANA	810	1933	William Fife III	A.M. Dickie and Sons, Tarbert	Aux. bermudian sloop	T. Gerald Tait Girvan	10	27.8	41.5		10.3	4.2
LOTUS		1934	William Fife III	A.M. Dickie Tarbert	Conway OD	James Kenneth		16		24.5	6.3	3
MAISIE		1934	William Fife III	A.M. Dickie Bangor N. Wales	Conway OD	A.H. Horrocks		16			6.3	3
COIMA		1934	William Fife III	A.M. Dickie Bangor N. Wales	Conway OD	W.L. Horbury jun.		16			6.2	3
SONAS	811	1934	A. Mylne & Co	William Fife & Son	Aux. bermudian cutter	Major J.G. Allan Helensburgh	25 / 15.76	37	46.4	53.5	11.7	7.5
FIONA	812	1934	William Fife III	William Fife & Son	6 metre bermudian sloop	Evelyn S. Parker Liverpool & Little Cumbrae	6		29.6		6.8	4.4
CARRON II	813	1934	William Fife III	William Fife & Son	8 metre bermudian sloop	J. Lauriston Lewis Templecombe	13	39.9			8.82	5.1
MERRY DANCER	814	1935	William Fife III	William Fife & Son	Aux bermudian sloop	(Stock) W.R. Law Glasgow	20	34.5	42.5	51.7	11.0	7.3
FAY	815	1935	William Fife III	William Fife & Son	Motor launch	Evelyn S. Parker	12.75 / 10.26		38		9.1	2.6
VANITY V	816	1935	William Fife III	William Fife & Son	12 metre bermudian sloop, composite	John R. Payne, Billericay	35 / 22.77		56.2		12.2	7.2
PEREGRINE	817	1935	Capt. O. M. Watts	William Fife & Son	Aux bermudian cutter,	H.F.B. Sharp Cupar	12.43 / 9.28	30.96	34.61	39.33	9.71	6.25
LATIFA	818	1935	William Fife III	William Fife & Son	Bermudian cutter composite	Michael James Mason Oxford	53.6 / 35.12	52.5	58.12		15.3	10.2
EOLE	819	1935	William Fife III	Auroux, France	6metre bermudian sloop	Monsieur Auroux	4					
GALENE	820	1935	William Fife III	Stockholms Batbygg, Neglinge, Sweden	Aux. bermudian cutter	Carl Wickstrom Stockholm	32		55.5		11.8	7.8
FELMA	821	1936	William Fife III	William Fife & Son	8 metre bermudian sloop	F.A. Richards Boldre	12.3		39.5	48.7	8.6	5.4
EILEAN	822	1936	William Fife III	William Fife & Son	Aux bermudian ketch	James V. & R.W. Fulton Greenock	59.05 / 31.57	50.9	62.4	72.4	15.4	10.1
EVENLODE	823	1936	A. Mylne & Co	William Fife & Son	BM sloop, composite	T.C. Ratsey Cowes	20	35	42.7	51	10.9	7.5
MARIELLA	824	1937	William Fife III	William Fife & Son	Aux. bermudian, yawl	James D. Paterson Thorntonhall	74	54	67.8	79	16.5	10.4
MERLIN		1937	William Fife III	A.M. Dickie Bangor N. Wales	Conway OD	John Hunter		16			6.3	3
SOLWAY MAID	825	1937	William Fife III	William Fife & Son	Aux bermudian cutter, part steel frame	Ivan Carr Carlisle	21		43.5		10.9	7
STEPHEN ROBSON	826	1937	William Fife III	William Fife & Son	Motor boat,	W.J. Darby	15	34.5	40.1	41	9.8	9.1
827	827	1937	William Fife III	William Fife & Son	Aux yawl,	Major D. Bengson Stockholm		35				
MADRIGAL	828	1938	William Fife III	William Fife & Son	Aux bermudian cutter	Campbell Paterson	17	33.2	40.2	48.7	10.5	7.2
FLICA II	829	1938	Laurent Giles	William Fife & Son	12metre bermudian sloop composite	Hugh L. Goodson Brixham	33		56	66.7	11.8	7

References

Chapter 1

Fairlie Past and Present, Revd Arthur Allan, 1914, Printed by J.R. Simpson, Largs.
Kelburn Castle Archives, bills, receipts, tacks, crop rentals 1707–1774.
Customs Letter Books, Largs, 1819–1833, 71/5/3 and 71/4/3.
Ordinance Survey Map, 1856.
Armstrongs Map, Cunningham, 1775.
Northern and Clyde News, Feb 1982 'Cruise of the Comet', extract from log of James Smith of Jordanhill.
The History of Yachting, 1600–1815 Clark A.H., 1907, Putnam, New York.
Smith of Jordanhill Papers: Mitchell Library Glasgow.
Naval Architecture, D. Steel, 1812, 2nd edn. Steel & Co., London.
The Royal Northern Yacht Club 1824–1974, A Short History, Hugh Somerville, 1974.
Glasgow Regality Club, Second Series, 1893, 'Industry', Lawrence Hill.
Diaries of George Parker 1827–1842.
Boating Journals 1833–1851, 920 Part II.
Liverpool Record Office, Libraries and Information Service.
A Century of the Scottish People, 1830–1930, Smout, T.C., 1986, Collins, London.
Statistical Account of Scotland 1970, 1796, vol. 17, John Sinclair.
A History of the Scottish People 1560–1830, 2nd edn, Smout, TC., 1970, Collins, London.
The Overseas Trade of Ayrshire, 1660–1707. Smout, T.C.
Topographical Accounts of the District of Cunningham, Ayrshire, compiled about 1600 by Mr T.Pont, 1858, The Maitland Club.

Chapter 2

Register of Sasines, Scottish Record Office.
Diaries of George Parker, 1827–1851, Liverpool Record Office, Libraries and Information Service.

Chapter 3

James Smith of Jordanhill Papers. Mitchell Library.
Yachting, Volumes 1 and 2. Badminton Library of Sports and Pastimes, 1894. Volume 1 editor, Sir Edwin Sutherland, Volume 2 editor, Pritchett R.T. Longmans Green and Co.
Glasgow Herald, 9 January 1884.
'The Development of Rating and Measurement Rules', Sambrooke Sturges G., in *British and International Yacht Racing Classes.* Ed. Whitaker H.E., 1954. Ward Lock and Co. Ltd.
Personal reminiscences of Mrs Jenny Cairns, 1993.
Cunningham Topographized. Timothy Pont (1604–1608), Illustrated notes by the late James Dobie of Cumnock, edited by his son, John Dobie, in 1876.
Notes on Old Fairlie, James Boag. Largs Historical Society.
Fairlie Past and Present, Revd Arthur Allan, 1914. J & R. Simpson Largs.
Kelburn Estate Records. 1773, 1869.
George Parker Papers. Liverpool Record Office, Libraries and Information Service
Glasgow Courier, May 7 1883.
Obituary of Captain William Jamieson. *Yachting World,* January 1902.
Scottish Record Office, Census Records 1851.

Chapter 4

The Royal Northern Yacht Club, 1824-1974, A Short History, 1974. Hugh Sommerville, RNYC,
Companies Registration Office, Edinburgh Records 1856.
Cruise in Company. History of the Royal Clyde Yacht Club 1856-1956. Blake G. and Small C., 1959, RCYC
    Glasgow.
'Early Yachting in Scotland', in *Famous Clyde Yachts 1880-1887.* Meikle J., 1888. Oats and Runciman.
Personal information from Mr Geaves on *Fiona.*
Hunt's Magazine, January 1867.
'Clyde Yachting', in *The Scots Pictorial,* 14 July 1900.
Famous Yachts, Hughes J.S., 1928, Methuen.
British Yachts and Yachtsmen. The Yachtsman Publishing Company, 1907.

Chapter 5

Largs and Millport Weekly News, 5 September 1885.
Largs Sexton's Records, Largs Historical Society.
Cruise in Company. History of the Royal Clyde Yacht Club, 1856-1956. Blake G. and Small C., 1959,
    RCYC Glasgow.
Scottish Sail: A Forgotten Era, Simper R., 1974. David and Charles.
Customs Records Greenock. *Register of Ships 1875, 1885.*
The Field, 9 June 1877, 'Collision of *Beagle* and *Nyanza*'.
Largs and Millport Weekly News, 30 June 1877. 'Nearly Fatal Accident'.
The Mohican in Iceland, 1886. James Clark. Private publication
Famous Clyde Yachts 1880-1887, Meikle, James, 1888. Oats and Runciman.

Chapter 6

Shipbuilding, Theoretical and Practical. McQuorn Rankine, W.J., 1866.
'The Evolution of the Modern Racing Yacht', Watson G.L., 1894 in *Yachting Vol.* 1. The Badminton Library
    of Sports and Pastimes, ed. Sir E. Sullivan *et al.*
'Five Tonners and Five Raters in the North', Blake G.L., 1984 in *Yachting Vol.* 1. The Badminton Library of
    Sports and Pastimes, ed Sir E. Sullivan *et al.*
The Corinthian Yachtsman or Hints on Yachting, Tyrrel Biddle, 1881. C. Wilson.
Largs and Millport Weekly News, 24 February 1883. 'Dinner at Largs YC'.
'The Development of Rating and Measurement Rules'. Sambrook Sturges G., in *British and International*
    Racing Yacht Classes, 1954, ed. Whittaker H.E. Ward Lock and Co. Ltd.
'The American Yachting Season of 1893 and Yachting in America'. Herreshoff L,. in *Yachting* Vol. 2,
    Badminton Library of Sports and Pastimes, ed. Pritchett R.T. *et al.*

Chapter 7

Glasgow Herald, 25 April 1879.
The Field, 13 June 1883.
Largs and Millport Weekly News, 5 September 1885.
Famous Clyde Yachts 1880-1887. James Meikle, 1888. Oats and Runciman.
The Mohican in Iceland, 1886, James Clark.
Personal reminiscences, Mrs Jan Howard.
Largs and Millport Weekly News, January 1878.
'Interesting Industry – an Afternoon Among the Toy Yachts', J. Meikle in *Yachting Yarns and Clydeside*
    Sketches, 1885, J. & R. Simpson.
The Firth of Clyde, Blake G., 1952, Collins.
Largs and Millport Weekly News, 16 May 1885.
Correspondence between William Fife and W.P. Stephen. Blunt Memorial Library, Mystic Seaport Museum.

Chapter 8

Largs and Millport Weekly News, 16 June 1978.
Hunts Yachting Magazine, 1865.

Personal correspondence with John Bilsey, owner of *Morna*.
'Kelpie. A Century Old and Still Sailing'. Pardey L. and L., *Classic Boat,* June 1992.
Yachting Monthly, 1934.
Correspondence with Daina Fletcher, Curator of the Australian Maritime Museum, Sydney, Australia, including correspondence from:
    John Wood owner of *Kelpie.*
    Cruising YC of Australia.
    Royal Perth YC of Western Australia.
    Royal YC of Tasmania.
    The Royal Prince Alfred YC.
Sydney Sails, Stephenson P.K., 1962, Sydney RSYS.
Yachting World, May 1931.

Chapter 9

Fife Correspondence, Scottish Maritime Museum, Irvine.
Correspondence between W. Fife and W.P. Stephens. Blunt Memorial Library, Mystic Seaport Museum.
'The Waterwags of Dublin Bay'. O' Brian T., *Classic Boat,* August 1995
'The Carving of Stemheads', in *The Field,* November 1890.
'Belfast Lough Classes', in *The Field,* November 1906.
'Belfast Lough Classes', in *Yachting Monthly,* April 1915.
Dixon Kemp's Manual of Yacht and Boat Sailing, 10th edn, 1904. Ed Heckstall-Smith, B., Horace Cox.
Yachting World, May 1907.
Maritime Museum, Barrow.
'The Sway of the Grand Saloon', in Brimnin J.M., 1986. 2nd revised edition. Arlington Books (Publishers) Ltd.
'Yacht Racing in 1893', Horn H., in *Yachting* Vol 2. The Badminton Library of Sports and Pastimes, 1894, ed. Pritchett R.T., reprinted 1985.
'The America Cup Races 1893', Sir George Leach, as above
Lloyds Register, August 1896

Chapter 10

The Lawson History of the America Cup. 1986 reprint. Ashford.
'The Romance of the America Cup 1899' in *Scots Pictorial,* July 15, August 15 1899.
The America's Cup. An Informal History, 1980. Dear I. Hutchieson.
New York Herald, 31 August 1903.
Lipton Collection, Mitchell Library Glasgow 5.25.795.
Leaves from Lipton's Logs. Sir T. Lipton Bart. Hutchinson and Co. Ltd. London.
Yachting and Boating Monthly, November 1907.
Yachting World, August 1907, September 1907.
'The Burgess Legacy Part II', Lwellyn Hewan III, 1986, *Wooden Boat* No 72.
Great Yachts and their Designers, Eastlard J., 1987. Adlard Coles.

Chapter 11

Cruise in Company: History of the RCYC: 1856-1956. Blake G. and Small C., 1959. RCYC Glasgow.
The Records of the Clyde 19/24 Feet Class 1926. Teacher, Professor J.H. Jackson, Wylie & Co.
Yachting News, May 1895, August 1895.
The Field, April 1896, December 1896.
Yachting News, 1897.
Yachting World, 1895.
The Field, November 1906.
Yachting World, October 1906.
Yachting World, April 1907.
Yachting and Boating Monthly, November 1907.
Yachting Monthly, August 1912.

The Sailing Boat, Folkard H.C. 1901, 5th edn. Edward Stanford, London.
Personal correspondence from Mr Terry Needham, Comber.
Classic Boat, December 1992.
Register of Sasines, 1900 and 1904. Scottish Record Office.
Yachting World, January 1902.
Largs and Millport Weekly News, December 1901, January 1902.

Chapter 12

'The Development of Rating and Measurement Rule'. Sambrook Sturges, G., in *British and International Racing Yacht Classes 1954,* ed. Whitaker H.E. Ward Lock and Co. Ltd.
Yachting World July, August, September and October 1907.
Yachting World, April 1908.
Classic Boat, June 1993.
Register of Sasines, 1904. Scottish Record Office.
Correspondence between W.Fife and W.P. Stephens. Blunt Memorial Library, Mystic Seaport Museum.
The Field, July 1908, August 1908.
'The Six Metre Class', Linton Hope, in *Yachting and Boating Monthly,* 1908.
The Field, December 1909, January 1910.
Personal reminiscences of Miss Ruth Swann, Edinburgh.

Chapter 13

Yachting World, January 1913, June 1913.
Classic Boat, March 1993.
The Field, January 1914, June 1914, September 1914, December 1914, May 1915, July 1915.
The Glasgow Herald, September 1915.
English Electric Aircraft and their Predecessors. Ranson S., 1987. Putman.
History of the English Electric Company, 1951. Basic Data.
The Field, May 1919, November 1919.
Largs and Millport Weekly News, September 1986.
Scientific American, November 1919.
The Institute of Engineers and Shipbuilders, 1944, 88 436.

Chapter 14

The Field, October 1920, February 1921, August 1921, July, 1922, August 1922, October 1922.
'The International Six and Five and a Half Metre Classes'. Sommerville H., in *British and International Racing Yacht Classes,* ed Whittaker H.E., 1954. Ward Lock and Co., London.
Stephen of Linthouse: A Record of 200Years of Shipbuilding 1750-1950. Carvel J.L., 1950, Robert Maclehouse and Co., University Press.
Correspondence between W.P. Stephen and William Fife. Blunt Memorial Library, Mystic Seaport Museum.
Yachting World, July 1928, July 1936.

Chapter 15

Correspondence between William Fife and W.P. Stephens. Blunt Memorial Library, Mystic Seaport Museum.
Glasgow University Marticulation Roll, 1907, 1908.
Fife Yard Correspondence, Scottish Maritime Museum, Irvine.
Companies Registration Office, 102 George Street, Edinburgh.

Chapter 16

Classic Boat, January 1991.
The Yachtsman, Issue No. 2, 1992, Clio.
'Kentra', Morgan A., in *Classic Boat,* September 1995.
Fife Correspondence, Blunt Memorial Library, Mystic Seaport Museum.

'Hallowe'en', Carles Serra i Nadal in *Classic Boat,* May 1994.
Yachting Monthly, 1925, Vol. 38.
'The Conway 16-foot LWL Fife Boat', Jones R.A., in *Yachting and Boating Monthly,* 1925 Vol. 40, 110.
Personal correspondence, Mr P. Dickie Bangor
Personal correspondence, Le Maire d'Epine.
Noirmoutier-en-Isle, local newspaper, 17 February 1995.
The Field, February 1925, September 1926, October 1926.
Yachting World, February 1925, August 1926, October 1926, November 1934.
Fife Correspondence, Scottish Maritime Museum, Irvine.

Chapter 17

Fife Correspondence, Scottish Maritime Museum, Irvine.
Yachting World, May 1928, June 1928, March 1930
Daily Telegraph, June 1961.
Largs and Millport Weekly News, 17 June 1991.
Classic Boat, January 1991.
Yachting World, March 1931, September 1931.
'With Fife at the Helm', Snider C.H., in *Yachting,* 1899.

Chapter 18

Fife Correspondence, Scottish Maritime Museum, Irvine.
Yachting World, February 1936, March 1936, July 1936.
The Field, May 1936, July 1936, October 1936.
Personal reminiscences of Mrs Jan Howard, Norwich.
Racing, Cruising and Design. Fox U., 1937. Peter Davies.
'Obituary: William Fife OBE', Institution of Engineers and Shipbuilders Scotland, 1944, 88, 436.
Personal correspondence with David Loomas.
Personal correspondence with Mark Ratsey-Woodroffe.
Classic Boat, August 1995.
Yachting World, March 1939.
Yachting Monthly, April 1939.
Chasse-Marée, No. 65, 1992.

Chapter 19

Custom House Register, Greenock, Largs Letter Books, 1821, 1825, 833, 1845.
Census Returns, Parish of Largs, 1851.
Kelburn Estate Records, 1773, 1869.
Fife Yard Records, Scottish Maritime Museum, Irvine.
Register of Sasines 1876, 1877, 1878, 1892, 1899, 1900, 1903, 1904. Scottish Record Office.
Companies Registration Office, 102 George Street, Edinburgh.
Racing, Cruising and Design. Fox U., 1937. Peter Davies.
Sail and Power. Fox U., 1936, Peter Davies.
Yachting World, November 1936.
Walking in All of the Squares. Thom A.S., 1995. Argyll Publishing.

Epilogue

Viola: La belle ecossaise. Gwendal Jaffry, Chasse-Maree, 2001, No. 141, p. 50.

Index